Tatyana's War

Escape and Survival on the Eastern Front in World War II

HELEN CHAROV *and*
TATYANA ARTEMYEFF

McFarland & Company, Inc., Publishers
Jefferson, North Carolina

Unless otherwise noted, all photographs
are from the family's collection.

LIBRARY OF CONGRESS CATALOGING-IN-PUBLICATION DATA

Names: Charov, Helen, 1952– author. | Artemyeff, Tatyana Borisovna, 1916– author.
Title: Tatyana's war : escape and survival on the Eastern Front in World War II / Helen Charov, and Tatyana Artemyeff.
Other titles: Escape and survival on the Eastern Front in World War II
Description: Jefferson, North Carolina : McFarland & Company, Inc., Publishers, 2024 | Includes index.
Identifiers: LCCN 2024031964 | ISBN 9781476693101 (paperback : acid free paper) ♾ ISBN 9781476651422 (ebook)
Subjects: LCSH: Artemyeff, Tatyana Borisovna, 1916–2007. | Soviet Union—History—German occupation, 1941–1944,—Personal narratives. | World War, 1939–1945—Personal narratives, Ukrainian. | World War, 1939–1945—Refugees—Soviet Union—Biography. | Russian Americans—New York (State)—Biography. | Donezk (Ukraine)—Biography. | Charov, Helen, 1952– | BISAC: HISTORY / Wars & Conflicts / World War II / General | HISTORY / Women
Classification: LCC D802.S65 A783 2024 | DDC 940.53/477 [B]—dc23/eng/20240809
LC record available at https://lccn.loc.gov/2024031964

BRITISH LIBRARY CATALOGUING DATA ARE AVAILABLE

ISBN (print) 978-1-4766-9310-1
ISBN (ebook) 978-1-4766-5142-2

Front cover image: Tatyana Artemyeff, née Fediay, age 16, 1933 (family photograph)

Printed in the United States of America

McFarland & Company, Inc., Publishers
Box 611, Jefferson, North Carolina 28640
www.mcfarlandpub.com

This book is dedicated to my grandmother, my mother, and my sister—three courageous and remarkable women.

Table of Contents

Acknowledgments

First and foremost, I owe a debt of gratitude to the heroine of this book, my mother, Tatyana Artemyeff, who despite all the obstacles she faced in her life, was compelled to keep diaries and preserve photographs, which she carried out of Russia in a single suitcase. She must have known their value to posterity even as a young woman. I am lucky to have had them in my possession, since so many others in my generation have missed out on the rich stories and legacies of their predecessors, relying on spoken words which are lost over time.

My sister, Natasha Schimkewitsch, who lived in Sea Cliff, New York, up until her death on February 16, 2023, was an invaluable resource and fact checker for me, having begun her life in Donetsk, Ukraine, as Tatyana's first child, and lived through her teen years during the war and beyond. Her remarkable recall of the minutest of details, even until the final hours of her own life, verified much of our mother's memoirs. I entreated her to hang on for their publication. Natasha's last words to me focused unselfishly not on her own life, but on the insistence that I should never doubt that my mother had loved me and held me dear.

I thank members of her family, her son Vladimir, beloved grandson Elijah and his mother, Tatiana, as well as our brother Yura Budishevsky's family for celebrating Natasha's life in remembrance of both of those courageous women.

I thank my brother Eugene Artemyeff for archiving photographs and mementos of our parents' lives. It was gratifying to learn that his wife, Connie, daughter, Natalie, and son, Andre, were ecstatic over the chronicling of their grandparents' journeys. My own children, Katia and her husband, Michael Ostertag, and Nik Charov, and his wife, Xanthe, supported me from the start of this project and my grandsons, Huck and Max, will now have a written history. Mission accomplished on that score. Special thanks to Howard Emerson, a family member, for exhorting me long ago not to give up the quest. His own musical creativity has been an inspiration.

My cousin, Anna Everest, shared family tree information. My Australian cousin, Larissa Belov, helped me contact the source of my late uncle, her stepfather, Leonid Artemieff's, published memoirs in Unification, West Ryde, Australia. Had those two "Bandit Brothers," Leonid and Sasha, not supported each other through the unimaginable privations imposed on POWs, my own history would not have existed. *Vechnaya Pamyat* (Memory Eternal) to the millions who perished in the POW camps, the death camps and genocides of the Holocaust.

Thank you to my fellow hikers, Natalia Szidon and Olga Novosilsov, and my extended family of St. George's Pathfinders, in exile worldwide, who carry the torch of serving a bygone and better Russia. Once again you are called upon to preserve what is best and admirable about our troubled second homeland.

On the professional level, the introduction to Barbara Ellis-Uchino by her agency partner, Jan Kardys, in late 2017 proved a fateful meeting. To call Barbara an agent would be to grossly understate her years of interest, encouragement, editing and sheer will to help tell my mother's story. Barbara is the literary world's gift to me—I will never be able to thank her enough for her belief in this book.

Thanks to Charlie Perdue and the exceptional crew at McFarland.

To a new writer, early readers who get pulled into the story and ask for more are a surprising but welcome drug. Suzanne Kitchings and Barbara Boyd-Ellis were ever constant, along with Mildred Devine, Joshua and Kathy Chasan, Susan Mostowy, Anne Bohsack, and Vassily Rajevski. Thank you to Dr. Steven Bruce for some early editing, in between masterly maestro rehearsals with Con Brio Choral Society. Thanks to John Williams for bringing the photos to life.

Teachers and mentors can never be sure of when their impact will be felt. My North Shore High School English teacher, the late, great Bruce R. Mooney, once scribbled a note in red on my Melville paper, asking if I was thinking of a writing career. I didn't need to have kept the paper, although I did for years; the words stayed emblazoned on my mind. Thanks also to Lary Bloom, a Connecticut journalist, author and writing teacher, who decades ago inspired in me a cautious ambition and later fueled it with thoughtful editing and critique.

Finally, to the tall Irishman who met me atop Mount Higby after much wandering, who gave me ne'er-before support and a quiet desk in Eastport, Maine, and then a proposal of *carpe diem* for the rest of our lives, thank you and all my love forever, Raymond Comstock, we wander no more.

Preface

As with many an aspiring writer, I had been walking around with this book in my head but never put pen to paper. I had been imagining the retelling of my mother's story for more years than I would admit. But it all began with the birth of a child I had long given up hope of ever bringing into the world.

Katia was born in December 1992, a few months after I turned 40 years old. Up to then, I had devoted 14 years to raising a son. After Nik, I had given up on having more children, it just wasn't happening. I had accepted that a stressful corporate job, which had required international travel, messing with biological clocks, had taken its toll on producing additional progeny. When relatives questioned me, I was defensive, arguing that I was glad to be long past all the diapering, that it would be burdensome to begin anew with another baby, then toddler.

Inwardly the regret of never nurturing another child again would sometimes stab at my heart, especially while holding my brother's newborn in my arms. But I didn't fight back at what seemed a decision ordained by Mother Nature herself, perhaps punishing me for years of birth control. So, when she reversed herself—and the little stick turned blue showing the pregnancy test was positive—I stared at myself in the bathroom mirror speechless, at once in reverence of life's miracle and yet uncertain of its benediction.

The shock wore off but was followed by a sense of the unfamiliar: it was to be a girl. After all those mother and son years, I was to have a daughter. The word "girl" itself was incongruous in our household, where even our Husky dog, Buck, was male. This would be uncharted territory.

In all respects this child, this daughter was different from the start, an easy pregnancy, an uncomplicated delivery. Katia arrived sympathetic to me; I was the nervous one. What would it be like to bring up a daughter? Was it different from bringing up sons? Katia's birth and then the days that stretched into weeks of looking into her tiny face removed any misgivings that I'd had before her birth. She was my adored Katienka, and most definitely and wonderfully a daughter.

I had not thought about myself as a daughter for a long time, if ever, in the same context of Katia and me. Motherhood was not novel—it had defined a big part of my life—this was something else, this was a different link. Katia was to me, as I was to my mother, as she was to my grandmother. But up to now, at mid-life, I knew little about either of the latter two and had not cared enough to find out, at least not until Katia connected us.

My mother and I did not have a strong bond; we had barely survived a rocky relationship through my 1960s adolescence, clashing in a new world vs. the old one that she had come from after the war. It wasn't until I became a mother myself that she accepted me, and even then, I never quite shook off the feeling of having been an unwanted child, appearing at an inopportune moment of harsh émigré beginnings in a new land. While still in Germany as a refugee, my mother had given my father a son; that should have been enough.

Katia's arrival came at a time when my own maturity allowed me more reflection than just reaction to life. I stayed home with her and did not return to full-time work, happily nurturing both a toddler and high schooler for a few years. It wasn't until I found myself as a single mother that I started thinking about what it must have been like for the women in my family who preceded me.

My grandmother, in her mid–30s, survived the Russian Revolution of 1917 and its aftermath. Widowed, grieving the loss of her beloved husband to political imprisonments and death, she was left alone to fend for herself and two small children, my mother, Tatyana, and her brother, Fediay. Babushka, as we would call her later, made her way from northern Russia to Ukraine, a journey of almost 1,500 kilometers, to seek solace and support from her family. For the next 33 years, she would be by my mother's side in surviving Stalin's repressions, Hitler's invasion and occupation of her homeland, and then retreat to Germany.

My mother, Tatyana, to whom I am profoundly grateful for having had the gift and compulsion to write, became the sole support of her family when her husband, Shura, was conscripted to fight the Nazis. She survived the war to meet and marry my father in Germany, and come to America where, unexpectedly, perhaps reluctantly, she gave life to me, her daughter.

When I started to write a book about Tatyana, translating her words and adding my own, I knew that her story, her telling of it, would stand on its own merits. She truly was a "Scarlett O'Hara" of the Eastern Front, with all that heroine's determination and beauty. But looking back on the days of working with her, I had another motivation. *I wanted her to be proud of me.* I wanted her to acknowledge that I had been worth keeping after all.

I had hoped that through my recognition of her life, she might see me as worthy.

But her past stood in the way.

She asked me not to go ahead with the revelations of her life that would make her uncomfortable, even fearful, in the twilight of her years. Ever the rebellious daughter, I rejected her plea and continued, without her knowledge or blessing.

Now with a glance at the heavens, I have found that there is more to the telling of her life than just my need for affirmation. It's too late for that, but I can still share the legacy of a brave mother, the story of a heroine who embodied all the positive attributes of being a true Russian woman. I don't think she thought of herself in those terms, she used to say that she had no alternative but to put one foot in front of the other every day, but her life was so much more than that. Here, her words will not "perish forever," as she predicted, and at least in these pages, I have honored her "to preserve them" for those to come.

—Helen Charov, Moodus, Connecticut

1

June 2001

"Did you know you were born on the same day as Vladimir Putin?"

"Really ... same day?" I asked.

"Same day, same year, even," my mother added.

That was puzzling. Was this good news? Or bad? It was hard to tell how long Mama had been keeping this information to herself, but today's visit held an air of triumph in it; she seemed proud to inform me that I shared a birthday with the president of Russia. Her pleased expression suggested this revelation ought to be relished for its historic significance. She waited for a reaction.

"Separated at birth, huh?" I muttered in English, knowing she would not understand the reference. It was not likely that Putin and I had come into the world simultaneously at Kings County Hospital in Brooklyn, New York. No doubt there was a Soviet hospital someplace, halfway around the globe, which held that distinction and had probably already marked it with a plaque at its entrance. Kings County Hospital was slower in acknowledgments.

"I'll put on the tea." She moved into the kitchen to light the kettle on the stove.

Of course, we would have tea, better known as chai, expected and served at any hour of the day, morning, noon, and night, and in between. I don't think I had ever even seen coffee in my mother's kitchen; maybe there was a jar of freeze-dried Maxwell House hidden behind the flour, to be fished out from the back of the cupboard and doled out by spoonful at the request of an infidel. A cup of tea was the welcoming gambit to family, to friend, to stranger. My Connecticut friends had long benefited by this inherited behavior in me as well.

"What will you have with it?"

"Thank you, just tea will be fine."

"*Goliy* [naked] tea? No, no, that won't do, let's see, what else is there, a bagel, perhaps?"

I seated myself at the dinette table, pushed against a wall, on which hung the monthly calendar from the Russian Orthodox Church of St. Seraphim, marked by Mama's teacherly penmanship, reminding her of upcoming services.

"How was your trip down? Any traffic?"

"Not bad at all, a smooth ride all the way on the highway and only a few delays on Throgs Neck," I reported.

Although it was only a three-hour trip down to Long Island, my mother still considered my life in rural Connecticut a forced exile to the hinterlands. She even feigned mock surprise at the availability of indoor plumbing a scant hundred and twenty miles northeast of New York. Years earlier when my Navy husband, Alex, and I had first moved close to the Navy submarine base in Groton, Tatyana Borisovna, as he called her formally by her name and patronymic, had derisively pronounced it the *derevnya*, land of the country bumpkins.

At least today, there was no rebuke for the distance I had driven. Over the past two decades, Mama had become reconciled with the reality that one of her four children lived more than ten minutes away. At first this was an imposition demanded by the Navy, but then the building of a home, the arrival of grandchildren who attended local schools, her son-in-law's startup businesses, all these created not a temporary condition to be tolerated, but a sad finality, a fact of life. Of course, I was still made to feel like the errant black sheep for having moved away, perhaps just a lighter shade by the passage of time.

No number of visits, tours of art museums and Hartford Symphony tickets had dispelled her prejudice. Yale University, the home of one of my parents' professor friends, was as far north as cultural life extended, and then nothing beyond. Where others were charmed by the acres of woodlands surrounding my home, Tatyana had pitied me for living in a town "which does not even have sidewalks!"

I was the only one of her children to have ventured so far away from the bosom of the family. "How can you live there, so far away from civilization?" she would ask, and then half seriously add, "Are there wolves?" My silent eye-rolling was the answer.

My parents' home, a three-story white house, was considered a late Victorian, but I had always thought of it only as old when I lived there as a child. It had changed little, even while the village, Sea Cliff, a small hamlet on the north shore of Long Island, had moved from middle class to gentry. The house sat on its corner of Sea Cliff Avenue and a side street. Across the street was Clifton Park, whose two baseball diamonds overlapped their outfields on either side of an 8-foot granite slab of a rock, on which were inscribed the names of the fallen from World War I. The only time anyone looked at the bronzed, worn names was when

Memorial Day parades of my childhood ended their brief march from the Fire House down Sea Cliff Avenue to Memorial Rock, with wreath-laying and speeches given by aged, watery-eyed men with red poppies in their lapels. Once the parade followers dispersed, shouts of "play ball!" would resume.

The house was set back from the street, hemmed by privet hedges and two ungainly pine trees that had grown too high to be trimmed, too expensive to be taken down. The pines obscured the northern side of the vintage structure, which my father had maintained in his frugal way—extra coats of paint, a patch here and there with a leftover plank—but no major work to the gray and white exterior for the forty years since they had moved from Brooklyn as first-time homeowners, eager to settle more permanently in the New World.

I remembered how, on the day we moved in, the narrow cement path leading to the back of the house had beckoned me to discover an apple tree, growing just outside what would become my bedroom window.

Today, when I arrived late in the afternoon, as I pulled into the space in front of the garage, I saw Mama standing there in the doorway, waiting for me to come up the back stairs. She had seen me drive up. She had been sitting in the library—her "cabinet," as she referred to it—at the small, varnished desk she called her writing table, looking through the lace curtains for my car. Her gray hair was neatly coifed with a permanent wave, and she was wearing a printed housedress and apron. She wasn't wearing lipstick, which meant she expected only me, and no one else.

Tatyana rose to pour the tea. At 85, she was still light on her feet. I looked at her as she crossed the tiny kitchen, a room which, like all the others in the house, had not changed since the 1960s renovations she and my father had labored at for over a decade. There were still the red-checked floor tiles, the ancient ceramic sink, the kitchen cabinets, painted white. There was no counter space, just a dinette table and chairs. It was clear that Mama was not interested in cuisine, haute or otherwise; she much preferred to read at the worn table than prepare meals on it.

The only thing that had changed in over forty years was the addition of a small television set perched on a shelf above the breadbox, recently wired for cable by my brother, who thought it would be entertaining for our parents to have access to daily broadcasts of Moscow television for news and arts programming. My mother's desire to link the president of Russia and me must have had something to do with Putin's appearances on the Russian news channel, showing him in the company of the high priests of the Russian Orthodox Church. She had probably even seen him bow under their blessing, kissing the cross they proffered to him.

Tatyana pretended not to hear my remark about separated at birth and went on with preparing tea. I had seen her attitude towards Putin gradually shift, from suspicion in 2000, when he was handpicked by President Yeltsin and all that was known was his "professional" background, to acceptance upon his recent election, to this new phase of admiration, a credit to Moscow Evening News, which often showed President Putin patting the blond heads of children in kindergartens, congratulating workers in steel plants, and strolling with the Patriarch of Moscow. The latter, of course, sealed the deal. All that was left for him was to reveal that he had been secretly baptized and was now a believer, and all would be forgiven.

"Yes, it's an interesting coincidence, don't you think, you and Putin having the same birthday?"

"Yes, such a distinction. But what about those three little letters," I asked. "K-G-B?"

"Ah." Waving them away, she said, "But he is doing a lot of good for Russia, and chasing out those bandits who have robbed the country, pocketed the money from her natural resources, sent it abroad...." She took on his defense more vehemently than I expected for someone who had probably been interrogated by Putin's predecessors more than once.

"And he's not doing that himself? Government-sanctioned corruption? Not only that, but where are the free elections, where is the democracy?" I countered.

I knew I was baiting her on a topic we had argued about before, that of American First Amendment rights, and what my mother saw as too much freedom in the U.S. She and my father, Sasha, often railed against the excesses of the free press, particularly indignant about the open availability of pornography. I had never been able to persuade them of the price to be paid to freely criticize the government without reprisal. Old habits never die.

She continued, "Huh, this so-called *democratia* ... who needs it if you don't have a job, or food to put on the table? Americans and their democracy, you hold it in such high regard, and all it brings is crime, movies and television shows that are ... well, worthless, or worse. That's what your *democratia* brings," she scoffed. And *I Love Lucy* and *The Honeymooners*, I thought, recalling two of their favorite sitcoms of the '50s and '60s.

It always amazed me that after almost fifty years in America, my parents had not come to any deeper understanding of constitutional rights, and for Mama, who had lived under Stalin's regime for all her life prior to World War II, freedom of speech would not have assumed a greater value when it had finally been secured abroad. But Russians admire and respect a strong hand that delivers law and order. They had both voted for Nixon. Now Mama saw those same qualities in Putin, blessed by the Church, restorer of Mother Russia, God, and Czar.

Suspicious of her motives, I wondered if Mama brought up the coincidence of my astrological birthmate, now atop the throne of Russia, as another poke at me. Was there some greatness expected of her daughter, which had remained unfulfilled? Was this to become another chance for her to remind me that she had wanted me to become a doctor, an opportunity she had never had herself? I had failed her in that regard, not even following in her footsteps as a teacher.

"So, what of it?" I asked. "Our birthday."

"Nothing, I just thought you might like to know. The Moscow Evening News said he was born in the morning, just like you."

Vladimir Putin was born in Leningrad in the same October of 1952 that I was born in Brooklyn. In January of that year, my mother, father, their three children and an aging grandmother, had stepped onto a west side pier in Manhattan after a rocky, eleven-day crossing from Hamburg, Germany. The days of Ellis Island were over because refugees were screened abroad before departure for U.S. shores, but they still steamed past the Statue of Liberty in New York harbor, overjoyed as much for her symbolic acceptance of them, as relieved from the seasickness which incapacitated most of them during the passage.

A few months later, settled into a cold, third-floor walkup on Vermont Street in the East New York neighborhood of Brooklyn, Tatyana discovered that she was pregnant. There were family jokes about a stork who insisted on making his delivery unbidden, but I still managed to be the first born in the New World, a strange and unintelligible place to my émigré family.

In far off Leningrad, Putin's mother surely had it easier with Vladimir. It is likely his father was there with flowers, much as mine had brought a bouquet to Mama in a multi-colored vase picked up at a dime store on Pitkin Avenue. Volodya and I had started our lives minutes apart, worlds away.

My mother dismissed my lack of enthusiasm for this bit of historical data, linking Putin and me. She switched over to the reason for the day's visit. "I have read over your translation of my old newspaper article about World War II. It's puzzling to me why you have shown an interest in my writing," she said, shrugging. She had sent me a yellowed clipping when I had requested it a few months ago. I hadn't told her then of my reasons for wanting a copy.

I hesitated. "Well, whatever. I have some questions about wording," she went on as she got up and went back into her study, which doubled as the library in our house. I followed her.

The library was her sanctuary. Floor to ceiling bookshelves lined the walls, leaving space only where a ten-foot gilded mirror, which had come with the house, rose from the carpeted floor to a cherub fluttering up by the patterned tin ceiling. A framed portrait of Count Leo Tolstoy hung on the opposite wall.

The books were all meticulously arranged by author, inscribed and numbered by hand on the inside, lovingly recorded alphabetically in a black composition book. As children, my brother Eugene and I were given a special task once a year: to remove, with great reverence, each book from its designated place on the shelf, wipe the dust which had settled on the top or sides with a cloth, and replace it in its slot with gentleness and care.

Oversized art books were given special attention. Mama would allow us to page through them, stopping at her favorite portraits or landscapes, while she described the stories behind the paintings of the Tretyakov Gallery in Moscow or the Russian Museum in Leningrad.

"Take a look at the expression on Ivan the Terrible's face," she would point out in Ilya Repin's depiction of the Tsar. "He has just killed his son." We would be directed to look closer at the bloody spectacle, perhaps as a warning. Turning to another page, we would recognize the playful bears in Shishkin's "Morning in a Pine Forest," from the reproduction on a decorative rug hung over Eugene's bed.

Then, Tatyana reached into a drawer of her writing desk and pulled out the marked-up, double-spaced manuscript. "It has some details I would like to add," she said.

We got down to the task at hand. I had come from Connecticut to work with my mother on my translation of a piece she had written about the start of the war. It was a pet project that I had conceived, which I hoped might bring us together, while answering some of the lingering questions I still had about her life in Soviet Russia.

Even with sixty years elapsed since the war's beginning, the bombing of Pearl Harbor, and later, D-Day, war anniversaries still generated interest. The war fought by the "greatest generation" had not faded into veterans' memories and was still an endless source of books, movies, HBO series and speeches. Much less was written or spoken about the war's Eastern Front, opened by Hitler's invasion of Soviet Russia in 1941, a cataclysmic event my mother had lived through as a young wife with two children, my older sister and brother.

Drawing on her remembrance of that day, she had written a short piece decades ago for the *Novoye Russkoye Slovo* (New Russian Word), a Manhattan-based Russian newspaper. It was the daily paper of Russians in the greater New York area, available by mail and even on the newsstand in Sea Cliff, which had a large émigré community. The paper had its heyday in the 1970s under Andrei Sedykh, its publisher, who had been the personal secretary to Ivan Bunin, and who had even accompanied him to

Stockholm in 1933 for the first Nobel Prize in Literature awarded to a Russian writer.

I recalled Sedykh's name mentioned at home, and the masthead of the paper was a familiar relic of my childhood, copies of it in the kitchen and library, but I hadn't paid attention to the fact that my mother had contributed bylined stories using a false name. The article I had translated, *The Day the War Began,* was one of them.

I was to find out much later why she had used a pseudonym.

2

June 22, 1941—The Day the War Began

The onset of war caught each of us differently, but certainly we were all caught by surprise. It all happened so suddenly, when we least expected it, on a beautiful June day in 1941. The weather was warm, but not yet hot. The spring floods had receded, the countryside was greening; flowers were blooming. Nature was celebrating its annual rebirth. Our pupils were celebrating too—final exams were over, school was out, summer vacation stretched ahead.

I remember that it happened to be a Sunday, that June 22. I had finished grading final exams on Friday and was getting ready to leave for Odessa where Natasha, then only six years old, was supposed to be discharged from the sanatorium for respiratory illnesses.

She had spent a month there, a benefit available to most children of the proletariat, and I couldn't wait to be with her, to hold her in my arms again. The trip itself promised to be a welcome change from the monotonous final weeks of school. Odessa, a sunwashed seaport on the Black Sea, beckoned me.

So off we walked to the train station on that beautiful morning. My husband, Shura, in a rare chivalrous gesture, had decided to accompany me as far as the junction station before reporting for his assignment on the railway. By 10 a.m. we were on the train to Jasinovataya, my switch point, happily chatting away about taking the family on a trip when I returned with Natasha the next day. Thanks to Shura's position, we had free passage from our town in the Donbas Basin to all points in the USSR, even as far as Kamchatka or Sakhalin Island. By 11 a.m. we had arrived at the junction station, where I would have to wait until 1 p.m.

We spent some time at the buffet with a late breakfast. Time dragged; it seemed like the minute hand had slowed on the platform clock. We strolled under the loudspeakers, paying little attention to the music, which was interrupted occasionally for announcements of arrivals and departures. At 11:30 a.m. the music stopped abruptly and there were a few seconds of crackling silence, then: "Comrades, at exactly noon there will be an important announcement from Foreign Minister Molotov. Remain by the loudspeakers. Listen for the announcement from Comrade Molotov." And then, just as abruptly, the music resumed.

I whirled around to Shura and asked him what it could be about. What could be so important that Molotov himself would speak? He was the Foreign Minister, so it had to do with something international, which sent goosebumps down my arms. Nothing good could come of this. Shura was silent for a few moments, and then he murmured just one word: "War." I looked over at him to see if he was joking. "Oh, come now, war? With whom? That's nonsense."

"You'll see ... just wait ... with Germany," he replied sullenly. I was irritated by his response. But then the seriousness of his gaze, his worried look, having realized that my train would carry me westward in the direction of what would be the front, silenced me. "It can only be war, and I know it's with Germany," he added.

At 11:45 the radio again blared the command to stay tuned or move toward loudspeakers at noon. The announcer's voice was solemn, somehow confirming Shura's prediction. The crowd of people on the train platform quieted and moved closer to the loudspeakers, putting their packages and sacks down by their feet, lighting up cigarettes, silently waiting.

I didn't know what Molotov was about to say, but I sensed it would be bad news. With that, my lighthearted mood vanished and the anticipated joy of being reunited with Natasha was replaced with fear. My thoughts raced from Mama at home with our young son, Yura, back again to Natasha. It seemed that time stood still those last few minutes before noon.

Finally, Molotov's voice came on the loudspeakers. There probably isn't anyone in my generation that doesn't remember his speech that morning describing Germany's attack on us, supposedly a complete surprise. Molotov spoke of cities that had been bombarded already that morning; he described the need for immediate mobilization of all resources; the coming difficulties and sacrifices. Less than confidently, he promised that we would soon defeat the enemy on his own ground, that our righteous cause would prevail, that victory lay ahead.

After Molotov finished, there was complete silence on the platform for several seconds. No one moved. Only after a few moments people started to stir about slowly, as if awakening from a deep sleep.

All I could think about was how can I now get to my child, how can I go in the direction of the front, the advancing army? Maybe the Germans already occupy Odessa, since it is so close to the border. But how to know? What to do? I tried not to think about the chaos and panic that must have engulfed the sanatorium where dozens of children would be stranded from parents too distant to come for them quickly, Natasha among them. Not only did I have to get to her, but I would have to return somehow. Passenger service, if not already canceled, would certainly be in a few days with Molotov's pronouncement, "All for the front! All for victory!" But there was no choice—I had to get there somehow and get back.

Shura nervously gave me the names of some friends who worked at Znamenka Station who might help with transfers. He wondered out loud what orders awaited him at the depot, but his fate would not be decided for several months. As for me, I had never traveled so far on my own before, still so young, in my mid-twenties. I was afraid to go, but eager to get started. I put my faith in God's will and boarded, taking a window seat, heavy in thought.

The countryside rushed by. The sunshine washed over the fields and pastures as the train passed through quiet villages. I saw a group of old women sitting on their hut stoops, shelling sunflower seeds with their teeth. A young man jauntily strolled down a lane. What was wrong with them? Didn't they know that life was now irrevocably changed and that the peaceful rhythms of sowing and tending the garden had vanished in a single morning? Hadn't they heard Molotov and his frightening words? What if I had imagined the whole thing? Maybe there was no war—from the window of the train there were no signs of anything amiss.

Znamenka Station was unusually quiet, probably because few would hazard travel westward toward the front. The connecting train to Odessa was late by only a few minutes, and again the clacking motion of the train wheels gently rocked me for hours, passing through a pastoral scene, while my thoughts raced ahead. Finally, Odessa.

But my God, what a sight at the station! The entire platform and the city square were teeming with people, pushing, shoving. Everywhere there were women and children, old people, even some young men, all with belongings tied in kerchiefs and packed into boxes and suitcases, everyone rushing to get out of Odessa, out, anywhere to the east, away from the advancing menace.

They were all trying to get on to something, anything—passenger cars, freight cars, even hanging on to the sides of the locomotives. I shuddered to think I would have to get through this mob in a few hours, and with a small child in tow. How would I possibly be able to push our way on board?

The loudspeakers announced changes and cancellations. "Last train to Crimea. All subsequent trains are for military use only. Last train to Kiev via Znamenka." My Znamenka Station! The crowds were pushing uncontrollably, people jumping on and off the platforms, hustling onto the railcar couplings, scrambling even on top of the cars and coal tenders. Yelling, swearing ... panicked screams as someone lost a child. I remember too well the face of an old babushka reeling by me, wild-eyed, kerchief pulled back on her gray head, clutching her rag-tied belongings. She is lost, separated from her family. Some conductors were hopelessly trying to push off the danglers, while others pocketed the bribes and shoved them inward.

I boarded a bus, almost empty since it was heading away from the station. Those approaching the station were packed tightly. Again, I thought about how to return with my little Natasha. The bus dropped me off at the sanatorium entrance and I rushed inside. It was a madhouse. The order had been given to evacuate, but not all the children had been picked up by their parents yet. Doctors and nurses were running around, trying to call mothers or fathers on telephones now out of service or ordered to be "All for the front. All for victory!" Crying children were all around me, unattended.

"Natasha!" She threw herself into my arms. "Mama, Mamochka, you're finally here! I thought that you had forgotten about me. The other children have already left with their mothers and fathers."

Everywhere there was frantic desperation, as if we were on a sinking ship, or on the second floor of a house on fire. We quickly packed up Natasha's clothes and thanked the nurses and doctors. Then it was back to the train station, before the last trains eastward get canceled, before the bombing attacks begin, before we are caught in the occupation of the city.

It was useless to even try getting on to a train, freight or otherwise. I went straight to the stationmaster and showed him my free pass and Shura's documents, explaining that I was trying to get my sick child home. Miraculously, it worked: not the plea for the child but the free pass of a fellow trainman. We were promised a place in a freight car away from the platform before the car came up for loading.

The stationmaster led us to the car in the yard, and we tucked ourselves into one corner. When it was opened for boarding at the station, for a moment I feared we would be crushed by the surging masses. But at least we would get to Znamenka, and there I would worry about the next leg of our return. Several times during the night-long trip, the train stopped for air raids. At other times it just stood motionless for long periods at various stations, creating the impression we were going no further. No one had any idea of when it would move again; there was no one to ask.

I constantly worried that there would be air strikes and then everyone would have to leave the car and I wouldn't be able to get myself and Natasha back on board. I was exhausted, hungry, and badly in need of sleep. There was nowhere to buy food and no water in the stifling heat. We reached Znamenka Station by dawn. The station was still in a relative state of order, since it was further from the front, with even some passenger service, though I was told it would be difficult to get a seat on board. I searched out one of Shura's friends who took one look at us and insisted that we rest at his home before traveling further.

The next morning when we walked to the station with him, we learned that the last train in our direction was leaving shortly. We boarded the passenger car the same way, but this time it was already full even before pulling up to the platform. Somehow, I managed to find a corner to put Natasha down on her little suitcase but I stood the entire way, knees buckling as I dozed off but held in place by the passengers squeezed beside me.

We finally made it home and were met with disbelief. Mama almost fainted when she saw us, she hadn't eaten or slept since I'd left, spending her time in prayers for our safe return. And God had answered them, as He would so many more times in the troubled years ahead.

I finished reading the translation to my mother as we sat in the kitchen. She was quiet while I made some corrections. She had been taken back to that day. "Windows were blanketed, goods disappeared from store shelves," my mother said. "The troop mobilization began almost immediately with the send-off of sons and husbands, including mine. War? How could it have been possible?" she shrugged. And yet, it had begun.

Like the Japanese attack on Pearl Harbor, Hitler's invasion of the Soviet Union began early on a Sunday morning and took the Russians completely by surprise, since Germany and the USSR had signed a mutual non-aggression pact in 1939. The invasion had been planned months in advance and Hitler was known to have said to one of his generals, "We have only to kick in the door, and the whole rotten structure will come crashing down."

The entire 1800-mile border, from the Baltic to the Black Sea, was attacked by a three-million-man deployment of German aircraft, tanks, and ground troops, bombing major cities with the intent to drive toward Leningrad and Moscow in the north, and Kiev and eastward in the south. The advance of the German troops was stunning, meeting virtually no opposition along the line.

We talked about how that day had changed the course of her life. Prior to then, my mother's life had been characterized by events internal to Soviet Russia. The shocking arrival of Hitler's war on her doorstep irrevocably changed its direction, separating her from her husband, Shura, and leaving her to fend for herself and her two young children, Natasha, six years old, and Yura, two.

The war became the defining event of her life, fought on the territory of her homeland. The theater of my mother's war was not some overseas continent, or a Pacific archipelago, but her town, her street, her house. Within several months of Hitler's invasion, she witnessed the German armies advance deep into Russia and Ukraine, overrunning and occupying captured territory, while Soviet troops retreated hastily to the east, taking her husband with them.

We finished our tea in silence. Tatyana returned to the present. "Tell me, why are you working on this now?" she asked.

I explained that there had been a resurgence of coverage of World War II in recent years, and there might be renewed interest in the upcoming anniversary of "Operation Barbarossa," the name Hitler had given to his opening campaign against the USSR.

"Interest. From whom?"

"Well, me, for one." I leaned on flattery to deflect her question. "You've always been a writer, but this piece was published in the Slovo. The kids should have this, too. Someday, they may want to know about that time in your life," I added. I was holding off for now in saying anything more. She had been hesitant from the beginning to work on this project, I didn't understand why. I knew there were several other articles that I had seen in a scrapbook of newspaper clippings.

"Well, all right then." She sighed, glancing skeptically at me before rising to rinse the teacups in the sink. "Let's leave it at this for now."

3

1937—The Elections

As the summer months of 2001 went by, I slowly gained my mother's confidence, and she entrusted me with the translation of more of her writing. I sent her the draft of a second article, which I knew she wouldn't be able to resist leafing through, if only to see how I rendered the vernacular of her compatriots into English.

On my next trip down, as we sat reviewing a passage about her teaching days in Soviet Russia, I reminded her that she had encouraged me as a child to become an interpreter, a profession she deemed less worthy than becoming a doctor, since it lacked the humanitarian aspect, but a possible fallback, nonetheless. Armed with a portable Royal typewriter, a gift from her on my eighth birthday, I had proudly presented her with my translation of a favorite Russian children's book, Korney Chukovsky's, *Dr. Aibolit* ("Dr. Ouchithurts"), which I later recognized as a loose adaption of Hugh Lofting's *Dr. Doolittle*, a 1920 English classic.

Chukovsky, a beloved Soviet children's author akin to our own Dr. Seuss in his rhymes, had given printed credit to Lofting in some of his editions for the adaption, but it had escaped ours, leaving me to believe that the stories about the good Russian doctor were original. With no Dr. Doolittle in our home library, I had unknowingly translated back into English Lofting's tales of the kind, bearded doctor who could understand and speak in animals' languages, traveled to far off destinations, and—in the Russian version—did battle with the famous pirate Barmaley. Although some of the stories were derivative, Chukovsky had added some original poetry which all good Russian children, me included, committed to memory by the age of six:

Добрый доктор Айболит!
Он под деревом сидит.
Приходи к нему лечиться
И корова, и волчица,
И жучок, и червячок,
И медведица!

Всех излечит, исцелит
Добрый доктор Айболит!

Oh kind Dr. Aibolit!
Under a tree he finds his seat.
Come to him to be healed,
Cow and she-wolf,
Mayfly and worm,
And she-bear, too!
Cures all, will he
Kind Dr. Aibolit!

Chukovsky had retained Doolittle's name for his monkey, "Chee-chee," but the Russian doctor's dog was "Ava," not "Jip," the owl was "Hoo-hoo," not "Too-Too." The two-headed llama, Pushmi-Pullyu, had made a full circle to Russian, then back to the English in my translation. I had meticulously pecked out the manuscript on my typewriter.

Seeking to further impress my mother, I had written to Bennett Cerf, then publisher at Random House, whom I had identified from his appearances on the 1950s TV game show *What's My Line,* to pitch this new children's book. He failed to reply. By the time Rex Harrison personified Dr. Doolittle in the 1967 movie version, I had finally made the connection although I may have suspected that it was Chukovsky who had been plagiarized.

For this visit, I had chosen to work on an article that made Mama more at ease with my contemporary translation efforts. We had worked our way back in time to 1937, when in another article she had described her added responsibilities as a schoolteacher during the historic electoral period in the Soviet Union, the first national elections in the 20-year rule of the Communist Party since the revolution of 1917. The entire nation was to go to the polls and vote for their representatives on the Supreme Council of the Soviet Union. The Council would consist of two chambers—the Council of the Union, with 569 members, chosen by electoral divisions based on one deputy to every 300,000 of population, and the Council of Nationalities, with 574 representatives. All citizens over the age of 18, without distinction of race, nationality, creed, or sex, had the right to vote.

"The Elections"

A teacher occupied a special position in the Soviet system I grew up in. He or she was the "cultural vanguard of society." Owing to this definition, the breadth of involvement required of teachers went considerably beyond schoolwork, extending into any facet of life that could be considered "cultural activities" by the government. That could include issuing passports, taking a census, LIKBEZ, an acronym for the "liquidation of illiteracy in the elderly," and even helping the collective farm workers bring in the harvest.

The teacher had to be right there, even though none of the activities, except for teaching literacy, were within the realm of the profession. These additional cultural responsibilities were given to teachers above and beyond their usual teaching duties, which included daily checking of pupils' notebooks, working with parents, catching up slower pupils after school hours, and sitting through endless pedagogical conferences. These added responsibilities, of course, earned no extra pay.

On December 12, 1937, the entire Soviet Union was to have open elections to the two houses of government: the Soviet of the Nationalities and the Soviet of the Union. These were to be the first elections in twenty years of Soviet rule. Up until then, no one had voted our leaders in, they had "elected" themselves, that is, they appointed, installed, and then removed their own. So, the people placed considerable hope on these elections, thinking that at least some representatives from their ranks would get a seat in government.

With the elections three or four months away, local planning by the Party hierarchy had already begun. In meetings at factories, schools and universities, the pomp was building. One of the goals was to show countries in the West, as well as our own people, just how truly democratic our system was. New slogans were posted, portraits were hung of the candidates, supposedly chosen at workers' meetings, but in reality, hand-picked by the Party. Loudspeakers blared from dawn to dusk about how the upcoming election would be the most democratic in the world, how we were the most fortunate citizens on earth, on and on.

At the time, I was a young schoolteacher, having just completed a two-year pedagogical program. I was drafted to be the "campaign propagandist" for our precinct. The town that we lived in was divided into four precincts, with twenty to thirty houses in each. The first step was to determine which of these homes had a room large enough to accommodate a meeting of our citizen-voters, most of them housewives, since their husbands attended campaign rallies at their respective places of work.

Right away, I was faced with my first obstacle—no one had a large enough room for that many people, and certainly no one had an adequate number of chairs, but most of all, not a single housewife wanted to allow thirty pairs of dirty boots to trample mud into her home. It was autumn, cold and rainy. Finally, one housewife agreed, and a home was selected under the condition that everyone brought their own stools to sit on. A meeting day was set.

When the day came, I made my first presentation. I described in simple words how the elections were going to take place and where, and the rules of voting. I stressed that we were being given the important job of casting our votes for the most democratic government in the world and how our form of government was superlative to the capitalist system of exploitation, etc.

After the presentation, a question-and-answer period was allowed. A hand shot up: "Is it true that on 'lection day they gonna be distributin' cotton cloth?"

"That's irrelevant, comrade." I responded. "Any other questions?"

"Who'll we be choosing among? How many *candidati* are there gonna be?" Good question? What was I supposed to answer, when in fact there was only going to be one and "electing" him from a field of others was not what the Party had in mind. I couldn't dismiss this as an irrelevant question; indeed it addressed the issue. I had to wiggle out of that one with all sorts of lies and half-truths about how the Party had already chosen its best man, it alone knew its loyal members better than we did.

"Next question, comrades?"

I thought we'd had enough of questions, when one of the women decided to get clever. "After the elections are over, are the Communisti still gonna to be in charge?" She dared me to answer that one, I could tell. Once again, as the campaign promoter, I had to weave in and out of hypocritical words and falsehoods, piling one on top of another.

By our next meeting, the name of our candidate had been announced and now the assignment was to put him in the best possible light. I had to present him as a trusted son of the people. He was a loyal friend to all, honest and true, a party member above reproach. The flattering and fawning words poured from my mouth, describing a person about whom I knew absolutely nothing. The candidate, by the way, was Latvian, which created a slight problem since Latvia was on the other side of the border in the enemy camp, so to speak. But the orders from above directed me to turn this into a positive feature about him and even to point it out as an extraordinary trait.

"This man would leave his own country in the name of Communism and its ideals, to serve the power of the proletariat. This man has understood and come to value the advantages of our free system and has devoted his life to it. Regardless of his nationality, he deserves our votes." And so on.

I took great pains to lay all this out, showing a photograph of our candidate to the assemblage. At least he was rather good looking, well-groomed, with an intelligent face. The women liked that. It didn't convince my audience, however. One Ukrainian woman spoke up. "Why are you braggin' about him, sister? How do you know he's a good man? Have you ever spoken with'm?"

That was more than a fair question. Not only had I never spoken to him, but I had never seen or heard of him before the day he was presented to me for my "campaign." I had no answer for the inquiring elector. At the third meeting, a face-to-face meeting with the candidate had been promised, but unfortunately didn't take place. I had to make excuses for him, he was too busy, he had had a change of plans—it all sounded so fake!

Finally, Election Day arrived. The local party bosses came the day before, on Saturday. Our community clubhouse was turned into a makeshift election headquarters with the addition of curtained voting booths and ballot boxes, and a separate room available for babysitting the children of the electorate while they cast their paper votes. Again, it was the teachers who had to devote their only day off to keeping the children occupied with games and toys.

In the large hall of the clubhouse, normally used for movie screenings or amateur drama productions, everything was ready as if for a big celebration. A band had been brought in for entertainment and the benches removed for dancing. In another room was the main draw—the free buffet dinner. Tables were laden with an abundance of appetizers obtained for just this occasion, who knew from where? Election Day was really going to be a holiday!

The campaign workers were gathered into a special meeting and sternly instructed to bring out our voters as early as possible. The bosses insisted on having all the ballots in by ten o'clock in the morning so that they could be tallied and sent on to central headquarters. However, all the newspapers and radio announcements had informed the people that the voting precincts would be open from six o'clock in the morning up to midnight. It was useless trying to point this out to the local bosses. The toadying in front of the Party big wigs had reached such a level that it would only have resulted in unpleasantness or a reprimand.

We had to be at the booths by six o'clock to check off our voters as they arrived. If anyone was late, we had to go to their homes and hurry them up. This led to some curious scenes: some voters, watching the approaching organizer through their windows simply refused to open their doors, or shouted back through them that there was still plenty of time left before evening to cast their ballots. Others cursed us, with reason, and one even let his dog off his chain as I came toward his house, making it impossible for me to reach the door. I had to stand on the picket fence and knock on his window to get his attention. I'm glad none of my students saw their teacher clambering over the fences.

It took all our persuading, from "Please go, do your civic duty and you will be free for the rest of the day," to "Do me a favor, I have to do this, I answer for the voters in my precinct." By ten or eleven o'clock, we had completed our rounds and could have finally relaxed, except then we were sent on to other, delinquent precincts to beg, threaten, cajole, and somehow get those electors to their polls.

The voting process itself was boring. Suffice it to say that both the most ardent Party members, showing off their unquestioning devotion to their candidate, and the timid and unaffiliated, fearful of being noticed, dropped their slips into the ballot boxes without entering the curtained booth. There was no point, anyway, since the pencil tips in almost all of them had been broken off early in the day, to prevent write-ins.

All the votes had long been cast; the festivities continued in the clubhouse late into the night. Children had finished reciting commemorative poems for the occasion, but the band played on for dancing and singing. The buffet had been consumed to the very last crumb by noon. The last voters finally straggled home, leaving the janitors to clean-up by morning.

The surprise finale came several weeks later. We learned that my praiseworthy "candidate," the one whose virtues I had extolled so highly, and for whom I had been willing, it seemed, to vouch with my life, that same one turned out to be a spy in the service of capitalist Latvia!

There it was. And that same woman who had questioned the honor of our candidate from the beginning, met me in the street one day and whispered, "And you, sister, you campaigned for him, you said all those good things about him, and he be an enemy of the people! Shame on you!"

I crept away. Heavy was the mantle of the teacher in our country that year.

Wondering what had prompted her to write that piece, I asked my mother what had made her recall that autumn, several years before the onset of World War II and Hitler's armies? Was it the political events in America in the 1960s, which I knew had polarized my parents in their own voting choices? They'd had staunch Republican sympathies since becoming American citizens in 1958, with the right to vote for any candidate. Along with most Russian émigrés, they despised FDR for what they saw as his capitulation to Stalin at the 1944 Yalta Conference, attributing to him the forced repatriation of refugees and POWs back to the USSR.

They had assumed that stronger anti-communist sentiments prevailed with Eisenhower and then Nixon, but the escalation of the Vietnam War had made my mother fearful that my brother would be drafted, and she turned pacifist, even against my father's insistence that the Domino Theory would bring Southeast Asia under Communist rule. For once I had sided with my mother, which she probably hadn't even noticed back then.

"It's what I remembered of being a teacher back then, it wasn't easy," she responded. She had attended a two-year pedagogical institute, which trained her to teach German as a foreign language, a skill which was to figure heavily in the years ahead.

4

Ukraine 1941—The Bookkeeper's Story

The trips to Sea Cliff became more frequent, and as I had hoped, the translation project drew my mother and me closer, after years of distance. I learned more about her life in Soviet Russia, but many questions remained. In the years leading up to the war, my mother taught in the city of Stalino, later renamed Donetsk, Ukraine, in the south of Russia. As the summer of 1941 approached, she had an encounter with an enigmatic character in her school, Pyotr Ivanovich, and his wife, Dusya, which she described in her article.

The Bookkeeper

He turned up at our school unexpectedly a few months before the war began—a quiet, calm man with a simple Russian face, a pleasant smile. He endeared himself quickly to the teachers and the schoolchildren, always finding something friendly to say to each one. Pyotr Ivanovich was our new bookkeeper. His wife was also given a job, scrubbing the classrooms daily, but somehow, she didn't seem to fit the role. There was something about Dusya, as she wanted to be called, that hinted of a different, more cultured upbringing.

They both seemed eager to help in whatever way they could, if not in a deed, then with a kind word. The two of them, Pyotr Ivanovich and his Dusya, managed to bring a coziness into our world, a warmth that was so lacking during those bleak years.

Before the arrival of Pyotr Ivanovich, we had had the pleasure of dealing with another bookkeeper. He was more the moody type and "disappeared" one day, as did many others during that period. If you'd ask him for a ten-ruble advance on your next paycheck (we never had enough money to last from one to the next), he wouldn't even discuss it, acting as if you had approached him to commit a crime, or had asked him for it personally. He would just slam shut the cash box right in front of your nose and walk away, without saying a word. Other times, he would give you an excuse about not having the money or requiring the signature of the principal. Once in a great while if he felt so inclined, he would push a twenty-ruble note over the table, but not without a curled lip of disdain.

Pyotr Ivanovich was not like that at all. He never refused anyone, and there were never any questions asked, or signatures required. For some reason he trusted us. Sometimes he kidded us about our spendthrift ways, but he always responded favorably to our requests for a little cash.

We became good friends with him and Dusya, who was an excellent seamstress and was happy to mend our scant dresses, even adding to our wardrobes when cloth was available. She refused our offers of a few rubles in payment, although we knew that she did all the work by hand and could have used the extra money. We had to resort to leaving her little gifts since she did not want to be paid for her efforts.

It seemed to us that for Pyotr Ivanovich and Dusya there was no greater joy than to be of help to us—even if only with some trifle, a few heartfelt words of advice or encouragement, or a small treat for a child. In a word, they were "not of this world," at least not of the world we lived in at the time.

When we met in the teachers' room, we often wondered aloud about these two people. I tried to ask Pyotr Ivanovich in passing where they had come from and where was their home. But each time, he skirted the question with a courteous but vague answer.

It would be several months of working side by side with Pyotr Ivanovich and many hours in the company of his wife before I learned their true identities.

The war started at the beginning of the summer of 1941 with Hitler's invasion from the West, and I lost touch with the other teachers over the summer break. I didn't see much of Pyotr Ivanovich or Dusya, either. When we returned for the start of the new school year on September 1, we were in for a big change. Our school, a new two-story building, had been commandeered by the Soviet armed forces as a field hospital for the growing number of wounded brought from the front lines. It was both horrible and strange to walk by and hear the cries of the soldiers, instead of the sound of children's voices.

The entire school population was squeezed into the old building that used to be the only school for the whole district. We had to work two shifts, but there were hardly any complaints. After all, the war was already requiring other sacrifices of us; shift work was the least burdensome.

Pyotr Ivanovich's office was moved into a space no bigger than a closet. Dusya was now given an added responsibility: she had to keep track of the clock and pull on the school bell rope to ring for class changes and recesses, since the old building had no buzzer system. She seemed to enjoy this job—it brought her closer to the children—and when the bell had sounded, she would bustle the children along with "Come now, enough play, time to get back to your studies." The children liked her. She always had a few sweets in her apron pocket for them; we noticed that she was particularly generous to the younger boys.

Pyotr Ivanovich and Dusya seemed to almost welcome the hardships of our new circumstances. "This is nothing, my friends," he would say, "just think of how much worse it is for the poor boys over there," pointing to the other school building turned hospital. "The real suffering, it's over there. As for us, we just must work a little harder, it's not that bad now, is it?"

But we didn't get to work for very long, only September and half of October. After that, the Soviets started to withdraw from the advancing German forces. Without a single shot fired, with no resistance whatsoever, they began their withdrawal through neighboring towns and villages, leaving our fate to the German army. They withdrew well ahead of the advancing Germans, who had trouble taking up the void left behind the retreat.

For seven days, it was a no man's land: no militia, no party committees, no city soviets, no one. We were left on our own. Whatever supplies the Soviets hadn't managed to take with them or destroy ended up disappearing instantly. The more enterprising thieves used carts and wagons to haul away rice, grain, and other foodstuffs, figuring that the Germans would probably show little generosity to the local populace. Surprisingly, there were no major outbreaks of crime, although the absence of authority would have allowed personal scores to be settled without reprisal. Everyone banded together to await the next cataclysm of our lives—the assault of the Germans.

The German army arrived in the second half of October 1941. We stayed indoors as much as possible, not knowing what to expect. They imposed a curfew immediately, and I had little chance to find out which of my teacher colleagues had remained in town, and which had fled with the Soviets.

As the weeks went by, the German authorities established their own rules. Everything they could get their hands on they shipped back to the German Fatherland. The townspeople were forced to labor at fixing the railroad tracks that had been damaged by the retreating army. The Germans reopened the coal shafts, and soon trainloads of coal mined by the forced labor of the locals were moving westward.

The Germans allowed us to reopen the school and we were instructed to assemble at the old school building. German staff headquarters were now in the new building, which had previously served as the hospital.

As I walked into the school on the opening day, the first person to greet me was none other than our kindly Pyotr Ivanovich. He was happy to see me; his face lit up with a big smile. "And you too have stayed behind! You're still with us then!" he cried out, embracing me. "I'm so happy!" he continued. "Somehow, I knew that you wouldn't leave with the Reds. Whatever happens now, it can't be any worse than it was." How sadly mistaken he was. For many people, very many, it became much worse.

I was a bit surprised; I wasn't used to this kind of candor. I started to wonder again as to his true identity. He and Dusya had chosen to remain under the occupation when it would have been easy for them to pack up and leave. And here he was, ecstatic that others had stayed behind also.

Day by day, we settled into the old routine of teaching. But life was becoming more difficult—we were paid next to nothing, and the price of a cup of flour soared to over thirty rubles at the open-air market. At least we could count on the bread rations at the school. Then the Germans decided to close all but the four primary grades, leaving many of us with no means of support at all. They reasoned that it was enough for Russian children to get only the barest essentials of reading, writing and arithmetic and no more, since German children would grow up to be the ruling class. The teachers were dismissed and left unemployed. One day I found myself at the home of Pyotr Ivanovich and Dusya. We got to talking and slowly at first, then more boldly, he related his story.

"To be honest with you at long last, I am a parish priest. I had a small congregation for many years south of Vinnitsa, not far from the border. How wonderful, how sweet it was for me to serve God. How joyful to my ears was the music of the church bells. How blessed were the hours passed in my service to the Lord. It was enough to know that I could serve Him by helping others in need. And to know that my family and I were loved in return. Our life was filled with the light of happiness that comes from helping our brothers and sisters. You cannot imagine how magnificent were the celebrations of the holy weeks of Christmas and Easter for us, how beautiful the services on those days."

He glowed, and then his face darkened. "And it was all destroyed by the Bolsheviks, all to dust. One day, suddenly, they descended on us. There was a battle for the church itself. The faithful tried to defend the church from the godless, but like the Tatars of the Middle Ages, they scaled the church walls and attacked the parishioners inside with sticks, beating them mercilessly.

"I could only stand by the side, with my wife, praying on our knees. In horror we watched as the *komsomol* youths toppled the high cross from our cupola, how it dangled for a few moments, swaying from their blows, and then crashed heavily to the ground. What I would have given to run and pick it up, to save it as some small piece of what had been my life, my very existence, everything for which I had lived.

"But what could we do, the two of us, against these marauders? They took the church by force. The wounded were taken away and never seen again. I was advised to go into hiding and we were given shelter by a kindly couple—we hid in their basement. They brought us food and water, and tried to help in what way they could, but we couldn't stay there long, we were a danger to them if found.

"But, as it is said, the world is not without good people. There were many that knew us, who had prayed with us in our church. Somehow, they managed to get us new identities, new documents. My real name is neither Pyotr, nor Ivanovich," he said, smiling at his deception.

"With these new papers, we were able to get away. We wandered, homeless, sleeping in train stations—Dusya, myself and our little son. Our little one, so beloved by us, was such a sweet child. We lost him during those years of homelessness. He fell ill from exposure to the cold and hunger, we couldn't protect him well enough, and he died in our arms one night. We had to bury him by the side of the road, somewhere between Vinnitsa and here."

Pyotr Ivanovich sat quietly, not speaking for a few minutes.

"Yes, we've lived through a lot," he began again. "We had to go begging at times, but we were never turned away, not even during the most difficult winters. May God bless and keep all our benefactors, I love them all. I love the goodness in our people. If you only knew how many kind souls we met along our way, how many times we were warmed at the hearth of a simple home."

Pyotr Ivanovich refused to speak more of those who had so brutally destroyed his church and plunged him into poverty and destitution. He spoke only of those who had helped them to survive, who in the darkest hour had stretched out a hand to him. "We managed to make it this far thanks to some good folks; first one job, then another, and now finally here."

I sat staring at Pyotr Ivanovich, struck dumb by his story. My mind was reeling with the realization of who this man was, and why we had felt the closeness of his affection, his attention, and his interest in each one of us. So, this was why Dusya, our dearest Dusya, lavished her kindness on us, and especially on the littlest boys in school, in memory of her son.

I realized then that it was his love of their fellow man, his burning faith in God and belief in the abiding goodness of people that had saved and sustained Pyotr Ivanovich and Dusya on their difficult journey. How few among us there were of their selflessness, their charity.

There were rumors later that Pyotr Ivanovich and Dusya were hiding a young Jewish girl in their apartment from the Germans for several months, sharing their scant bread rations with her. I had no way of verifying this, but I didn't doubt for an instant that it could have been so. It would have been like them to do that.

I don't know what became of them afterwards. As the tide of the war changed and the Soviets began to regain lost ground, the Germans retreated westward, and we were scattered to the wind.

I looked over at my mother—the story had touched both of us deeply. I re-read the last paragraph, word for word. This time I ventured a question: "What did you mean by 'we were scattered to the wind?'"

"Exactly that. After Stalingrad, the Germans began to retreat from the East. They had been stopped by the Soviet Army and started to pull back. It was in the fall of 1943."

"Had you heard anything from Shura?" I asked. I held back from adding the words, "your husband" to his name. I couldn't picture her married to anyone but my father, whom she met later.

She gave a low sigh. "Well, there was no way for us to receive any news from outside the occupation. All radios were confiscated. We hardly even knew where the front was from day to day."

The Soviet Army casualties at Stalingrad exceeded one million men, and she had assumed the worst case had befallen him, although not knowing his fate, she had kept a slim hope alive. I asked what seemed an innocent enough question. "Why didn't you wait for his return?"

She took her time to answer. "We had to evacuate with the German army, we moved west with them."

I knew I had touched a nerve by the way she got up from the table and moved to the other side of the room, busying herself, rearranging some papers. Of course, I had always known that my mother emigrated from Russia to Germany by the end of the war, where she met my father, where my brother Eugene was born. She had also brought out with her Natasha and Yura, her two children by Shura, and her own mother, Nadezhda. But what I wanted to know was why. "Why couldn't you stay?"

There was another long pause before she answered. "I am not going to go into that with you." She stared directly at me "And you are not going to write about it."

I was taken aback by her finality. I could see that she had become more agitated than I had expected from this turn of questions; her mouth had worked itself into a straight line. Then she turned away. What Mama said next took me by surprise; she never quoted Scripture. And she didn't address me, but the sky. *"Авва, Отче, Чашу эту мимо пронеси."* ("Abba, Father, may this cup be carried past me.")

With that plea, our work was over for the day. On my way home, I kept rolling those words around in my head, they sounded oddly familiar, but not from the Gospel reading of Jesus in the Garden of Gethsemane, which my mother would surely not have committed to memory. When I returned home, I hunted up my yellowed, college paperback of Boris Pasternak's novel, *Dr. Zhivago*, and, on a hunch, flipped to the back of the book to the cycle of poems he attributes to his protagonist, the poet-doctor, Yuri Zhivago. In its time, the novel was banned in Russia, but I recalled it occupied a prominent place on my mother's bookshelf. The first poem, "Hamlet," included these lines (translated here by A.Z. Foreman):

Hamlet

The tumult fades. Out of the wings, I enter
Leaning the doorway to the stage,
I seek to catch within a distant echo
A sense of what shall happen in my age.

On me a thousand theater glasses focus.
My figure in the dark of night they spy.
If it be in Thy power, Abba Father,
Pray let this cup of torment pass me by.

I love Thy high unwavering conception,
And have agreed to play this part as tasked,
But now another drama is unfolding.
So, just this once, release me from the cast.

But every act has been already written.
And journey's end irrevocably marked.
I am alone. All things fall Pharisaic.
A mortal life is no walk in the park.

Our project had stopped abruptly, but the questions remained. What secrets had my mother been hiding, for all those years? And what could possibly cause her such worry in revealing them now? I wondered but hesitated to go back to that time with her, she was so visibly set against revisiting it.

5

December 2002— Finding the Journal

What makes us think about the meaning of the past—not the history we learn in school—but our personal past? Some philosophers say it is a question of elapsed time: We must be old enough, we need to have at least twenty adult years to make some sense of our own history, and only then, that of others. But when do we stop to reflect on our experiences when we are busy rushing away from our past and into the future? Often it is the onset of a serious, perhaps life-threatening illness, or a divorce, that is enough to pause the business of living and open us to reflection. On occasion, it is a chance stumbling upon something long forgotten.

One morning, a year later, I went up to the garage attic of my Connecticut home to bring down the boxes of Christmas tree ornaments. I surveyed the clutter of more than twenty years' accumulation, mentally dating the junk: remnants of computers that read eight-inch floppy disks from college days; dust-laden printed circuit boards from our first company.

In the corner stood the original two green suitcases which had been all our earthly possessions when Alex and I had moved to New England as newlyweds. On a whim, I stepped over to the smaller one and flipped open the hinges. Inside among musty clothes and old Navy uniforms was a collection of letters and papers I hadn't looked at in years. I stuffed them into a larger manila envelope I found at the bottom of the suitcase and, throwing it all in with the Christmas ornaments, descended the steep stairs.

Later that evening, I fetched the envelope and sat down to look at its contents. The manila envelope was filled with thin, almost onionskin pages, densely typed, from top to bottom. I could tell even without picking up the first one that they had come from the Cyrillic typewriter that my mother had used to correspond with her pen pals. The typed "e's" and "o's" were unevenly dark; a sign that the mechanically striking keys needed cleaning. I fanned the manuscript; it looked to be close to 100 pages, single-spaced, neatly stacked, and paginated at the top. Some of it appeared to be fading, difficult to read, but the topmost pages were clear and dark. The first page was headed in capital letters (in Russian): **Remembrances of the Major Highlights of My Life.** Intrigued, I continued. The opening paragraph was sub-headed:

Introduction

> It is now 1978. I will be 62 years old the 2nd of November of this year. I am determined, while I still have the energy and the will, to write down what I remember in my life, although there is little hope that my children, to say nothing of my grandchildren, will ever have an interest in reading these words.
>
> Today, young people are not interested in the backgrounds of their ancestors, their great-grandfathers, grandfathers, and care little about the history of even their own fathers and mothers. But perhaps someday in the future, affected by the passing of time, or life's changes (for everything in life is subject to change), there will awaken in them a desire to understand where they came from and what happened in this world before their arrival in it.
>
> If they never develop this desire, so be it. All the words written here will perish forever; no one will have thought to preserve them. It will matter none to me by then. I will have left this world, I hope for another where, in the words of our Saintly Fathers, "there is neither sadness nor sighs, only everlasting life." I will have no thought to what has become of these notes and albums left after me when I am gone.

My mother's opening paragraph carried me back in time to that year in my own life, one that I remembered well. Nik, our son, had just been born in the summer of 1978 while his father was away for several months, serving on a U.S. Navy submarine, based out of Groton. All alone with our first child, I had asked my mother to come up from Long Island and help me for a few weeks; I was struggling to manage on my own in our unfinished house in Moodus, Connecticut.

She agreed, and when I met her at the train station in Old Saybrook, she was holding the handle of a portable typewriter in one hand and pulling her wheeled suitcase with the other. On the ride home, we talked about how long she could remain. As a young mother for the first time, I was still trying to adjust to sleepless nights and unstructured days, so I was happy to hear that despite her disdain for the rural setting, she would stay for as long as I needed her.

Settling in, she set up her room in the roughed-in second floor of our house, amid open beams and stapled insulation. Her bed was flanked by a makeshift writing table and chair. By turns she and I would change or bathe little Nik, or just sit and rock him into a blissful sleep, his belly filled with milk.

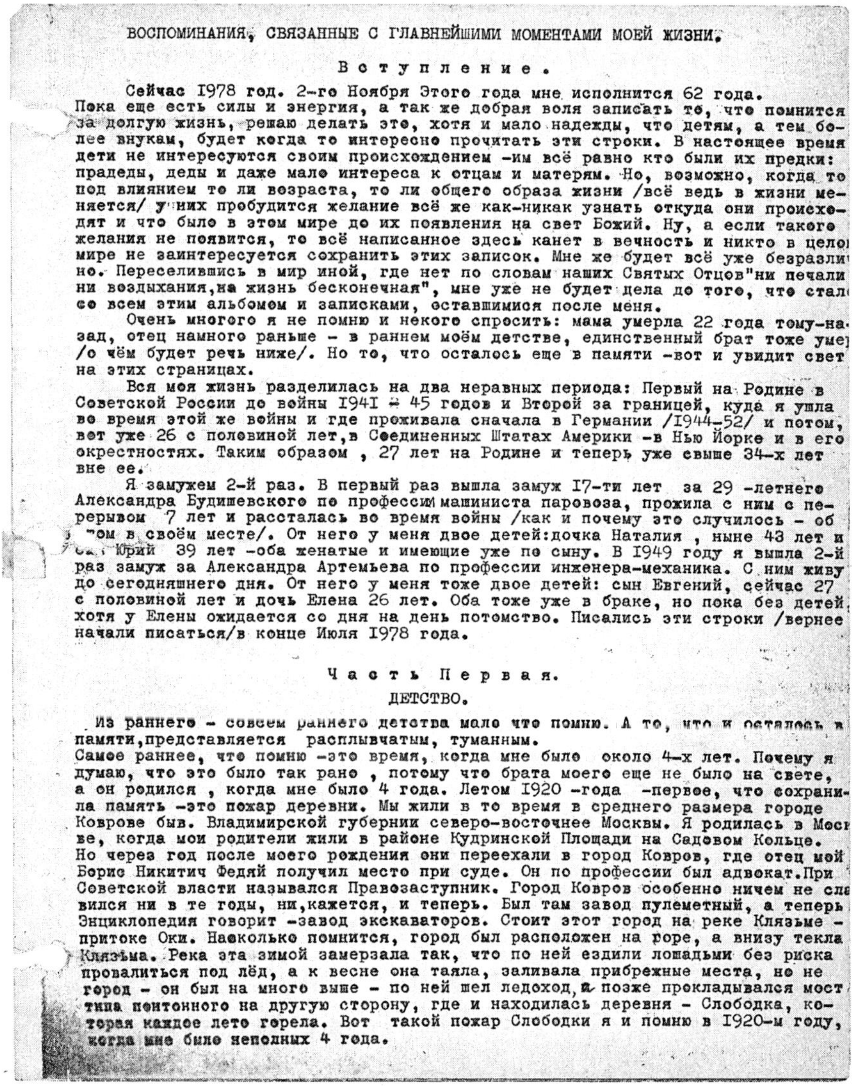

ВОСПОМИНАНИЯ, СВЯЗАННЫЕ С ГЛАВНЕЙШИМИ МОМЕНТАМИ МОЕЙ ЖИЗНИ.

В с т у п л е н и е .

Сейчас 1978 год. 2-го Ноября Этого года мне исполнится 62 года.
Пока еще есть силы и энергия, а так же добрая воля записать то, что помнится
за долгую жизнь, решаю делать это, хотя и мало надежды, что детям, а тем бо-
лее внукам, будет когда то интересно прочитать эти строки. В настоящее время
дети не интересуются своим происхождением -им всё равно кто были их предки:
прадеды, деды и даже мало интереса к отцам и матерям. Но, возможно, когда то
под влиянием то ли возраста, то ли общего образа жизни /всё ведь в жизни ме-
няется/ у них пробудится желание всё же как-никак узнать откуда они происхо-
дят и что было в этом мире до их появления на свет Божий. Ну, а если такого
желания не появится, то всё написанное здесь канет в вечность и никто в цело
мире не заинтересуется сохранить этих записок. Мне же будет всё уже безразли
но. Переселившись в мир иной, где нет по словам наших Святых Отцов"ни печали
ни воздыхания,на жизнь бесконечная", мне уже не будет дела до того, что стал
со всем этим альбомом и записками, оставшимися после меня.

Очень многого я не помню и некого спросить: мама умерла 22 года тому-на
зад, отец намного раньше - в раннем моём детстве, единственный брат тоже уме
/о чём будет речь ниже/. Но то, что осталось еще в памяти -вот и увидит свет
на этих страницах.

Вся моя жизнь разделилась на два неравных периода: Первый на Родине в
Советской России до войны 1941 - 45 годов и Второй за границей, куда я ушла
во время этой же войны и где проживала сначала в Германии /1944-52/ и потом,
вот уже 26 с половиной лет,в Соединенных Штатах Америки -в Нью Йорке и в его
окрестностях. Таким образом , 27 лет на Родине и теперь уже свыше 34-х лет
вне ее.

Я замужем 2-й раз. В первый раз вышла замуж 17-ти лет за 29 -летнего
Александра Будишевского по профессии машиниста паровоза, прожила с ним с пе-
рерывом 7 лет и рассталась во время войны /как и почему это случилось - об
том в своём месте/. От него у меня двое детей:дочка Наталия , ныне 43 лет и
сын Юрий 39 лет -оба женатые и имеющие уже по сыну. В 1949 году я вышла 2-й
раз замуж за Александра Артемьева по профессии инженера-механика. С ним живу
до сегодняшнего дня. От него у меня тоже двое детей: сын Евгений, сейчас 27
с половиной лет и дочь Елена 26 лет. Оба тоже уже в браке, но пока без детей,
хотя у Елены ожидается со дня на день потомство. Писались эти строки /вернее
начали писаться/в конце Июля 1978 года.

Ч а с т ь П е р в а я.

ДЕТСТВО.

Из раннего - совсем раннего детства мало что помню. А то, что и осталось в
памяти,представляется расплывчатым, туманным.
Самое раннее, что помню -это время, когда мне было около 4-х лет. Почему я
думаю, что это было так рано , потому что брата моего еще не было на свете,
а он родился , когда мне было 4 года. Летом 1920 -года -первое, что сохрани-
ла память -это пожар деревни. Мы жили в то время в среднего размера городе
Коврове быв. Владимирской губернии северо-восточнее Москвы. Я родилась в Мос
ве, когда мои родители жили в районе Кудринской Площади на Садовом Кольце.
Но через год после моего рождения они переехали в город Ковров, где отец мой
Борис Никитич Федяй получил место при суде. Он по профессии был адвокат.При
Советской власти назывался Правозаступник. Город Ковров особенно ничем не сла
вился ни в те годы, ни,кажется, и теперь. Был там завод пулеметный, а теперь
Энциклопедия говорит -завод экскаваторов. Стоит этот город на реке Клязьме -
притоке Оки. Насколько помнится, город был расположен на горе, а внизу текла
Клязьма. Река эта зимой замерзала так, что по ней ездили лошадьми без риска
провалиться под лёд, а к весне она таяла, заливала прибрежные места, но не
город - он был на много выше - по ней шел ледоход, а позже прокладывался мост
типа понтонного на другую сторону, где и находилась деревня - Слободка, ко-
торая каждое лето горела. Вот такой пожар Слободки я и помню в 1920-м году,
когда мне было неполных 4 года.

The first page of the manuscript which looked to be close to 100 pages, single-spaced, neatly stacked, and paginated at the top. It was headed in capital letters (in Russian), "Remembrances of the Major Highlights of My Life." The Introduction was followed by the First Section, Childhood.

After dinner she would fix herself a cup of tea with a piece of bread, her "dessert," as she called it, and retire upstairs, typing late into the evening while Nik and I slept. I remembered hearing her two-fingered clacking on the manual typewriter, sometimes pausing for long periods in thought, then bursting into a lengthy paragraph. When I would ask her in the morning about her efforts, she passed it off as long overdue responses to friends. As it turns out, she wasn't writing letters; she was working on something else. It was this work I held in front of me now. I continued to read:

Part One: Childhood

I remember very little from my early childhood, and even that I recall dimly, as if peering into a mist. My earliest memories are from a period when I was not quite four years old. I know it was no later, because Fediay, my brother, had not yet been born. It must have been the summer of 1920.

My first memories are of the burning of the Slobodka village across the river from the city of Kovrov, northeast of Moscow. My parents had moved to Kovrov from Moscow, a year after I was born in 1916. By profession, my father was an attorney and had secured a position with the court in Kovrov as a "pravozastupnik," a defense attorney.

The city of Kovrov was not particularly renowned, neither then nor now, it seems. Kovrov is on the Klyasma River, a tributary of the Oka River. As I recall, the city sat on a hilltop, and the Klyasma ran below it. The river froze so thickly in the winter that horse drawn carriages could be driven on it without the risk of falling through the ice. In the spring the river thawed, flooding the banks but not the city which stood on higher ground. An icebreaker would come up the river and later a pontoon bridge would be laid across it for access to the other side and the village of Slobodka, which burned to the ground every year.

I remember it was a clear evening at the end of the summer of 1920. The shouts of "Slobodka is on fire!" announced what was apparently an annual event, much like summer fireworks.

Mama and I walked to the boulevard that was high up overlooking the river and watched with the assembled crowd as towering brush fires swept through the entire village in the distance. I remember her consternation that every year the village would burn, and every year its inhabitants would rebuild it in exactly the same spot, with no thought to moving it or otherwise preventing the next year's conflagration, as if resigned to the will of God.

I cannot recall whether my father was home on that summer evening or in prison. In the two years since Lenin's new regime had taken over the government in Russia, my father, Boris Nikitich Fediay, had become an "undesirable" citizen on at least two counts. The first strike against him was that he came from a lineage of nobility. His father had an estate in Poland and Boris was educated in the law, which made him unacceptable to the new order of the proletariat. Secondly and worse still, were his activities in the Socialist Revolutionary party, one of several political groups which had enjoyed a brief life during the Russian Revolution when the Provisional Government was in power from March to November 1917.

Mama had begged him to stay out of politics, but the draw of newly found democratic ideals was too strong, and Boris Nikitich was elected a delegate of the "SR" (Socialist Revolutionary) Party from Kovrov to Kerensky's Provisional Government in Moscow that spring. I remember my mother kept an oversized, framed photograph of the entire group, of the full assembly in the vast Hall of the Duma, Kerensky seated and my father and the other delegates standing, until it became dangerous to have such a photo in the house and she burned it.

Elections, conventions, all these were possible during the six months of the Provisional Government, and then, of course, were forbidden when Lenin set out to eradicate all opposition to the Soviets, or Bolsheviks, as they were then known. The single party system was instituted somewhat severely, shall we say. Members of political parties other than Lenin's were executed or imprisoned, as in the case of my father.

Because of his frequent imprisonment, my memories of my father are few, but vivid. He was held at Vladimir Prison, infamous for its brutal treatment of political prisoners then and for decades to come, but luckily close enough to allow my mother to visit him and bring him much needed supplies.

With no notice, he would suddenly be released, because at that time a lack of evidence was still enough to set a political prisoner free, if only until the next week when they came to search the house and take him away again.

I can recall one morning being awakened by voices in the next room, my mother speaking quietly with someone. I lift my head; a heavily bearded man approaches my crib and picks me up. I'm standing barefoot in my bed, he is hugging me close to him, and Mama is saying, "It's Papa, go ahead, kiss him," and I embrace this man, my father.

Boris Nikitich Fediay was married to Nadezhda Robertovna Brand with whom he had two children, Tatyana and Fedor. Boris Nikitich lived in Poland, Moscow and Kovrov, Russia, where he was active in the Socialist Revolutionary (SR) Party during the Alexander Kerensky period of the Provisional Government (March to October 1917) of the Russian Revolution. Because of his political activity, which was not approved by the Bolsheviks after November 1917, he was incarcerated in the infamous Vladimir Prison and died of typhus in 1922. Nadezhda gave birth to their first child, Tatyana, in Moscow in 1916, after which they moved to Kovrov.

My father adored me, his Tatyana. I sensed this even then in my child's heart, long before Mama would tell me it had been so, after he was gone. I was his beautiful little girl; blonde hair set off by eyes that were dark brown, like his. In the mornings, he would gather wild strawberries for my breakfast, or surprise me with the chocolate he knew I loved. He would take me everywhere he went; his walking cane on the right and my hand in his left as I skipped along, barely keeping up with his long strides.

I don't remember much more of my father directly; only what Mama told me about him later. She said he did have one weakness, and that was card gambling. Sometimes he would win, and then he would be ecstatic; more often he lost everything, leaving us almost destitute. Mama, who as the wife of a prominent public defender in the city's courts and expected to keep up appearances, was forced to wear torn shoes because she couldn't afford to have them repaired. I would have to go without milk sometimes.

But I don't want to dwell on this aspect of my father. I don't want to spoil my memories of this beautiful person, especially since I was not aware of this flaw, and I don't remember personally being the worse off for it. More than anything else, I remember his boundless affection and love for me. I want to retain this radiant vision of him in my memory.

Mama was madly in love with him. She had left her first husband for my father during Czarist times when it was almost impossible to get a divorce without taking all the blame and waiting for seven years to remarry. A woman who did this became a social outcast, much like Anna Karenina, and was shunned by society, surrounded in shame. Perhaps this was the reason that my parents left Moscow and moved to the smaller city of Kovrov. My mother took all of this in stride because she was so in love with him. Theirs was a common law union—in those days not accepted by many—and their marriage wasn't even registered anywhere, which made my birth technically out of wedlock. I was only able to get a legitimate birth certificate later, when the Soviets didn't care about such matters.

My father was an avid disciple of Count Leo Tolstoy. He had made several trips to visit Tolstoy at his estate home in Yasnaya Polyana before the writer's death in 1910, each time returning more persuaded by Tolstoy's rationalism and renunciation of church practices. Papa refused to be married in the Church when it was possible, after Mama's first husband had left for Paris, or for us to be baptized. On his deathbed, he exacted a promise from my mother to forego any last rites. But in her grief, her friends hastily arranged for the church services and a Christian burial.

Mama mentioned that afterwards, whenever she dreamed of him, my father always appeared angry at her for having allowed it. Her devotion to him made her a willing acolyte of his convictions. The steady anti-religious propaganda the Soviets rained on us for decades only served to distance us further from the church.

Late in 1922, my father contracted typhoid in prison and was released. Although he was extremely ill, he managed somehow to make it home, where he collapsed. I contracted typhoid from him and was semi-conscious in a fever for six weeks. He died while I was in a delirium.

By the time the crisis had passed in my illness, he was already gone. I remember waking up and asking Mama to hold up a mirror to my face, since I had run my hands over my head and felt only short hair in the place of my long, thick braid. Hopelessly tangled, it had been shorn as close as a boy's.

To my questions about Papa, she replied only that he was back in prison again, which seemed a plausible explanation except that she started to cry. I thought her tears strange since I knew she believed the house searches and the arrests would eventually come to an end. She told me the truth only after I had fully recovered.

The winter of 1922–23 was a bitter one. Our apartment had been subdivided so that we now shared it with several other families. We were hungry most of the time. When my father was alive, he used to barter clothes for flour and salt, but that was difficult for Mama with small children to tend.

By the summer of 1923, widowed at the age of 41 and left alone with two children, she decided to leave Kovrov and seek spiritual solace and shelter closer to her three sisters, who lived to the south, in Ukraine.

We visited Papa's grave at the cemetery in Kovrov several times that summer before we left. I could still probably find my way to

At the far right (circa 1923), Tatyana, seven years old, stands next to her mother, Nadezhda Fediay, and her seated brother, Fedor (Fediay, three years old). They were living in Yenakieevo, a suburb of Stalino, now Donetsk, in Ukraine, having traveled down from Kovrov, through Moscow, after the death of Tatyana's father/Nadezhda's husband, Boris N. Fediay, in 1922. (Others pictured are unidentified.)

the cross that marked his grave—it was on the left past the entrance behind the chapel, that is, if the hallowed ground withstood the later bulldozing of church cemeteries by the Bolsheviks.

We prepared to leave Kovrov and to journey to the Donbas Basin of Ukraine. Our suitcases were loaded onto a horse and carriage and Fediay and I were seated on top of them, swaying back and forth on our way to the train station.

I stopped reading there. I had read only three pages from the thick stack. I mentally calculated the number of years between what I had just read about my grandmother, my mother, and myself. Exactly eighty years had passed since that winter of 1922. I tried to imagine my mother as a child, bereft of a father who cherished and adored her for the few short years given to them, yet still embraced by his love and affection in her memory of him. I thought of my grandmother's plight—alone in the world with two small children to raise—grieving for her husband, yet still struggling to make her way to something better.

6

1956—Brooklyn

My earliest memories of my own mother, true memories unprompted by family album photographs or home movies, are of walking with Mama holding my hand along the streets of East New York, a neighborhood of Brooklyn. We walked everywhere then, or rode the subway, since an automobile was beyond my parents' means for the first few years in America. The urban community we lived in was one of multistoried apartment buildings, corner groceries, small city playgrounds, public schools, churches, all accessible on foot. Our walks took us to these destinations almost daily.

I remember the feeling of my mother's hand in mine, of having to stretch my arm upward to maintain her grasp. I felt secure tethered to her; nothing would happen to me as long as she was there. Even as that was a normal four-year old's reaction, it was exacerbated by the stories I overheard at home about *bombardirovki,* the World War II nightly bombings in Europe of civilian centers, the frantic dashes to shelters, often separating families in the rush.

This talk spawned in me a mortal fear of being away from my mother, even in daylight, long into my childhood. I thought that if I could only follow her closely, not necessarily holding onto her hand but keeping her within sight, then, if we perished from the bombs that were sure to fall here too, at least we would die together, and I wouldn't be left alone. I shadowed her from room to room sometimes.

Although we didn't have handwritten addresses pinned to us, my brother and I were instructed to head for Australia and find my uncle in the event that both our parents perished in a cataclysmic event. That reminder heightened my desire to hold onto at least my mother. So off on our rounds we would go—my brother Eugene, two years older, flanking her on the other side.

In those early years we spoke only Russian at home, none of us knowing any English. So, when Eugene started kindergarten at the local elementary school, he was terrified to be left in a classroom where children spoke a language totally incomprehensible to him. Mama and I would walk him the several city blocks to P.S.182, up the stairs and into his classroom. Then at the signal from his teacher, we would bolt for the exit door, my mother gripping my hand as we raced down the wide staircases, flying down the stone steps to get out of the school, his screams ringing in our ears.

Outside, she would stop to catch her breath, angry and upset that the teacher wouldn't allow us to stay with him through the morning. A schoolteacher herself, she knew that it would take a few weeks before a new child adjusted to joining a group, but her mother's heart sought some way to make it easier on my brother. This routine continued until he finally learned a few English words.

At the end of the school day, we would return for Eugene and continue our tour of the butcher, the grocer, the baker, with whom Mama could easily converse in German or Polish, Ukrainian or Russian. English was optional for many years, a condition both comforting and crippling for new arrivals. In my memory, the ethnicities of the shop owners were their names. We would stop at the baker, "the German," then continue to "the Polack," the butcher, and end the day at "the Ossetian's" for sweets and ribbons.

Throughout my entire Brooklyn childhood and for years later, I thought that "Ossetian" was the man's name, not his nationality. He was a towering, imposing man, with a horse-like head atop his aproned torso. I came to dread the "Ossetian's" huge, callused fingers as they reached down to pinch my cheek, a suffering rewarded by a chocolate-covered jelly ring. In all the grocery markets, it seemed normal that my mother could easily switch from language to language.

One such outing for the three of us stands out from the rest. It began as a subway ride on a stretch of the train that was elevated above the streets. My brother, six years old at the time, refused to sit quietly in the seat next to Mama and kept jumping up to look outside at the passing apartment buildings, shops and streets below. Sitting next to the sliding doors, he would pop out of his seat when the subway car would start to move, swing around the pole, watching through the windows.

At one stop of the subway, something made Eugene step across the threshold of the sliding doors as they opened at an unfamiliar station. Had something caught his eye on the subway platform, or had he finally summoned the courage to play chicken with the doors? A split second before Mama turned to put a stop to his antics, it was too late. The doors slid shut, leaving him standing alone on the elevated platform, Mama and me inside the subway car, pulling away. I can still see his face with that look of surprise, turned to terror.

God knows what must have gone through Mama's mind at that

moment, but her sense of order prevented her from rushing to pull the handle of the emergency brake. She and I rode anxiously to the next station, luckily only several city blocks away. It all happened so fast, I don't recall panic in her, only haste as we descended to the street level and started to race back in the direction of the previous subway stop, where we hoped that Eugene had had the sense to remain waiting for us.

We had walked only a block when we saw them in the distance: a little boy being led by the hand by a tall, thin man. As we rushed to them, we could see that my brother was crying, and that the smiling Black man gently leading him was trying to comfort him by pointing toward us, as if to say, "Don't worry, here they come, it's all right now, sonny." He approached Mama, gesturing back to the train station, trying hard to explain it all to Mama, which of course she didn't understand, other than his kindness.

"'Thank you, thank you," she kept saying to the man, over the wails of my brother, as I looked on. He waved us off, laughing, and went on his way, patting Eugene on the head. I remember the grip on my hand being tighter after that.

We would return daily to the fourth-floor walk-up on Vermont Street where our family enjoyed the spaciousness of a one-bedroom apartment, the rent of which had been discounted in exchange for providing the services of building superintendents, or "supers," as they were called. While Papa went off to work at the machine shop in the mornings (he gradually worked his way up to draftsman, designer and then engineer), it would fall to Mama to haul the building's trash cans out to the curbside on pick-up days, and when emptied, to roll them back into the alley.

We usually accompanied her, but when inclement weather kept us inside, Eugene and I would be left upstairs on our best behavior, giving us an uninterrupted ten minutes of dropping pencil erasers on the pedestrians below; later we would escalate to crayons. Sometimes his sibling rivalry would flare, and Mama would return to find me wailing, imprisoned beneath the heavy brown cover he had lifted off the portable sewing machine and placed on top of me. But mostly I would be unharmed, at least in the physical sense of the word, oblivious to what must have been the adult trauma of starting over again in a strange new world.

Especially for my mother, the early years of immigrant life in America were a difficult adjustment, even after seven post–War II years of being a "displaced person" in Germany. In Europe, she still felt somehow closer to the *Rodina* she had left behind, even as she knew there would never be a return to her motherland. There was a term for it in the émigré community, *toska po rodine*, "nostalgia for the homeland," so there must have been other sufferers of this malady, but Russians seemed to have it the worst.

Growing up, I could never understand how one could be homesick for the brutal life in Soviet Russia, for its famines and repression, the bleakness and hopelessness which characterized the first twenty-seven years of my mother's life, but the sadness was something that I recognized in her, even as a child.

By late afternoon, before my father's arrival home from work, the errands of the day would be done and she would be in the kitchen, while Eugene and I played in the bedroom. Then she would walk into the living room, and I would hear the click, the dropping of the first in a stack of three of four LP records on to the turntable, and the rhythmic scratching that signaled the opening measures of the war ballad or love song. The melodies were familiar by now, some catchy and waltzing to the accompaniment of an accordion, the refrain easily repeated. Mama knew them all and would sing along, sometimes adding a little two step as she circled the kitchen.

The trouble would start when the next selection was a slower, lilting tune crooned by a baritone in that half-spoken, half-sung style meant to evoke nostalgia and longing. Unfortunately, in her it did. Whether the lyrics described the undying love of a soldier for his faraway girl, or in the case of patriotic ballads, mourned the separation from home, the effect on Mama was the same. She would start bravely, her voice sounding like the same one that we were accustomed to hearing at bedtime, yet now focused somewhere else, not on us. She would get through to almost mid-song, and then her voice would break. Still, she kept on. To see Mama crying was disconcerting to us, and we stayed away, making believe we didn't hear, leaving her to herself. But on a particularly gloomy afternoon, when she had sat down and hidden her face in her hands for what seemed an unbearable amount of time, I came up to her and lay my head on her lap, looking up questioningly.

"*Chto takoye?*" ("What's the matter?") I asked in a tentative, imitative way.

"*Nichevo.*" ("Nothing, never mind.") She sighed. "You wouldn't understand," she added, wiping her eyes, and getting up.

She was right, I couldn't understand it then. As a child, I could only think that it was some physical injury, some hurt that must have brought her to this unaccustomed state, and that she would be soothed by a kiss. It would take a long time before I would learn the nature of her grief, and years before I fully understood her pain.

Russian émigrés, at least those whom I knew had arrived in America after the Second World War, were different from the legions of other ethnic immigrants who landed on these shores. In elementary school, my German and Italian school mates were exhorted by their parents to learn English with, "You're in America now, speak English! Be proud to be an

American!" in the hopes that they would more quickly blend into the melting pot and avoid the stigma of foreignness.

For Russians, however, the word "assimilation" was an unspeakable curse. The dreaded *assimilyatsia* was to be avoided at all costs, with every effort made to guard against the normal process of adaptation. We were not to become American. We were to remain Russian. This directive was manifested through seeking out other Russian children to play with, reading Russian children's books, sending us to Russian Sunday school, and of course, strict orders to speak only Russian at home, on pain of death or possibly no TV. Answering back in English to a question posed by a parent in Russian, who might, above all else, struggle to understand the response, was a major offense and garnered a swift reprimand or even a nasty cuff on the nape, the humiliating *podzatil'nik*.

With some émigrés, this attitude stemmed from the belief that one day, when the hated Communist rule of Mother Russia was toppled, we would all return to the motherland. This was a false hope that even my parents understood to be unrealistic. More likely, it was the comfort they took from preserving some familiarity, customs, and above all, pride in their heritage. Not much else is left to the stateless and displaced when there is no possibility of return.

Later, when we had moved out of multilingual Brooklyn to Long Island, we found ourselves in more of an English-language environment. Stanley Goodwin, the principal of our Sea Cliff Elementary School, agreed to my mother's request for a parent conference about the name-calling that a small band of us were subjected to in the school yard during the Cuban Missile Crisis in October of 1962. "Dirty Russians! Commie Reds!" were just some of the names flung at us.

Back home, when I complained of being called "Khrushchev's daughter!" by a fifth grader from a politically astute family, it was the last straw. My mother walked the three blocks to the elementary school with resolve. "But we are *White* Russians," she explained to Mr. Goodwin.

"Yes, I understand," he answered slowly. "But these are difficult times. Have you thought about speaking English at home?" he asked, hoping she might see the value of becoming more integrated into the community. Anathema! She stood up and marched out of his office.

Epithets unbecoming to an educator were attached to Principal Goodwin's name thereafter at our house. He clearly had not understood my Russophile mother or her pedagogical support for a bilingual education.

To further her goals, my mother engaged a private tutor, Madame Nadezhda Ilyinishnaya Epanchin, to expand our Russian reading and writing skills, as did several other parents of Russian kids in the community. Weekly attendance at her home-based lessons was mandatory, but also fun. A group of eight of us, seated around Madame Epanchin's big table, were assigned roles in Nikolai Gogol's 19th Century play, *Marriage*, giggling as we read aloud the parts. A large woman, with eyeglasses suspended on a chain, Nadezhda Ilyinishnaya would look over the top of the frames to admonish Grisha or Vitaly to please return to the reading of the play without further mischief.

There was safety in numbers, and as a group in school, we fended off the bullying which ended in peaceful coexistence on the playground. After all, if there was anywhere that Russians could bring up their children in peace, with not one but two churches, a deli, annual bazaars selling nested dolls and meat-filled *piroshki*, it was Sea Cliff.

7

Summer 1923—Leaving Kovrov for Ukraine

I toiled on with translations, without my mother's knowledge, not knowing what the outcome would be and not wanting to further draw her attention to my work. With only a Russian-English dictionary to aid my efforts, the progress was slow.

It seemed strange that she hadn't recalled the typed autobiography when we had worked together, but it might have been long forgotten by her over more than two decades, or maybe she had wanted it to remain buried, along with her secrets. I continued to read passages from her memoir, which both fascinated and educated me on what had been her life in Soviet Russia before the war.

Tatyana, her mother, and brother left Kovrov in the summer of 1923. The journey south to Ukraine passed through Moscow, and my mother's first impressions of the capitol city in which she had been born in 1916 were captured from a child's view:

> We arrived in Moscow by train to spend the night with my Uncle Pavel, Mama's brother. He was an attorney who lived with his wife and daughter in an apartment which had been subdivided, now shared with other families. We went to the Pushkin Monument, on Tverskiy Boulevard, which I circled, amazed at how immense the bronze poet was, how huge was the hat that Pushkin held behind his back. The pedestal of the statue was surrounded by cast iron garlands of laurel leaves, attached to short granite posts, which I sat on and tried to use as a swing, but the chain pressed into my flesh.
>
> My mother bought me a doll in Moscow, which I kept with me on our train travel to our destination, Yenakievo, northeast of Donetsk, then called Stalino, where Mama's sisters lived. We arrived at 23 Leningradskaya Ulitsa, the home of one of her sisters,

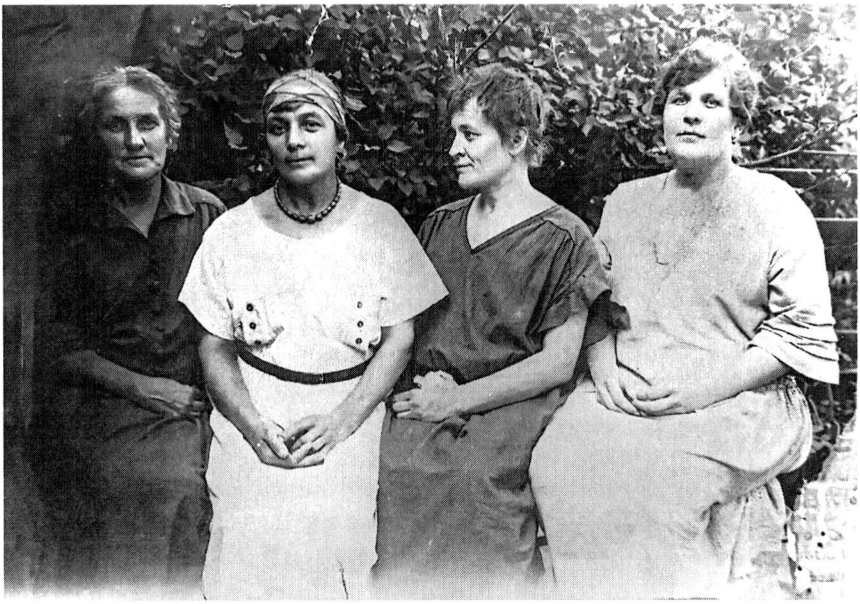

Nadezhda Robertovna Brand and her sisters. Left to right: Olga, Ekaterina, Maria and Nadezhda. Maria, known as Marusia, had her right eye removed as a child due to severe headaches. It was replaced by a glass eye. Because of this perceived "deformity," she never married and spent her life dedicated to family, in particular her widowed sister Nadezhda and Nadezhda's children, Tatyana and Fediay. Maria died of starvation in 1943 during the Nazi occupation.

Ekaterina, known as Katia, and later that day, Mama was met by her other two sisters, Maria, nicknamed Marusia, and Olya, in a happy, but tearful reunion.

The three sisters decided that we would live with Aunt Olya in her government apartment, with her husband, Evgraf, a surly, quiet man who was none too happy with his new tenants, especially my brother, Fediay, who as a toddler got into everything and cried when he didn't get his way, disturbing the peace and quiet of my uncle's life.

Aunt Marusia was a big help to us, and she played a major role in our lives for years to come. She was an old maid; her life having taken a tragic turn at the young age of three years. In the late 1800s, my mother's family, Robert Arnoldovich Brand, his son and four daughters, one of them, my mother, Nadezhda, lived on the estate of Count Dolgorukov, where my grandfather managed the estate for the Count. One day, little Marusia was afflicted with a headache, and the pain reached such levels that she cried incessantly day in and day out.

My grandfather took her to a specialist in Kharkov, which was the capitol of Ukraine from 1919 until 1934 when it was moved to Kiev. The doctor said that there was no other course of treatment but to remove her healthy right eye. The pain subsided immediately, but Marusia was left for the rest of her life with an artificial eye. She was deeply affected by this and never married, because Russian men did not see the need to wed a "defective" woman, when there were plenty of healthy ones to choose from.

Aside from the false eye, Marusia was an interesting, educated woman, well-read in Russian and French, and by nature a kind and giving person. In the years that followed, it was she who took us under her wing and cared for us no less than our own Mama. I am getting ahead of myself, but her terrible fate during the German occupation of our city, on my watch, burdened my soul then, and hangs heavy on me even to this day.

The first years after the Revolution in Russia were hard not only because there were famines, hunger, and arrests of those who had come under the suspicion of the Bolsheviks, but because most of the industrial base had been destroyed and it was difficult, if not impossible, to find a job. This was especially true for someone like my mother, who had no profession. We lived at one aunt's, helped by the others, but that was not a long-term solution and we had to find another way to get by.

Mama wrote to her mother-in-law, Vera Pavlovna Fediay-Silvestrova, who lived not far from Poltava, in a village called Horol. This was the heart of Ukraine. Vera Pavlovna felt sorry for us, her grandchildren, and in her letters invited my mother to come and live with her, away from the factories, in a good climate. She insisted that living with her would be wonderful for us children, who would thrive on the fresh air and healthy country food.

For a long time, my mother hesitated, knowing that her mother-in-law had a reputation for her stern temper and had not gotten along with her other daughters-in-law, neither Vera, the wife of Aleksei, nor Maria, the wife of Vladimir. But Mama still hoped that the mother of her beloved late husband couldn't be as bad as all that. She needed to bring up her children and it was not possible to rely indefinitely on the support of her sisters, so she decided on the move to her mother-in-law. Once again, our trunks were loaded on the horse-drawn cab, and we were underway. (For some reason I remember all those drays from my childhood.)

Our grandmother, Vera Pavlovna, then around sixty years old, was a squat woman full of energy. She lived in a three-room railroad apartment; all the rooms were connected to each other in a line. That wasn't very convenient for us, because as it turns out, Babushka Vera was a country midwife, earning her living providing illegal abortions. They were illegal because she had no medical training and took no responsibility for the health outcomes of her patients, who were mostly farm women, arriving on foot or in a wagon at her door. In exchange for her services, they brought flour, chickens, eggs, meat, and other produce, which is how the promised "healthy country food" appeared for us.

She conducted her clinical procedures in the middle room of the apartment, which required that Fediay and I had to stay with our mother for the duration in the last room, with no exit other than the window, through which my mother would pass us to play outside as best we could, while she remained inside.

As expected, it was hard for my mother to get along with Babushka Vera, although as children, we didn't see any problems. She constantly watched Mama to make sure she didn't find herself a suitor, or had too fine a time with other people, not that there were many opportunities for entertainment. There were some distant relatives of my father living in the same town, cousins twice or even three-times removed. One of them was even named Fediay—Uncle Vladimir—who was subsequently sought for trumped-up charges by the GPU (State Political Directorate) and I was brought in for questioning about him, but that was much later, as I will write here.

I recall him to be an impressive man, with a mustache, in hunter's garb and a feathered hat, a rifle on his arm. He had a hunting dog. I remember him in detail because he brought a great sorrow to my brother Fediay and me. We had a dog, *Zhul'ka,* a backyard mutt whom we loved and played with in the yard. But Babushka Vera was against keeping her and made us give her up to the peasants who came into town. We were saddened by that, and I can still remember taking her by cart to the edge of town, tearfully bidding her farewell, and then walking home.

But *Zhul'ka* found her way back to our house, trailing a piece of frayed rope. What joy! Such a display of canine loyalty earned her yet greater love from us, and Babushka Vera even showed us some mercy in letting her stay.

But then a new misfortune befell us—our puppy was bitten by a rabid dog. We had to either take her to Poltava for shots or put her down. Uncle Vladimir stepped in to end this tragic episode with his rifle. Fediay was especially heartbroken, although the truth was hidden from him, and he was told that she had been taken to Poltava. Later, he forgot about her.

By the age of 8 years, I loved books and was already a good reader. Babushka Vera had a huge trunk of books, most of which were for an older age, including an illustrated book about beekeeping, a thick volume of the writings of Sir Walter Scott, and many others. There were some children's books, too. I would take these and climb up into the branches of a tall pear tree which grew in the middle of the yard to escape from Fediay. Sitting on a limb, leaning my back against the tree trunk, I would read for hours.

I had to stop reading there and reflect on the scene she painted for me: my mother up a tree, looking down on her toddler brother with both scorn and teasing, and then returning to a passage from Walter Scott's novel, *Ivanhoe*:

"Fight on, brave knights! Man dies, but glory lives!
Fight on; death is better than defeat!
Fight on, brave knights! For bright eyes behold your deeds!"

The romanticism of a bygone era would have appealed to her. I could see the seeds of her adult reading habits being sown in the roots of that pear tree, but it was hard to imagine her scrambling nimbly upwards, a feat she would probably later deny as unladylike, along with playing sports of any kind. That was for boys!

I realized that I had not once, in my entire life, seen my mother in a pair of pants; she was always in dresses or skirts. That day, too, no doubt, she was in a summer frock, her bare legs dangling from her high perch, a ribbon in her hair. She was never able to ride a bicycle because of a problem with balance, so she said, but perhaps it was unbefitting of a damsel in distress, awaiting her knight in armor. Yet as she grew older, there was no one to come riding in to save her, but herself.

I read on to learn that the disagreements between my grandmother and her mother-in-law became untenable and once again, they had to move. Vera Pavlovna, who did not approve of this decision, could not be expected to pay for their return passage as she had for the incoming travel. My grandmother struggled to find something of value to sell. Her one possession, a sewing machine, was sold for forty-eight rubles, a sale that was regretted much later when Aunt Marusia needed it for her seamstress work, which helped to keep them alive through the years of the famine. The money bought the train tickets to leave Vera Pavlovna and return to her sisters in Yenakiev, passing through Poltava again. This time they settled with Aunt Katia, and her daughter's family.

My mother recalls the death of Vladimir Lenin, on January 21, 1924:

Suddenly, the sirens in all the city's factories started blaring loudly, non-stop, in an alarming, long, single blast. People poured into the streets, not knowing what was happening, and rumors spread the news that Lenin had died in Moscow. For me, at the time, these were meaningless words, I had no idea who he was, and no one had taken it upon themselves to enlighten me. Later I learned all too well who this Lenin was, thanks to whom my father had been imprisoned and died.

8

September 1925—School Days

At age nine, late even by Soviet standards of starting school at seven years of age, my mother was finally enrolled in *Semiletka No. 2* (Seven Year School No. 2), entering the second grade. Because she had been home-schooled, she was already a good reader and writer, and became an excellent student.

There must have been a big emphasis on proper penmanship, because all through my life I marveled at my mother's flawlessly penned cursive letters, perfectly aligned, each letter always well formed, not leaning left or right. Compared to my scrawl, her handwriting was calligraphy; the capital "T" of Tatyana was a work of graphic art. Even the shortest note, or a shopping list left on the kitchen table was not just easily readable, but exactly conforming to cursive standards. Years of practice as a teacher must have honed those skills on the blackboard and on student papers. She writes of her first experiences in second grade:

> I had already learned how to read and write; I would have been bored in first grade. I knew addition and subtraction from my mother, so when I started second grade, I learned the multiplication and division tables, not easily at first, but then I mastered them. I had a good teacher, Nadezhda Gladush, whom I liked a lot, and my schooling went well.
>
> It was a long walk to school, which was on the outskirts of the city, and I had to walk the length of the Leningradskaya Ulitsa, then turn right to the Tenth Line and proceed its full stretch, and then cross an enormous football field, and there, diagonally, was *Semiletka No. 2.* But I made some friends, girls who lived in my direction: Sarah Berdisheva, a wonderful Jewish girl, who lived on a street parallel to us, and Tonya Karnaukhova, who lived further away, and who had to pass my house on the way to school. Tonya was a good pupil and she and I always competed for top grades.
>
> Tonya introduced me to two of her friends, sisters, and they

were my first initiation to the subject of sex, since they had an older sister who was married and lived with them. They would observe and report on certain things and she didn't hesitate to share her impressions of married life with us.

By fifth grade, I started to receive instruction from several teachers, which was part of the three-subject system at the time: language, which included reading, writing and grammar; arithmetic, and *complex*. What was *complex*? It was a random assortment of topics. Here were social studies, which included civics, current events, the story of the Communist Party and Comrades Vladimir Lenin, Trotsky and others, as well as the study of nature, plants, animals, biology and a smattering of chemistry and physics. I am not sure how a teacher created a lesson plan in this hodgepodge, and which subjects were presented.

Only later at the Teachers Technical Institute did I learn more about the history of pedagogy. As a student, I recall that one day we went out to catch butterflies, on another we practiced pencil drawing of blast furnaces, and then on other days we were presented with lectures on the Revolution, the "Damnable Tsarism," and the uselessness of religion, which received a heavy emphasis. That was all called *complex*.

And then a new method of learning was introduced to us: group work and group responsibility, no doubt meant to prepare us to be good members and "work in the collective," a tenet of Communist ideology. Divided into groups of five or six pupils, we designated a leader who answered for the group. We were assigned homework, which had to be completed as a group, requiring us to meet at each other's houses to work on it together. The teacher would call on a member of the group to report for the rest, and a grade would be earned for all, depending upon one student's preparedness. One for all and all for one.

Often whoever knew the lesson best would get up to present without any objection from the teacher. The rest of us, with no knowledge of the subject matter, would receive a good grade. It's not hard to guess that we all played off that and assigned lessons to members of the group, not burdening ourselves with unnecessary learning. Our group met in the apartment of young Fira Kudasheva, whose family had a large flat by the then standards, and her parents usually disappeared somewhere during our meetings, so activities that had little to do with schoolwork prevailed.

It was in our group that I first met Yasha Aronov. Daily, we would meet in our group for lessons. We fell in love and started "dating." I use the term loosely because I was only 14 years old, and I had no idea of what it meant to be in love. But we started meeting at other times as well. He played the violin beautifully and earned some money by providing the musical accompaniment to movies—which were silent at the time—joining up with a pianist. Thanks to him, I gained entry to the movie theatre since Yasha brought me in to the shows when he played.

After the cinema, we would go strolling through the gardens across from where I lived, deserted in the evenings, and sit on the park benches, kissing and enjoying the open air. In school, the students had noticed our attachment and started teasing me with "Madame Aronov," but I didn't pay any attention to it. Our love blossomed.

This teenage affection went on for quite a while and, I should add, it was to the detriment of my studies—I went from being at the head of the class to bringing up the rear. I finished school with only

Tatyana (left), age 14, in 1930, and her friend and schoolmate, Valya Golovkin, with whom she later studied at the Pedagogical Teachers Institute.

satisfactory grades. Mama, of course, was very unhappy with this situation, knowing that I was smart enough to be an outstanding student, and the more so because I was in love with a boy who didn't have much to recommend himself to her, neither good looks nor good standing.

My first love ended completely unexpectedly. On one of the evenings that Yasha and I spent on our park bench, we got up to walk over to the gate at my house, where we typically did not linger because my mother would come out and shoo us apart with her broom, sending me to bed. As we approached the gate and started our goodbyes, I involuntarily put my hand into his pocket, and felt a condom! My God! I felt the heat rise up to my face, I didn't know what to do or say, I was dumbstruck.

When I came to myself, I screamed at him, "What are you doing with this in your pocket?"

"So, what of it? Just in case."

"In case of what?"

But he didn't answer me, shrugging.

"Get away from me, I never want to see you again!" I yelled, shutting the gate behind me. Our love evaporated into the ether, just like that.

After that, in school I didn't pay any attention to him, passing by him as if he were an empty space. Soon it was the end of the year and graduation, and we parted like ships in the sea. Nowhere, and never again did I come across my first love.

And so, I finished the *Semiletka* when I was only 15 years old, in the spring of 1931. What would come next? My life's dream was to become a doctor, not for all the reasons that medical students here want it now—a good income—but because I have always believed, and still do, that the medical profession is a prestigious occupation in which a doctor must have a unique, incomparable sense of responsibility for the lives entrusted to him or her, and be willing to be rewarded mostly by the satisfaction of having saved a dying person.

I wasn't at all put off by the possibility of having to be sent to distant rural areas, likely to have to make middle-of-the-night visits in the cold to aid the sick in their poor huts, *izbas*. On the contrary, this evoked in me a sense of purpose, regardless of the hardships. But unfortunately, I wasn't able to realize this dream.

In Yenakiev, not only was there no Medical Institute, but there wasn't even a Technical Institute for Health, from which I could then continue to a medical institute. The nearest one was 60 kilometers away, in Stalino, now Donetsk, which was not that far, but my mother couldn't afford that for me, however minimal the expenses.

There were only three choices in Yenakievo: A Technical Institute for Construction, one for Chemistry, and a Pedagogical Technical Institute, with a department for the study of Foreign Languages. Not strong in chemistry, and not interested in construction, I decided to enter the Teachers Institute with the intent to study the German language.

Looking ahead, that decision ended up being a fateful one, since the knowledge of German saved myself and my family more than once and made life more tolerable on many occasions. Without it, we probably would have perished in the fog of war.

9

September 5, 1931—Death of Fediay

The Bolshevik Revolution and the ensuing Civil War in the Soviet Union had damaged the economy and measures had to be taken to restore at least food production for the population and light industry through capitalist incentives. During the years 1921 to 1924, Lenin put in place in the USSR what was called the New Economic Policy, or *NEP*, for short.

Tatyana's mother, Nadezhda, my grandmother, was able to find a job as a registration clerk in a medical clinic, earning a salary of 32 rubles a month. This allowed her to move into an apartment with Aunt Marusia, the spinster sister, on Mezhevaya Ulitsa, No. 73 in Yenakiev. A normal life seemed to return.

After the death of Lenin in 1924, however, when Joseph Stalin came to power, the *NEP* was reversed and the "collectivization" of agriculture began in earnest, with the forced relocation of the peasantry into *kolkhosy,* collective farms, taking away their incentives to grow and harvest their own lands.

The richer peasants, who owned land, were called *kulaks,* and were considered enemies of the state by Stalin. They resisted the collectivization and Stalin mounted a campaign of dekulakization, *raskulachivanie,* characterized by repression, arrests, deportations, and executions between 1929 and 1933, which led to mass starvation and the deaths of an estimated 11 million peasants. Massive food shortages resulted, both artificially created by Stalin to punish the peasants and through the drop in productivity. The famine reached the cities as well. My mother writes of herself and her brother, Fediay:

> Before I started the Pedagogical Technical Institute, not more than a week before I entered, an event took place in my family which left an indelible mark on me, my aunt, but most of all, on my mother. Now, 48 years after this tragedy, I still cannot remember it without sorrow overwhelming my soul.

I need to start with the fact that both my brother and I were neglected and unsupervised, almost like homeless children. We had no father and my mother had to work to provide at least some kind of life for us. Food was scarce because at that time in Russia there was what was called the "artificial hunger," the result of "Widespread Collectivization and Liquidation of the Kulaks as a Class," as Stalin had ordered. I will not explain here what that consisted of because much has been written in books and articles, both factual and literary.

The famine affected children as it did everyone at the time—we were in a state of perpetual hunger. The meager rations, for which we went to the *narpit,* a government cafeteria (abbreviated for *Narodnoye Pitanye*, i.e., People's Nutrition) to collect and bring home, did not even begin to satisfy our stomach's hunger pangs. The meals we received were calorically deficient, providing nothing to our growing bodies. For years we did not even see sugar, or any kinds of oils or fats. We subsisted on the scant rations and dinners taken from the *narpit.*

At night, before going to sleep, Fediay would beg my mother: "Please, go and search in all the kitchen cabinets, in the corners, maybe there is a misplaced piece of crust there, it doesn't matter if it is dry and stale. Please go look."

But there wasn't a crust, not even a crumb of bread anywhere in the house. My brother and I looked like starved children in India or Biafra.

May the powers of the Soviet Union be thrice damned for the hunger, poverty, and homelessness that was the lot of its children! The posters of that era should have read:

MAY COMRADE STALIN BE ETERNALLY DAMNED
FOR OUR HUNGRY, NEGLECTED CHILDHOOD

instead of the noble, fawning words about our happy childhoods.

Fediay spent his days hungry, shoeless, in just a shabby shirt and pants, which were hardly held up on his thin frame. He had a friend, Borka Shkrabo, one of the sons of a poor, even poorer than us, family of a widow. She herself was just a skeleton, skin stretched tightly over her tiny frame, yet she still kept a job. Her middle son, Shurka, went to school with me, and we got together as a class and bought him a pair of shoes for the winter, otherwise he wouldn't have been allowed to attend. I should add that my brother and I were allowed to wear shoes only from September 1, when school started, to June when it ended, to preserve them for as long as possible. So, for Shurka, without even a single pair, this was the abject poverty in which he lived.

At center, Tatyana's brother Fedor ("Fediay"), with his "band of brothers" who ran together as children in Yenakievo in the late 1920s and early 1930 before his death in 1931. In 1938, Borya Shkrabo, second from left, would admit to witnessing the accident that took the life of his best friend. (Others pictured are unidentified.)

Borka and his brothers lived lives of neglect, just as Fediay and I did. But as a girl, and older than them, I found ways to spend time with my girlfriends and not loiter in the streets or entertain myself by sliding down the wet chutes of factory waste disposals. Fediay and Borka did just that, splashing down the gutters of warm water combined with the harsh chemicals. As a result of this child's play, Fediay developed sores on his body, which Mama was able to heal with great difficulty. But the toxic slide was not enough for the boys, and they sought out other adventures, like clinging to the freight cars as they were shunted back and forth at the railroad depot. And so, on one unfortunate day, they set off for the rail yard.

What exactly happened is not known. In all likelihood, Fediay, while jumping up on the edge of a moving freight car, was knocked off while passing a pole and fell. He was pulled under the wheels of the railcar. He may have been knocked unconscious when he hit his head on the pole, but witnesses later reported that they saw him sitting up against a pole that he had crawled to, swatting away flies with his one remaining arm, unless it had been only an involuntary movement. The rest of him was in … pieces.

Borka, who was there and saw everything, admitted nothing to us. (Only after several years, when I was already married and he came to visit us, did he confess to being there the whole time.) We were at home and knew nothing of Fediay's whereabouts. Evening fell, and he hadn't returned. Mama started to worry and sent me over to Borka's house to find him and ask if he knew where Fediay might be. Borka was home but told me that he hadn't seen Fediay all day, and that he didn't know where he was.

Then Mama sent me to the police station to find out if there had been any incidents in which Fediay might have been involved, but they told me that nothing had been reported which would have included an 11-year-old boy.

The evening passed, the night arrived, with still no sign of Fediay.

Later that night, my Aunt Marusia went again to the police station, and they told her that a boy fitting Fediay's description had been crushed under a train. His body was in the morgue.

She returned home with this news, unsure of how to tell my mother. But one look at her and my mother knew that something fateful and irreparable had happened. When she understood the horror of it, her face changed perceptibly, immediately. If a person can become older in the space of a few minutes, that was what happened to her, she aged decades in place.

It was one of the worst nights of my life. I didn't recognize my mother in the morning—before me was an old woman, a *starushka*. Her hair had turned gray during the night, her face had become lined with deep wrinkles, she was shrunken. From that day forward, she stopped looking after herself.

There was still a tiny hope—what if it wasn't Fediay, what if it wasn't him, there in the morgue? There are miracles in this world, after all. But that hope was not to be realized. Arriving at the morgue, my aunt Katia went inside. When she came out to us, we could tell by her face that it was Fediay. Aunt Katia begged my mother and me not to go in to see him and to this day, we don't know what his body looked like, or more so, what the pieces of him looked like. They nailed his coffin shut right there, and we prepared to take him to the cemetery.

There was no funeral. The churches had been shuttered or bulldozed; the parish priests sent to labor camps. My little brother, this wonderful boy, was neither baptized nor given his last rights in the Russian Orthodox tradition.

And so died my only brother, a clever boy, first in his class in school, my Fediay. We buried him in a graveyard outside the city. May he dwell in the Kingdom of Heaven in Eternal Peace. We walked there together, the coffin hoisted on a cart by a tearful Mikhail Ivanovich, a driver who lived with Aunt Katia, and who loved Fediay and used to give him rides up and down the street.

It was impossible in those days to mark the gravesite with a cross, but we remembered the place where we laid him to his rest, near the fencing of another mound. It was September 5, 1931. My brother missed his 11th birthday by six days.

To add to our family's tragedy, when we returned in the spring to visit his grave, we were shocked to find neither his grave nor the cemetery itself. The grounds of the cemetery had been leveled and apartment buildings were going up in their place. How the workers could dig up the earth for the building foundations is beyond understanding—with every shovel they must have come upon the remains of the dead. Why couldn't they have built further out and not touched the grave sites? It must have been the decisions made by some Communist Party City Committee members, and not the builders themselves. We didn't find my brother's grave, which only added to my mother's suffering.

Later, when the buildings had been completed and were occupied, the residents said that no one could live there. Supposedly, as soon as anyone moved in, strange sounds emanated from somewhere, ceaselessly. The occupants were kept up all night. Terrified, they would leave as soon as they could and not return. I don't know how true these stories were, I am relating what we heard from those we encountered while searching for Fediay's grave.

And so, we were three of us—Mama, Aunt Marusia, and me.

There is a German saying, *Das Leben geht weiter,* which is translated as "life goes on." Whatever tragedies befall us, in time we overcome them and move forward. Whether we want to or not, we become resigned to getting on with life, we immerse ourselves in the bustle of daily concerns. We continue to live, and so Mama lived on. But how, that's a different question. She often said that God was punishing her. Perhaps it was so.

10

Pedagogical Technical Institute—1931–1933

After the description of the tragic end to Fediay's life, I laid aside the translation of my mother's writing, and as with her, allowed my life to go on until I could move forward again, hopefully learning about happier times in her youth. She had seldom talked about her brother when I was a child, only to mention that she was certain that he would have grown up to be a talented, smart man had he survived his childhood and later, his certain conscription into the Soviet military during World War II.

In June 1941, the standing army and navy of the USSR was 4,900,000 men, but after Hitler's invasion, more than 29,000,000 men were drafted into service. A staggering 8,668,000 men died over the next four years, over half of which were young men under 30 years of age. The chances of 21-year-old Fediay's surviving as a soldier to the end of the war would have been slim. My mother carried a wallet-sized photograph of him, his laughing eyes peeking out from a cap, all the way to America.

Tatyana's only sibling, a brother Fedor (known as Fediay), at age 10. He died five days before his 11th birthday on September 5, 1931, in a tragic accident playing with his friends in the rail yards as trains were switched back and forth. The incident is described by Tatyana.

Less than a month after Fediay's death, a new chapter opened in my mother's life. In 1931, when she was 15, she had entered the local pedagogical technical institute to become a teacher of the German language. The institute, which had an intensive six days-a-week, seven-hour school day, compressed its three-year program into two years, due to the demand for teachers in the region.

As part of a total immersion in the language, the students studying German, including my mother, were sent to live with families in a German mining community for two months. They traveled there to study and observe the classroom instruction of children of the German workers; these classrooms served as a training site for the institute's language learners. (A decade later, when Hitler invaded Russia, many of these German miners, who had settled in Ukraine, were accused of spying, and were sent to prison and perished in the Gulag.)

The language immersion consisted of thirty students auditing the classes taught in German, which gave them little in the way of hands-on practice speaking or teaching but was combined with daily study of the language with their native German instructor. The institute students were supposed to speak exclusively German to accelerate their mastery, but as expected, they reverted to their native tongue when in each other's company.

For the first time, I read about a time when my mother was happy. Carefree, fed, not hungry. Those two months away in the coal mining community gave Tatyana some of her most pleasant memories of youth. As a bonus, while she was away, her mother was allowed to use her ration card for meals back home, which was a godsend. She wrote about her young life:

> The focus, of course, was the German language, which we studied intensively between 2 and 4 hours every day, in addition to our learning from the classroom. In the evenings, when our German instructor had gone to sleep, we kept ourselves amused as best we could. The young men came over from the adjoining barracks, our dormitories, and we created our own entertainment.
>
> I remember one night I wrapped myself in a bed sheet and performed a dance called the *Shamila*, singing the words:
>
> *"In the Caucasus there is a mountain,*
> *There is found Shamila dancing,*
> *Shamila prays to her God,*
> *Fighting for her freedom!"*
>
> Everyone picked up on the words and sang along with me. I raised my hands upwards and whirled faster and faster around the room.

More often, we experimented with spiritualism using a home-made Ouija board, in the form of small china plate inverted downward on the table. We would ask the spirits different questions, which frightened one of our younger girls, Dora Zeiger, especially when we threatened to call forth the ghost of her formidable grandmother! Dora rushed out of the room, clamping her hands over her ears, and dove under the covers of her bed, pulling the blankets over her head.

Outside the winds were blowing the snow with gale force. We kept our coal stove roaring, not only to warm us, but as the only source of light in the room, since the power station would shut down intermittently. We sat surrounding the stove's open door, the flames throwing a half light into the room, creating a mysterious, supernatural ambiance, and watched as the answers were channeled to us by the spirits of the Ouija board, remarkably logical in their content, it seemed to us. I don't think that one of us was directing the Ouija plate to the letters, because first of all, we didn't know the answers to our questions, and secondly, we were all dying of curiosity as to the ability of the Ouija to propel itself in response to us. We swore that none of us was moving it.

Regardless of the harshness of the times, I recall those days of my youth with pleasure. I had many good friends—Valya Golovkin, Nina Ishenko, Sarah Berdishev, the same girl who went to school with me for the first six years in Semiletka No. 2. My best, kindred-soul friend then was Olga Brilyeva. We were friends for a long time and visited each other's houses. I knew her mother, a worker in one of the factories, and her sister, Nusya, who married her childhood sweetheart, and whose fierce, mutual love had begun from the age of five, when they had sledded down hills together. She died delivering her first child.

Olga and I not only shared the students' bench at the Institute, but we also liked to stroll in the evenings together, hoping to attract the attention of young men. In the wintertime, we sidled back and forth in front of the movie house, called The Illusion, and in the summer, we visited the municipal gardens. There were two city parks in Yenakievo—the Alexandrovsky Garden, which was a distance from the city, and the Poitier Garden in the center. The latter was named for a Belgian who had created it in the days of old, when the Belgian-Russian Society built the Yenakievo Metallurgical Factory. It was renamed The Peoples Park by the Soviets, but no one called it anything but Poitier.

During summer evenings, Olga and I took ourselves to the parks, where the sounds of music would carry forth from a rotunda.

Tatyana, 16, and school friends, December 24, 1932. Right to left are Tatyana Fediay, Olga Brileva, Nadya Kudareva and Valya Golovkin. Tatyana's written comment on the reverse of the original photograph reads, "It would be better to jump off a 5th story building and die, than to appear as we do in this photograph, especially me!"

Walkways were lit and park benches were crowded with couples. We begged our mothers for the 25-kopek admission fee and headed for Poitier, walking side-by-side with our elbows interlocked, followed by a bevy of young men trying to catch our eye. Depending upon whether we thought them worthy, we would engage in conversation or slip away.

On one such outing, I met a young man, Grisha Bikovsky, who despite his working-class background, was well-mannered and bright. One of his legs was just a bit shorter than the other, which made him walk with a barely perceptible limp. He was polite and never allowed himself to act untowardly, not even seeking a kiss without my permission. Our courtship lasted all through my years at the Institute. I don't recall it exactly, but I think that we quarreled, and he disappeared from my life.

Much later, when I had completed the Technical Institute and had moved to Mushketovo for my first job and had married, Grisha suddenly came to my mother's apartment one day to ask about me. He had returned from Moscow, which explained his absence, where he was attending the Petrovsko-Razumovsky Academy, and had come home for the summer, hoping to find me. He was very disappointed to learn that I wasn't there, as my mother related to me, and she said that his face changed on finding out that I was married. She was sad for him, as she had liked him and thought him to be a well-spoken, widely read young man, with many interests.

"You should have married *him*!" she said to me then. But what of it? Fate had come between us, as it happens, and no one could have predicted that Grisha, the son of a workman, and who himself had toiled as a metalworker during our time together, would attend an academy in Moscow and become an educated, intelligent person.

Tatyana (right) and friend Valya Golovkin, May 26, 1933.

11

Fawn Lake, New York—2002

"I can't believe you wore flip flops to hike to Fawn Lake!" Natalia said over her shoulder as the three of us made our way up the muddy, abandoned Jeep trail in upstate New York.

"I *always* wore flip flops to Fawn Lake, even at night!" answered Olya, snickering.

"It's amazing that we found the trail, and that it's still here after what, forty years?" asked Natalia, walking up ahead by a few yards. "It doesn't look like it's been used much by anyone."

"We're almost there, I think," I said, looking up for the patches of blue where the trees would open over the lake, buttressing the high, cathedral sky.

The rugged, overgrown trail gave me hope that Fawn Lake had remained undefiled by developers. It was one of hundreds of small lakes dotting the map of New York's Adirondack State Park, left alone and wild, eclipsed by the larger, gentrified Saranac and Tupper Lake areas.

"I did the third day of the Three Feathers merit badge up here," I added, knowing that both Olya and Natalia would remember their own attempts at that outdoor challenge at St. George's Pathfinders, the Russian summer camp we attended every July in the early 1960s, along with several dozen other Russian émigré children and youths.

Three Feathers ("*Tri Pera*") was a coveted merit badge of the Russian scouting organization. The first of the three-day badge requirements prohibited any speaking for twenty-four hours; the second day, no food, and the third and final "feather" could be earned by not being seen, which meant hiking solo away from camp with a pup tent and provisions and spending the night alone in the woods.

Most of the chatty campers failed by the first morning. But my best friend, Tania, and I had managed to remain silent for day one, despite the expected provocations, then persisted through a hungry second day. For the third day's challenge, we had been allowed to go no further than Fawn Lake, a half mile from the girls' and boys' camps. The lake was sufficiently far for 24 hours of seclusion, but close enough for a 12-year-old to run back with the jitters or dead-of-night regrets.

I had pitched camp on one side of the mile-long pond, Tania on the other; our only communication was the sight of smoke drifting up from our fires. The night passed with only an occasional hoot from an owl. At dawn, we headed back, a hundred yards apart.

Triumphantly, we returned to girls' camp in time for the flag raising of the imperial Russian tricolors—white, blue, and red—accompanied by the singing of the Russian Empire's 1794 anthem, *Kol Slaven Nash (How Glorious Is Our God in Zion)*. At the camp gates, we were met with three cheers of "Ura!" by our fellow campers, relief on the faces of the counselors, and congratulations at breakfast for earning the highly respected Three Feathers badge that year.

"Well," Olya winked, her joking bringing me back to the present, "I didn't stay more than a few hours with that cute guy from Syracuse."

"And luckily you didn't get caught by Scoutmaster Boris Lusin!" chuckled Natalia, who had probably made more than one romantic excursion herself to Fawn Lake in the half dozen summers that we spent in that Adirondack idyll.

We walked on, skirting puddles, until we were out of the woods and stepped onto a thin strip of beach, barely ten feet wide. Fawn Lake was before us, quiet and serene. No cabins ringed the opposite shore. No sign that anything at all had changed in four decades, except perhaps the crowding in of the trees over the water's edge. The effect of time travel was breathtaking. We were speechless.

"Wow, it's exactly the same," said Natalia.

"Even the beach is as I remember it, maybe just a bit less wide," I murmured, looking up and down the sandy strip.

Otherwise, it seemed that Mother Nature alone had ruled this domain since our youth. It felt supernatural for everything to have remained exactly as we had left it, following a cycle of summers and winters at its own pace, on its own life's plan. Of course, this was true of other natural splendors, but here it was the total absence of anything human, not a trace of even a visitor, that awed me. It was other worldly, yet so completely of this natural world. I was glad we had come.

The three of us had taken a day off from the summer camp reunion an hour south, and fueled by nostalgia, had set off to see if we could still find the original site of the camp on Sacandaga Lake, about 50 miles north of Amsterdam, New York. After we asked some locals for directions, one of them recalled a "Russian Beach" which fit the description, and we followed the directions to the trail head.

Like me, Olya and Natalia had been shipped off in our teens for four weeks to a camp which was promoted as a "Scout Camp," in the tradition of England's Lord Baden-Powell, the founder of the scouting movement, but with a decidedly Russian bent. My mother, having conducted her own survey of summer camps, had insisted that both Eugene and I give it a full month, "in the lap of nature," as she described it to us.

Although we were required to tie our fair share of rope knots, hike, set up field kitchens and latrines, and build campfires, the organization's true mission was the preservation and promotion of Russian culture, history, and religion to its young campers, all of whom came from émigré families like our own. We were all expected to speak only Russian at camp, although our native English crept in automatically in private and in post-curfew conversations in our tents.

Now, of course, we were speaking English to each other, with a few Russian words slipped in.

"Do you remember that time we made *pilmeny* [dumplings] for the entire camp?" asked Natalia.

"We had more flour covering us than in the dough," I added, laughing, recalling the day-long feat of shaping and boiling thousands of meat-filled *pilmeny* for the hungry campers at supper, especially for the boys, whose teenaged appetites were insatiable in the outdoors, even for food.

Unlike American boys' and girls' scout camps, which were held on separate dates and locations, our camp was co-ed. This was intentional. The boys' camp was situated only 100 yards up the overgrown Jeep trail we had just followed, from the girls' camp. The proximity of the camp tents raised teen interest in attending the summer camp, as much as it fanned the hopes of parents who fervently prayed that good Russian boys would meet nice Russian girls and, in their union, hold back the tide of that dreaded assimilation for at least one more generation. In my case, it did. I met my future husband on the shores of Sacandaga Lake, downstream from Fawn Lake.

The St. George's Pathfinders summer camp was not unlike the Ukrainian or Polish-American, or even Jewish youth camps of the Catskills of that time, which gently promoted their ethnic cultures, but ours had a more vigorous political ideology running through it. Alongside the customary woodcraft, nature lore, and canoe building exercises, we grudgingly sat through lectures on topics such as: "*The Purpose of the Struggle Against Communism, How the Russian People Have Fought and Continue to Fight It.*"

These open-air tutorials were led by well-educated, graying adults, wearing the green cloth kerchief of Scout Instructors around their necks, who in their own wandering émigré lives continued to burn in fierce opposition to the Soviet regime. Twenty years had passed since the end of World War II, yet their anti-Communist fevers were as hot as ever, finding expression in the "training of the new cadres of leaders"—meaning us—who presumably would return to the Motherland.

Standing at attention on the parade grounds, lined up by height with the youngest of the girls, the seven-year-old *belochki* (squirrels), and boys, *volchata* (wolf cubs), flanked by the pubescent *razvedchiki* and *razvedchitsi* (boy scouts, girl scouts), we would be exhorted in Russian to: "BE PREPARED!"

This was the familiar Baden-Powell motto in scouting, encouraging readiness in mind and body to do your duty. To which we were required to respond in a loud unison: "ALWAYS PREPARED, FOR RUSSIA!" We would shout in our loudest voices into the surrounding forest canopy. Exactly what we were being prepared to do "for Russia" was unclear in the 1960s—the Soviet regime was firmly in control—but building our resolve was the first step.

Looking back at those summer sojourns in the beautiful Adirondack Mountains, I am struck by the ease with which we, a bunch of happy kids, accepted the anachronism of anti–Soviet propaganda. Except, of course, that we had been hearing it all our lives; this was just a continuation. We were comforted in our numbers, knowing that we shared the experience and here we were not shunned for it, the way we were back home. We made it our own. Having the ideology slipped in was a small price to pay for bonding with buddies on a three-day hike over Mount Marcy, gallons of ice cream under a rainy tarp in the mess tent, and a first kiss on Big Rock.

After a week of woodland activities, alternating with Russian heritage lessons, the Saturday night *kostyer* (campfire) was a momentous occasion, the wood pyramid built up one story high, with no "cheat" dry paper to ignite it, just white birch bark and a single match. After dark, the entire camp population was assembled around it. Standing silently while the blaze crackled and rose inside the wooden structure, hands crisscrossed to neighbor on left and right, a hundred young voices would begin by singing a hymn to scouting, universal in its appeal to be ready to take on the hard road, to help the sick and unfortunate, to answer the call of those suffering, and led by our holy faith, to "stand on guard for truth and goodness."

After a handshake and release, we would sit down on tree logs in concentric circles around the fire, whose flames now reached upwards to the sky, sparks flying. There was a primal feel to our communal gathering around this huge bonfire, its light throwing shadows into the darkness beyond. It drew us together for ceremony, storytelling, and singing.

The first song was always *Long Ago in Pavlovsky Park*, about the beginnings of the scout movement in Russia in 1914 in St. Petersburg, when Tsar Nicholas II had encouraged the formation of a scouting organization. Even his young son, Alexei Romanov, had briefly joined. The song's lyrics were composed by scouts in exile, after the Russian Revolution and Civil War, and were probably never heard in the USSR by the red-kerchiefed Young Pioneer organizations formed by the Communists to extol the virtues of Marxist/Leninism.

Indeed, we not only sang of the suffering and bloodshed which had extinguished that first scout campfire in Russia, but also of our duty to keep it burning "in the forests, mountains and plains" of exile, for the sake of Russia. It was a call to "never forget!" and even to return, as the last stanza underscored:

> *"Его берегли как святыню,*
> *Хранили под каждым дождем,*
> *Когда же покинем чужбину,*
> *Костры по России зажжем.*
>
> We guarded the fire in its sacredness,
> Protected it from every rain.
> When we leave these foreign lands
> We'll light the fires in Russia again."

The traditional opening song of the campfire was followed by a speech from an elder Scoutmaster, who addressed us as "dear brothers and sisters" on a moral theme of honor and friendship, punctuated by references to our love of Mother Russia and unity in our mission to reclaim her. In the meantime, the campfire's sparks burned in our hearts.

Finally, in a lighter vein, a young guitarist would strike up one of the happier songs I'd heard on the gramophone at home as a child. We continued to the rousing classic, *Borodino*, set to the famous poem by Mikhail Lermontov, about defending Russia from Napoleon, which seemed a popular theme. We also sang military marches from the Russian Civil War, which had inspired General Drosdovsky's White Russian army to return from Rumania, and oddly, World War II ballads of Soviet soldiers longing for their girlfriends back home, or stranger still, liberating the west in 1945, in *Under the Balkan Stars:*

> "Bulgaria is a wonderful country.
> But there's nothing better than Russia!"

The final words recommended the song to all, regardless of origin, and the fast tempo made it a perennial favorite. We sang it here with gusto, and on hikes to maintain our stride.

The singing, the fireside skits, even some "long distance" signaling to scout groups across America, Canada, and even Australia through rhythmic clapping and thumping, ending in a simulated launch of a rocket upwards ("WHOOSH!"), would continue for several hours before the youngest scouts would be sent off to bed.

At the conclusion of the campfire, we would all rise to sing the Russian words to *Taps*, and then end with a prayer. Solemnly, an elder Scoutmaster would intone, and we would repeat:

> "God Grant" (All: "God Grant"),
> "That Tomorrow" (All: "That Tomorrow"),
> "We Shall Be Better" (All: "We Shall Be Better"),
> "Than Today" (All: "Than Today").

We would add the words, *Spokoynoy Nochi (Good Night)*, in a peaceful, final exchange before heading off to our respective camps' tents and bunks to whisper and fall asleep.

Sitting now on the beach at Fawn Lake, Olya and Natalia were humming one of our favorite songs about being both "happy" and "sad." How Russian that was, the refrain adding that it is a happy and sad Russian song, just like the Russian soul. We pulled out sandwiches and water bottles. I was still in the thrall of the lake's wild and pristine beauty. "Why do you think this was such a special place?"

"Fawn Lake? Or camp?" asked Natalia.

"Both," I answered.

"We were so young, so happy to be here," mused Olya. "We were brought together by the good intention of our parents, but it ended up being so much more for us."

"The first time I came when I was ten, the first week, I was homesick," I admitted, "but by the end of the fourth week, I dreaded leaving to go home. I cried."

"We all cried," Olya said.

"I couldn't wait until the next summer," said Natalia. "And seeing everyone again."

"To this day. Look at us, we're here."

We lingered by the lake for a while, reluctant to bid it goodbye. I wanted to take it into myself, to tuck it away somewhere inside until another pilgrimage would bring me back.

As we headed back toward the trail, I mentioned to Olya and Natasha what I had learned recently. "You know, my brother told me he wants his ashes scattered here."

We stopped to take one last look back. Maybe in our hearts, we all did.

12

The Harvest—1933

Joseph Stalin's harsh policy of *dekulaktivization* in the 1930s was decimating the agricultural workforce and the general population, claiming millions of lives, and leaving the collective farms without the hands to harvest the wheat.

Tatyana graduated from the Pedagogical Technical Institute with high marks and was issued her diploma. But before she could be assigned to a school, she and her fellow students were sent to a collective farm for five weeks to help bring in the harvest. The future teachers were ordered to help. She wrote about her experience with farm work:

> In the first years of the collectivization, when the most hardworking peasants in the countryside were accused of being *kulaks* and sent to the "places not so far away," meaning, of course, the gulags, the villages were left empty. The collective farms, or *kolkhozi*, as they were known *(Kollectivnoye Hoziastvo)* were not able to operate without the farm hands needed for their operations.
>
> Our "wise" government found a solution—sending its young students out into the countryside during the summer vacation to fulfill various labor needs, as a help to the *kolkhozi*. What sort of help this might have provided was in question, since students didn't have the least understanding of agricultural work, and never having worked the soil, couldn't even tell the difference between oats and wheat.
>
> In the summer of 1933, a few months before I would turn 17 years old, we were called together into the student union of the technical institute and ordered to prepare for a trip to the countryside.
>
> We gathered up our belongings and changes of clothes into rucksacks and were off on our journey! In all, we were 27 students—14 girls and 13 boys between the ages of 17 and 18 years. We were herded into train cars usually reserved for cattle, since there was no room for us in the passenger cars, and seated on straw. We were underway.

We traveled through the night, then stood still for another half day while our train car was attached to another train, and then edged forward until we arrived at the station which was nearest to the *kolkhoz*, where there was no further railway. Night was falling and no one was coming for us, so we had to spend the night in the waiting room of the train station.

It was a busy place, an ant hill of constant activity, with bags and trunks everywhere, children crying from tiredness, or more likely hunger, and their angry parents moving them around. Hearty fellows from the militia were supposedly there to maintain order. The din of the crowds was incessant. Since there were no benches available for us, we had to sit and sleep on the dirty, spat-upon floor.

In the morning, the next stage of our trip was in the back of a truck that the *kolkhoz* had sent for us, which could fit all of us—standing up. But youth, of course, being what it was, we didn't mind. Even not eating since the day before, having consumed the meager rations, it was not worth dividing what we'd been given, nor sleeplessness, nor the uncertainty of where we were going and what the conditions we would encounter, affected us. Songs and jokes emanated from the open truck load, interspersed with the happy squeals of the girls as the truck bumped over the uneven dirt road.

We rode for an hour, and then suddenly stopped. Something had happened to the truck's motor. The driver got out of the cab with a handle, which looked like the crank of a huge gramophone, and tried to start the motor, but with no success. He kept fussing, opening and closing the hood, and then announced that it was useless, the truck would go no further. He calmed us by saying that the village was no more than 12 to 15 kilometers and should not be hard to reach on foot.

Nothing could be done, and we set off. At first, it was just overcast, dry, with no rain, but in a while, dark storm clouds started to move in, the thunderstorm coming closer and closer to us. It approached us from all sides, the huge lightning bolts zigzagging across the sky, the raindrops dropping on us at first lightly, and then starting to pelt us unmercifully with full force.

We were totally exposed in an open field, no sheds, or barns nearby, nothing to give us shelter. The rain kept increasing and then, to our horror, turned into hail. The hailstones were the size of cherries, pummeling our bare arms and legs, necks, and heads. Water streamed down from our hair in rivulets.

We removed our shoes, of course, because we only had one pair and we had to save them, and anyway, they were useless in the rising water, which was flooding the fields and in places came up to our knees. It became difficult to move forward; we made our way slowly.

We were drenched to the bone, everything on us was soaked through, including our rucksacks, which were cheap cloth and not waterproof. The clothes inside absorbed the water, making the rucksacks even heavier to carry. Underneath our clothes, streams of cold water ran down our bodies. The hail had brought the cold; the water through which we slogged was icy.

We were pelted this way all the way to the village, the hail stopping occasionally, but then starting up again with new energy.

When we finally made it to the *kolkhoz*, sodden, cold, and exhausted from our battle with the elements, we were met by the chairman of the *kolkhoz*. He billeted us at first in the school, although he promised to provide us with other housing later or to put us up in the workers' houses.

The school, of course, had nothing resembling beds, not even benches, since it was undergoing renovations and had been completely emptied. He suggested that we spread some hay on the floor for the night in the classrooms. But how were we supposed to sleep, in what? There were no blankets, not even army issued, to say nothing of pillows, and not a stitch on us that was dry.

We lay down in our wet clothes, squeezing out the excess water from our hems, and slept on the soggy hay. Had we not been young and invincible, we would have probably come down with colds, bronchitis or worse from the chilling journey, but in the morning, we arose just fine, not even a sniffle. God had protected us.

As we were hanging out our clothes, the sun came out and a wind picked up to help us dry them. The Chairman returned to announce that we must head over to the dining hall for breakfast, and then to work. "The wheat will not wait," he said. "It must be threshed, and there is no one, all hopes are on you. This evening I will find you lodging, you can't stay in the school."

The breakfast was scant. We were given bread, baked from the first threshing of the wheat and replete with sharp pieces of the chaff which scratched our lips and tongues, and tea. But best of all, and nourishing us throughout our five weeks stay, there was honey. It came from an enormous apiary maintained by a stooped, elderly man who, likely because of his advanced age, had been overlooked by the *dekulakivization*. He had probably surmised in advance the oncoming changes, and had gifted the apiary to the collective farm, knowing that it would have been taken from him and put into the care of inexperienced hands. In this way, he could remain with his bees.

So, we were served honey, by the glassful. It saved us from what would have been a debilitating hunger. But you can't just eat honey by itself. You need to have something with it, and there wasn't much of that. All that we received was a watery soup, made with boiled onions, not even a single potato, but dumplings made from the same threshed chaff and then tea with honey, endless honey.

As promised, after the first night in the school, the Chairman found some lodging for us, in two barns, which were empty except for the straw on the floors. There was not a single window. The door to the barn was high up and could only be reached with a ladder, which of course was not available. We could only enter it by standing on each other's shoulders and pulling ourselves up and into the barn.

Exiting was easier—we just jumped! However, these jumps without a parachute weren't always successful. One of our girls took a leap which on landing turned her ankle and she was out of commission for a few days. After that, we were supplied with a ladder consisting of two poles with two or three cross ties.

What can be said about the work? It was threshing, which we barely understood. We threw the sheaves of wheat into the threshing machine, and out came the grain and chaff from one side, the straw from the other. We had to then separate the wheat from the chaff into sacks. The chaff stayed on the collective farm as feed for the livestock; the grain was sent to the city for milling.

The girls were tasked with making sure the grain did not mix with the chaff in the bags, and the boys were given pitchforks to move the straw into haystacks. During the day we were more or less attentive to these processes, but we were forced to work through the night as well, by moonlight, because the Soviet holiday of International Youth Day was coming soon, and it signaled the end of the harvest campaign.

As we knew, the Soviet government was always excited to announce the Fulfillment of its Plan just in time for a predetermined date or a holiday. They announced that "Red Carts" weighed down with wheat grain must reach the city and be turned over to the government by the first of September. For that reason, we were forced to work days and nights, in shifts, and did we *ever* work.

We likely filled many of the sacks of chaff with wheat, unable to separate them adequately in our haste, but the only one who saw us do that was the chairman of the farm, who told us one day: "That's all right, my fine young friends, don't worry, go ahead and fill the chaff sacks with some grain. In the winter, when we have nothing to eat and are starving until the next harvest, we will re-sift the chaff for the grain. Go for it, God give you strength!"

> So, the village would go hungry in the winter, with one of the best harvests ever that year? But he spoke the truth—the government took the lion's share of the grain and left only crumbs for the hungry collective farm workers. How many of them died in the cities, when they came with their entire families and begged for food and mercy from city dwellers, as they swelled from hunger and fell to the wayside? Russia had not known such a shame in all its centuries of history!
>
> We stayed at the collective farm for a month and a half. We did not have a single day off the entire time. We had no place to wash, except for a small stream that had water up to our knees, where we would run quickly because of the limited time allotted. Many of the girls developed head lice.
>
> One can imagine our happiness when after a month and a half of this forced labor we were finally told we would be leaving the next day. Now that was a real holiday!
>
> As our only compensation for our work, we were provided with a truck ride to the train station, so that we didn't have to walk back on the washed-out roads we had navigated at the beginning of our visit to the *kholkhoz.*

My mother's forced labor at the collective farm had at least one positive aspect—it provided my grandmother with the food rations allotted to Tatyana, while she was away on the work detail. The stress of Fediay's death, combined with chronic malnutrition and poor working conditions, had caused my grandmother to contract tuberculosis. There were no health treatments locally, other than trips to sanatoriums in warm climates, which were expensive or provided free by the unions for party members, but not available for "elements foreign to the Soviet," as she was.

The tuberculosis had become acute; the "galloping" consumption had caused my grandmother to lose weight and even start wearing my thin mother's dresses, unusual for a woman who had been big-boned and full-figured all of her life. The doctors had given her eight to nine months to live.

Tatyana did not know in what condition she would find my grandmother upon her return from the work detail, or if she would even find her alive. It was with great surprise and joy that she returned to a healthy, glowing woman. It was a miracle! My grandmother had added beets to the rations she picked up at the student cafeteria, along with additional bread. She had regained some of her weight and was well. Some good had come of my mother's toils. They would support each other through many more years together.

13

The 1960s

The first movie I recall seeing with my mother and father, in a movie theater, was *Taras Bulba,* a 1962 action film based on Nikolai Gogol's short novel of the same name, starring Yul Brynner in the title role, and Tony Curtis as his son, Andrei. Set in sixteenth-century Ukraine, it tells the story of the swashbuckling Cossack colonel, Taras Bulba, and the conflict of national identity vs. the love of family and honor. Bulba hopes that Andrei will learn the ways of their occupying enemy, the Poles, but instead the son falls in love with Natalia, the daughter of a Polish nobleman. A fateful choice ensues.

My parents shifted uncomfortably during the movie and exited the theater at the end, disgusted with what they called *klukva* (literally the word for "cranberry," but also the colloquial expression for "full of baloney"). There must have been some inconsistencies with Gogol, or more likely, overtly sexual innuendos. As for me, I couldn't decide if I was more smitten by the bald 'n' buff Brynner, with his scalp knot spinning as he rode bareback in the steppes, exhorting the Cossacks to victory over the Poles, or Curtis, a less Slavic but attractive blue-eyed golden boy of Hollywood. ("I'm a man before I'm a Cossack!" … You sure are!)

It was a memorable outing—my camp buddy and best friend, Tania, and I reacted to every appearance of Ostap, the faithful brother, with paroxysms of laughter, having dubbed him Oscar. The love scenes weren't lost on our pre-teen sensitivities either, despite my parents' stony silence, but it was Brynner's authentic Russian accent and machismo that captured my heart. I became his lifetime fan, returning to watch his portrayal of the smoldering Soviet Major Surov in *The Journey,* a 1959 movie about the Hungarian uprising, starring him and Deborah Kerr. Even as he was the King of Siam for the multitudes, he would always be a courageous Cossack ataman for me.

The other movie which stands out in my childhood is a long-forgotten drama called *One Potato, Two Potato,* which my mother and I, just the two of us, went to see in 1964. I have no memory of why she would have taken me to this film about an interracial marriage of a white, Midwestern, divorced woman in Ohio and a Black man. Especially memorable was the courtroom battle the wife wages to keep custody of her first marriage's child in the face of prejudice against her new family. It was released the same year Congress voted in the Civil Rights Act of 1964 and Martin Luther King, Jr., won the Nobel Peace Prize.

The film was first screened at the Cannes Film Festival to what was reported as stunned silences from the audience at the gut-wrenching ending where—spoiler alert—the Ohio judge rules in favor of removing the little girl from the embrace of her loving family to her wayward father because of the perceived harm of growing up in a racially integrated home. The film ends with the girl in the back seat of a car, being driven away from her family.

My mother sobbed as we left the theater house. She didn't speak to me on the way home, or ever, about the film's message. The ending must have caught her unexpectedly and she was embarrassed by her emotional reaction and her inability to control her tears. I was surprised at her sobs, which struck me as caused more by separation of a child from her mother, than the theme of racial injustice, although I can't be sure from the distance of so many years.

I knew that my mother respected Martin Luther King, because he had adopted his philosophy of nonviolence partly from the teachings of Count Leo Tolstoy, one of my mother's heroes, but I would not have supposed that she carried that into support of King's civil rights movement. While still in Russia, she had read *Uncle Tom's Cabin* in translation, and empathized with the plight of the American slave, but it didn't connect her with the racial reality of 1960s America, or the practice, not just the theory, of civil disobedience. "*Besporyadok*." Disorder. Unrest was unnerving to her.

My parents did not accept the liberal politics of their adopted New York City, in fact, they gradually shifted to the opposite stance. In the dozen years since they had arrived in America, they moved from the Soviet-propagandized portrait of a nation rife with beatings and lynchings, which evoked horror and sympathy for the southern Negro, to a headline-induced fear of Harlem and the Black neighborhoods of Brooklyn they had left behind.

Years later, when the dark-skinned father of my daughter's school chums walked into my dining room, where my mother was sipping tea with the children at our Easter gathering, she was gripped by a "fear that left her breathless," because, as she said, "he was as black as coal." When she confessed this to me hours after the visit, I cringed, both for her frank, unapologetic admission and in recognition of the power that the media had played in forming prejudice in my mother where none had existed before.

But not so for me. No longer the little Russian girl my mother had tried so hard to create, by my teen years, adept at moving through the culture of my time, I adopted the cause of my favorite folk singers, especially Joan Baez, Bob Dylan, and Peter, Paul and Mary. My brother played acoustic guitar and with another strumming friend, Greg, we formed a trio that performed many of their songs at school shows, including "If I Had a Hammer" and "When the Ship Comes In."

As I sat glued to the TV, watching the rendition of "Blowin' in the Wind," performed on the steps of the Lincoln Memorial during the August 1963 March on Washington, the seeds of protest stirred within me to advocate for social justice. The nightly news clips of water hosing, beatings, Black children my age and younger prevented from entering school, had fed my impressionable mind. Later that day, when Martin Luther King delivered his "I Have a Dream" speech, I was filled with passion to act. But unless I ran away from home, I was too young to travel to Selma.

I watched from the safety of my living room as the events of Bloody Sunday on the Edmund Pettus Bridge unfolded in 1965 and tried to find hope in the signing of the Voter Rights Act later that year by President Johnson. When riots erupted in the Watts section of Los Angeles, and Stokely Carmichael coined the term Black Power, I found myself unable to counter my frightened parents' rejection of the means justifying the end.

We stopped watching the news together, we stopped talking. I wrote them off as out-of-touch fossils; they prayed that the political and sexual revolution wouldn't camp out on our doorstep.

It did. It was my mother's turn to wonder what had become of her youngest Russian child, when on April 4, 1968, I was inconsolable over the death of Martin Luther King. I locked myself in my room and didn't come out. It seemed like the end of the world to me, and that we would spiral into some kind of hell, when the earth would "turn to ash," as I wrote in my diary that day. In the next few days, I took solace from my New York senator, Robert F. Kennedy, who was running for the Democratic nomination for President that spring. I had already been following his 1967 travels through Mississippi to check on the War on Poverty and recalled his dismay at seeing thousands of hungry children.

Kennedy was on a flight from Memphis, Tennessee, to Indianapolis and was told of Martin Luther King's death upon arrival. Despite the threat of riots and bloodshed, he still went to an African American neighborhood and delivered the news to the assembled people, who, in anguish over this tragic loss, listened to his impromptu words:

> *Ladies and Gentlemen, I'm only going to talk to you just for a minute or so this evening, because.... I have some very sad news for all of you, and, I think, sad news for all of our fellow citizens, and people who love peace all over the world;*

and that is that Martin Luther King was shot and was killed tonight in Memphis, Tennessee.

Martin Luther King dedicated his life to love and to justice between fellow human beings. He died in the cause of that effort. In this difficult day, in this difficult time for the United States, it's perhaps well to ask what kind of a nation we are and what direction we want to move in....

So, I ask you tonight to return home, to say a prayer for the family of Martin Luther King—yeah, it's true—but more importantly to say a prayer for our own country, which all of us love—a prayer for understanding and that compassion of which I spoke....

He echoed the hopelessness I felt, at age 15, to be living in a country bent on self-destruction. He gave voice to my fears that this land, my land, was on the brink of disaster. Yet, only five years after the assassination of his brother, Robert Kennedy could end his emotional appeal with these words:

"And let's dedicate ourselves to what the Greeks wrote so many years ago: to tame the savageness of man and make gentle the life of this world. Let us dedicate ourselves to that and say a prayer for our country and for our people."

Source: Papers of Robert F. Kennedy. Senate Papers. Speeches and Press Releases, Box 4, "4/1/68–4/10/68." John F. Kennedy Presidential Library.

So profound was the effect of Kennedy's words on me, that I sat down in the next few days and wrote a letter to him, a copy of which I didn't keep in my haste to post it. I must have asked him to do what seemed impossible—bring equality and justice to the world.

Miraculously, in the space of a few weeks, I received a reply from the Senator's Washington office on May 6, 1968. I will never know if it was signed by a machine, or by the eloquent statesman himself, but I kept it in my jewelry box forever, where it is still tucked into a pocket.

Robert F. Kennedy
New York

United States Senate
May 6, 1968

Miss Helen Artemyeff
Sea Cliff, New York 11579

Dear Miss Artemyeff:

Thank you for your letter about the tragic death of Dr. Martin Luther King, and the need for civil rights legislation and effective action to alleviate the problems of extreme poverty and deprivation in the United States today. I appreciated your taking the time to write to me and let me know that you share my deep concern in this vital matter.

I believe that the time for bold and imaginative action is now. We must not delay efforts to eliminate the deprivation and alienation of the ghetto, and must take steps to ensure that Negro Americans, and other victims of poverty in the United States, have an adequate diet, improved education, opportunities for employment, and decent housing. We must act to break the vicious cycle of dependency and hopelessness in which too many of our fellow Americans are trapped, and all of us must make a greater commitment to the achievement of these goals.

We can, of course, be encouraged by the passage of civil rights legislation. I was pleased to have your words of support for the Civil Rights bill recently passed by Congress and signed into Law. As you may know, I supported cloture motions and the open housing provisions considered during the Senate debate on the bill and voted for final passage of H.R. 2516. I am sure you were pleased, as I was, that the House adopted these open housing provisions.

This legislation will help, but Congress and private citizens must also take action to ensure that other effective means to deal with these problems are developed and funded. You may know that I have introduced legislation to encourage private investment in housing and industrial development in urban areas. I believe that this is one of the steps we must take. I am glad to know that I shall have your support for programs which will help to make quality of opportunity a reality for all Americans. Again, my thanks and my best wishes to you.

Sincerely,

Robert F. Kennedy

A month later, on June 6, 1968, Robert Kennedy was assassinated in the Ambassador Hotel in Los Angeles. I felt the world change for me that day. All hope was gone. And all trust in authority had fled with it.

If the departure of law and order, the withholding of civil rights, and anti-war protests (all to the soundtrack of Iron Butterfly) weren't enough, my mother and I had a complete falling out over my virginity, or the presumed loss of it even after being made to kneel in front of our living room's Holy Icons and swear to the contrary. I am still surprised that lightning didn't strike me dead right there and then!

In their own protest, my parents refused to attend my graduation and went on vacation even as I received my diploma at North Shore High School. I couldn't wait to leave home. In late June, I sublet an apartment and left for a temping secretarial job in New York City, several months before I enrolled at NYU.

Unforgiven.

Russia was the furthest thing from my mind.

14

A Married Woman—June 1934

In the fall of 1933, my mother was 17 years old. Having completed the Pedagogical Technical Institute that spring, she was sent on her first teaching assignment. It was in Mushketovo, a suburb of the city of Stalino (now called Donetsk). She taught German to children in the 5th through 8th grades. She shared a room with another teacher in a private house, because she couldn't afford it on her own, sending half of her monthly salary of 150 rubles home to her mother.

At the time: Tatyana's height was 5'8". Her weight was 52 kg. (114 lbs). She described herself as a "skeleton."

Her attire: She had one blue suit, which she had inherited from her cousin during her student years. It was so threadbare that it was close to wearing through in the sleeves, elbows, and the back of the skirt. She wore it every day.

Her shoes: She had one pair, ragged and worn so thin that she permanently sewed galoshes to them and wore them during both wet and dry weather, never removing them in company, since her stockings were riddled with holes.

Her meals: She could only afford one meal a week at the cafeteria by the railroad yard, and otherwise survived on sardines, the cheapest canned goods available in the food store, plus bread. Her landlady set aside salted cabbage for her, in an act of mercy for her condition of perpetual hunger.

It was in this state of subsistence that Tatyana met her husband, Alexander Budishevsky.

> We would have to attend Pedagogical *sovets*, which were teacher meetings, scheduled at least once a week, to discuss questions of pedagogy, methodology, and lesson plans, which were purely teaching discussions, unless it was a union meeting, which covered different topics.

The local *Partorg* (Party Organizer) of the railroad workers had a habit of attending these teacher meetings. In those days, the Party made it its business to meddle in everything; the so-called "Party Eye" was present everywhere. It was impossible to discourage these intrusions as one could pay heavily for denying them access.

Our Mushketovo Partorg was an uneducated self-promoting worker who, even if he might have had some experience in the management of the railroad, had absolutely no inkling of the educational world. It was somewhat humorous to observe—an unskilled, country bumpkin, totally lost in the discussion of teaching methods and unable to put two intelligent words together on the subjects at hand, sitting there with a learned look on his face and occasionally inserting what he deemed to be a valuable comment.

The Director of the school would have to listen to the Partorg patiently, as if his instructions were worthy of consideration, while he thought to himself, "What a blockhead, a useless distraction!" But he didn't dare interrupt him or dismiss his suggestion, for how could he? This was a Party Big Cheese, we had to pay heed, after all, the Party ruled above all else.

This Partorg, Krilov by name, arrived at our teacher meeting one day with another railroad worker in tow, a man by the name of Budishevsky. It was disconcerting that our teacher meetings could be invaded by all sorts who hadn't the least understanding of educational issues yet could have a seat at the table. The discussion covered many topics, I don't recall them now, during which Comrade Budishevsky sat there and stared at me, all evening long. I didn't know how to escape his burning gaze.

At the end of the meeting, he came up and asked if he might walk me home. He must have known something about me since he knew where I lived, in the home of another railroad worker, Rengevich, with whom he worked. Rengevich was a diesel engineer and Budishevsky was a locomotive instructor. Rengevich had probably told him about me.

And so, our courtship began. To say that I loved Alexander (Shura) Budishevsky would be an overstatement. At 17, I probably did not yet even know what real love was or could be. It was a diversion.

Shura Budishevsky was an interesting, cheerful, resourceful man, enlivening any group. Among his pluses was that he was an unselfish, kind person, never stingy with his money and loaning it to friends, often without it being returned. He was from a humble, plain-spoken family. His father was a train conductor in

Mushketovo; his mother was a simple Polish woman. Both were uneducated and even Shura had only attended school through the third or fourth grade; he was close to illiterate.

The environment in their house was, of course, completely counter to that in which I had grown up; I had been raised in a different way from his family.

He was an only child. He was 12 years older than me. In Mushketovo, the Budishevsky family was considered well-to-do. By standards then, they had a respectably sized house, with a garden and orchard of fruit trees—apples, pears, cherries and even apricots. Some years there was such an abundance of apricots that the father dragged buckets of them to sell at the bazaar. They raised a pig which they butchered in the fall. They kept a goat which provided a few liters of milk every day.

Shura dressed well and earned a good living. In Mushketovo, he was considered a rich bachelor. Throughout the town, he was known for his courtships which progressed almost to marriage but for his mother's objections to each potential bride, finding enough faults to oppose the union, and sending Shura once again in search of a new mate.

Madame Budishevsky, if one could ascribe that title to her, was particular in her behavior. If she wanted to endear herself to someone, she used all her charm, but if she didn't like someone, she spared no effort to cover them in dirt. His father, the old man, on the other hand, was much simpler—a taciturn being, wholly subordinate to his wife, with no say in the household. Mother and son made all the decisions.

This was the "situation" I would face. My courtship by Shura Budishevsky lasted all of four months. We met in February and were married on the 3rd of June 1934.

The school year ended at the end of May. I was readying to leave for Yenakievo, back to my mother, and had mentioned that to Shura on one of our dates. If I had said nothing and just disappeared to Yenakievo, perhaps my entire life would have unfolded differently. Returning home, maybe I would have met someone more interesting, more intelligent than Shura. After all, Yenakievo was a metallurgical center, with a large factory which employed many young engineers. I might have met a new group of friends and perhaps made a match with a more worthy and respectable partner.

Fate did not have that in mind for me. As soon as I mentioned to Shura that I was departing to join my mother, he began to implore me to stay. I told him I had good reasons to leave. I would not have to pay my room rent for the summer months, with no working wages, and my mother was alone.

He proposed immediately.

As his wife, I would move into his home.

Even now, I cannot account for my rash decision. Why did I take that step? Why did I agree to become part of a family which was completely alien to me, where not only was I not welcome, but I would be met with hostility?

On June 3, 1934, Tatyana married Alexander ("Shura") Budishevsky. He was 12 years older than Tatyana, who was then 17 years old. Her mother, Nadezhda, was against the union, but Tatyana was tired of the wretchedness of poverty, starvation, and need.

Shura's mother was hoping for a daughter-in-law who would take over the house and barn duties: milking the goat, mucking the pigsty, weeding and tending the garden, and picking the fruit in the orchard. I was completely unprepared for that kind of work, physically, and had no experience with it in my entire life. Moreover, my mind was set against becoming a milkmaid and farmhand.

My mother, when she found out what kind of life awaited me, was horrified and opposed it immediately, urging me not to succumb to any of the conditions. "I didn't raise you, educate you, go hungry, go without everything for years, for you to clean pigsties for them!" she insisted, and of course, she was right.

Aside from that, I feared that I would have no time for domestic duties, since there were more classes being added in the next school year in the upper form, for which I would need to prepare. Where would I find time to milk the goat? But that all awaited me in the future. Right then, however, I foolishly agreed to this marriage.

Still a child at 17 years, I was lured by the promise of a full belly and decent clothing, worn out as I had been by years of poverty and endless shortages. Malnutrition had tortured me for so long that I fell headlong forward, bowed.

The entire town of Mushketovo anticipated a happy wedding celebration, but sadly, there was none. The mistress of the house, from whom all decisions flowed, disapproved of our union, and refused to organize the celebration of it. Neither myself, nor my mother, had the means nor intention for it.

Our marriage consisted of going to the local ZAGS office (*Zapis Aktov Grazhdanskogo Sostoyaniya)* which was the registrar for marriages, on June 3, 1934, and signing the required marriage documents. In my sheep-like submission, I agreed to his request to take his surname, which was not required by Soviet law at the time and became Tatyana Budishevskaya.

Later, however, this name change served me well, because the occupying Germans did not accept this rule and it would have taken a great effort on my part to prove that my children were legitimately from a marriage. Too, this union with the proletariat was useful in hiding my background from 1937 to 1939, when merely being a member of the intelligentsia led to the camps, or prison terms. I was protected by a loyal member of the Party and the proletariat.

I had known many women who had relinquished their first husbands to the gulag or exile, and then were forced to marry simpletons to hide their former status as a "member of a family of the enemy of the people."

Our marriage documents in hand, we split up to return to our respective homes, me to my rented room at the Rengevich's, he to his house. Holding the marriage license behind his back, Shura told me later, he announced to his parents that a big change had come to his life, which his mother correctly asserted was his marriage. This time, she was powerless to do anything about the done deed. Mindful of her objections to earlier engagements, Shura had gone ahead without her permission.

Day followed day, but I still did not show up at my new husband's home. I shut myself in my rented room. My landlady laughed at me, the women at the bazaar tried to make sense of it, and my mother-in-law even sent her dimwitted niece, whom I had taught at school, to fetch me, but I still couldn't bring myself to move to my husband's home. Whether I was afraid of this marriage, its conjugal obligations for which I was totally unprepared, or my mother-in-law, I don't remember, but only on the third day, the 6th of June, did I finally venture to his house.

I was met warmly by the old man, his father, but his mother's reaction towards me was lukewarm.

I arrived in time for a dinner of steaming borscht soup and

heaping portions of cheese pierogis with sour cream. My God! How many years had it been since I had even seen the likes of such a feast! I gulped down the pierogis, one after another, in an unladylike manner. I just could not stop myself!

15

Motherhood—March 30, 1935

Less than a year after her marriage to Alexander "Shura" Budishevsky in June of 1934, my mother gave birth to her first child, a daughter, Natasha, on March 30, 1935.

Her unwelcoming mother-in-law had tried to talk her out of the pregnancy, arguing that someone so young need not be burdened with a child, and hoping, that in the absence of children, the marriage might be easier dissolved, that Shura would leave her if there were fewer ties. When she didn't succeed in her persuasive efforts, she then held back on providing an adequate diet for her daughter-in-law, feeding her only potatoes day in and day out, which Tatyana hated, in the hopes of a miscarriage.

But Tatyana was intent on keeping the baby, having heard that aborting a first pregnancy, although legal in the Soviet Union at the time, could lead to an inability to conceive later. The baby was due in May, at the end of the school year. Tatyana looked forward to having the summer off to care for her child, before returning to work in the fall, but it was not to be.

Unexpectedly finding herself in labor more than month ahead of the due date, and miles away from her own mother on whom she was relying to get her through childbirth, Tatyana left a note for Shura and traveled several hours by train, pacing through a two-hour wait on the station platform for the rail connection to Yenakievo, and then a trolley ride and uphill walk to her mother. She finally arrived, walked in, and burst into tears.

Surprised by her sudden appearance, my grandmother quieted Tatyana and put her straight to bed. After a night of intermittent contractions, which grew stronger by the hour, Aunt Marusya was sent to the clinic to fetch a buggy to take my mother to the hospital. There were no phones to summon a doctor or an ambulance, it was all done by walking to the clinic and requesting help. Many an expectant mother delivered at home, unable to wait.

My mother barely made it to the hospital in time to deliver her first child. Natasha, or Tusya, as she was nicknamed, was premature by at least a month and weighed only 2.2 kilograms (4.8 lbs.). "She'll never survive," the nurses and doctors predicted. My sister Tusya lived only because of the ministrations of our grandmother, who swaddled her in cotton to keep her warm in a makeshift incubator next to the stove during her first month and augmented her feedings with milk from a pipette.

When those same medical workers saw Natasha skipping gaily down the street at age three, they were in wonder but still skeptical. "Is this the child that was born at eight months?" they marveled. "She won't live past the age of ten or twelve," they cautioned, typically pessimistic. "We've yet to see one make it past that!" But Natasha grew and thrived.

A son, Yuriy, followed in four years, in a marriage that was characterized more by its unevenness and separations than by domestic harmony. The constants in my mother's life were her children and her mother, Babushka. This theme would play out later, under much harsher circumstances.

In the following article, Tatyana describes being a young mother, awaiting the birth of her second child, and at odds with an economic system inequitable at literally, every turn:

My Number Is 11

By now you probably have come to understand that one of the virtues of our so-called socialist system was economic stagnation, which in turn created shortages for every imaginable product. These shortages resulted in endless queues.

In the first years of the new regime this was to be expected: a new order brought with it new rules, no one knew what would be allowed or forbidden, or how freely trade would continue. So, it was normal to have had temporary shortages. But in Russia this was a permanent condition. Year after year, decade after decade, nothing changed. Just as our mothers queued numbly in the years following the Revolution, so did we, right up to the war.

It was the summer of 1939. I was expecting my second child. The due date was drawing nearer, yet I still didn't have a single blanket or swaddling in which to bring the infant home from the hospital. I know that this is difficult to believe that a teacher with a paying job should not have had the means to buy at least these indispensable items, but nonetheless it was true.

We didn't have a spare bed sheet or tablecloth to cut up into diapers either, everything was worn threadbare, and there was no place to purchase cloth. If there were deliveries of textiles to our local government store, the lines were so long that if I did manage to get to the head of the line when there was anything left to buy, I tried

Tatyana and her first child, Natasha, born on March 30, 1935. Natasha was born prematurely and was kept in cotton and fed from a pipette by her grandmother. Despite the dire predictions of doctors and nurses regarding premature births, she survived and thrived.

to get the rationed ten meters in dress materials, rather than cloth for undergarments. We desperately needed the outer garments, what was underneath didn't matter, it was hidden from view.

But what was I going to do for this new child?

Four years before, when I had given birth to Natasha, I watched as a new mother was detained in the hospital for days on end because she had nothing in which to take home her newborn son. The hospital staff refused to loan her a single diaper, insisting that if every new mother were given even one, it would soon deplete the hospital's meager supply and there would no diapers left for their in-patients.

The unfortunate woman pleaded with the nurses, promising to return the loaned diapers to the hospital as soon as she got home, but to no avail. It must have been less costly for the hospital to keep her there, occupying a bed even though she had fully recovered from her delivery, than to donate a few diapers to her, if only for a few hours. She remained there until some of us finally gave her a few diapers just to get home.

Now I was afraid to be in the same predicament, and with the baby's due date approaching at the beginning of September I began to worry even more. Soon after, when I heard a rumor that cloth bolts were being delivered to the local store and would be "distributed" the following day, I resolved to queue up for my ten meters' worth, come what may. My girlfriend next door advised me to take up a place in line the evening before, so that having stayed the night in the front of the queue I would be one of the first inside when the store doors opened in the morning.

Luckily it was the month of August, a warm moonlit evening. When I approached the storefront at around 9 p.m. there were ten to fifteen people already queued, most of them women. I asked the usual "who's last in line?" and then added the familiar refrain, "I'm after you, then," establishing my place.

It was not appropriate to say "Who's *last*?" since that somehow implied that the last person was a *lesser* person in our jargon. This gaff would elicit the response from some political watchdog to the effect, "There are no last persons here, we're all the same." We were all equals. To be proper one had to say, "Who is the 'edge' person?" or the person at the 'end.' We were supposed to be familiar with these nuances of Soviet phraseology.

Soon others began to take their places behind me, one after another, until the line snaked a city block long. As the night wore on, various proposals for keeping our line in order of arrivals were suggested. Someone proposed that we inscribe our number in line on our palms; others that we affix paper numerals to our backs. The latter suggestion was soundly rejected; it didn't instill enough confidence in the integrity of line holders, eager to move up. Providentially, an ink pen turned up and we accepted the first proposal.

The job of numbering the queue fell to the owner of the ink pen. He proceeded with this task masterfully, considering that each palm first had to be spat upon and rubbed before being presented to him (it was common knowledge that ink would take better to a moistened surface). Either the right hand or the left would do. Soon my palm had a medium-sized number "11" inscribed on it.

We had just finished being enumerated and were standing calmly in line, secure in the knowledge that we were indelibly fixed in our order, when a militzianer, a policeman, came around the corner. That was when the trouble started. At first, he appealed to us peaceably in an attempt to clarify the situation. He cited a law that forbade the forming of queues more than half an hour in advance of the opening of the store, to say nothing of an entire night before.

"Comrades! I'm asking you to disperse!" he pleaded. The crowd stood silent, motionless.

"It is against the law to assemble alongside a store at night," he continued louder. "You are breaking the law!" Still no movement.

Then the militzianer started threatening to make arrests on charges of disorderly conduct. The line continued to stand in place.

Only when he grabbed the arms of the first two in the queue, as if to take them away to the police station, did the rest of the line break up and start drifting slowly away. But not for long.

As soon as the militzianer was gone from the scene, the queuers slipped back out from the alleys and doorways and reassembled in correct order. Despite the way the crowd had dispersed, no one tried to jump the line and invalidate the previously established order, starting over again, which would have clearly benefited the later arrivals. There was an unspoken agreement that the numbers appearing on the palms were true and fair.

I retained my place in line as number 11.

We stood chatting quietly, afraid of drawing the attention of the defender of law and order, but our peace of mind was short-lived. He was obviously familiar with the habits of the day and did not wait long before returning to confront the reassembled queue. No friendly discussions this time. He flew into us mercilessly and with the aid of a partner began yanking us out of line. A few stout women dug their heels in and had to be forcibly ejected into the street. One lost her footing and slipped, landing with a loud thud. She picked herself up and hobbled off, muttering curses under her breath.

The matter did not end there. No, we are much too stubborn a folk. Over and over, as soon as the militzianer disappeared, the line reformed, only to be chased off again on his return. No one went home. We would slink off into the side streets, waiting for him to leave, and then float back again to resume our places, a game of "hide and seek," in slow motion.

Finally, either the militzianer tired of us or more likely his watch was over. The relief officer did not seem committed to enforcing the policy. After standing some hours undisturbed, some hopeful voices in line offered the opinion that perhaps the new one couldn't be bothered with us, or better yet, felt some sympathy for our plight.

The morning events convinced us of the opposite. The new watch simply employed a different strategy to make his point. At precisely half an hour prior to the store's opening, exhausted and disheveled as we were from the night's dashing about but standing firmly in our places, we looked on as the new militzianer walked to the very end of the queue, some two hundred people back. He took the very last person by the arm and motioned to the next to last, and so on from there to do an about-face and follow him. He thus reversed the queue, looping it around and marching it toward the entrance of the store. Those of us who had come the evening before now ended up at the very back.

I was now number 11 from the *end* of the line.

The crowd started to shout and hoot at him, pointing to the numbers on their palms and swearing at him. The morning's arrivals, pleased to have wandered into such blind luck, chuckled to themselves. Once the single file reached the store entrance, however, the crowd pushed forward in total disregard for any order, bunching up to get to the door. The stronger women started shoving and elbowing each other. Some of the women started to cry, as much from the unfairness of this outcome as from the sheer exhaustion of having spent a night in vain.

I tried to get in closer to the door, foolishly thinking that maybe I could still manage to get inside the store, but the crowd was pushing so hard that I suddenly became afraid for the child I was carrying. I was eight months pregnant, after all. Close to tears myself, I begged for God's sake to be let out from the pushing crowd. A stalwart lad saw my plight and parting the crowd, pulled me out by the hand to safety.

Tatyana and her second child, Yuriy ("Yura"), born on September 26, 1939, less than two years before Hitler invaded Russia on June 22, 1941.

"The likes of you should be home! This is no place for you in your condition!" he chided me angrily. He was right, of course. I should not have been there, and that ended any further attempts on my part. I returned home empty-handed.

Luckily for me, my cousin came for a visit soon and brought me several meters of cloth, not white but a flowery design. Her husband had got it for her through his connections, a much more reliable "distribution" system.

Tatyana's life was difficult beyond what most of us can imagine, exacerbated by a set of impossible regulatory rules, and underscored by the pervasive fear of getting on the wrong side of the "state."

A lifetime of living in anticipation of the midnight knock on the door had lasting effects on everyone, as she was to experience during a brush with the secret police.

16

Donetsk, 1938—The Belobandit Uncle

The Great Purge, or the Great Terror (Russian: Большóй Террóр) was perpetrated by Joseph Stalin and the Communist Party leadership in the Soviet Union from 1936 to 1938. As many as 1,750,000 people were rounded up, tortured, imprisoned, and executed, with hundreds of thousands more—some estimate millions—sent into the prison system of the Gulag.

Gulág is an acronym for the Russian term ***G**lavnoye **U**pravleniye Ispravitelno-trudovyh **Lag**ere* (*Главное Управление Исправительно-трудовых Лагерей*), or Chief Administration of Corrective Labor Camps, the name of the governing board of the Soviet labor camp system. In the period between 1934 and 1947, an estimated 10 million people were sent to camps.

Stalin's goal was to purge the country of those accused of various political crimes, including espionage, sabotage, "Anti-Soviet activities," or just being "enemies of the people" by their status as intelligentsia before or after the Russian Revolution.

Here in America, my mother and father rarely spoke of the Soviet security organizations, first the CHEKA, created in December 1917, then the NKVD (People's Commissariat of Internal Affairs), but the bookshelves in our family library contained paperbound émigré descriptions of the Gulag with titles like "*Unforgettable,*" even before my mother's hero, Alexander Solzhenitsyn's work, *One Day in the Life of Ivan Denisovich,* was published in the west in 1962, and then his *The First Circle* and *Cancer Ward* in 1968, and later, *The Gulag Archipelago,* smuggled out to Europe and America between 1973 and 1978.

I only learned later, through reading her journals, that there were members of Tatyana's family who had disappeared into the camps, with euphemisms such as "Kolya is far away" to explain the absence of a cousin's husband, likely forever.

It may have been the lingering fear of the KGB's reach, even into her

American home, that prevented my mother from talking about the widespread Soviet repression and scares, which as she describes below, affected her as well:

The Belobandit Uncle

One day, sometime early in the 1938–1939 school year, the principal of my school called me into his office and said that there had been a call from the regional *Spetz-Otdel* (Special Department) requesting that I report to them that day. He was relieving me from my lessons, without a loss of pay, and I needed to go immediately to the *Oblast Spetz-Otdel.*

The principal, it should be noted, was not a person who might sympathize with members of his staff or his subordinates. He gave me this news in an official tone, with even some strict overtones, which might make one wonder, is he perhaps a *spetz*-worker himself?

My thoughts swirled with suspicions, guesses—what could it be, why were they bringing me in? Those were difficult years; one after another, friends and colleagues were "taken" every day, new "enemies of the people" were uncovered, wave upon wave were arrested and sentenced to the camps and exile in the East. There was plenty to think about.

Frightened thoughts, wildly unrealistic, filled my consciousness. I couldn't find anything derogatory about myself, except that they might have finally found evidence of my parentage, after having searched for years, even during my student years. But I knew that the archives had burned down in the city where I lived as a child and where my father died, so when asked, I had always been purposefully vague in stating that I was the daughter of a worker.

I was living and employed using my maiden name. In Soviet Russia before the war, when married you could keep your maiden name, and your husband could even take *your* name if he found it had a better sound to it.

In our village, a man named Konovalov took his wife's name, Koch, when they married, but regretted it bitterly when before the German advance in 1941, all the families of German extraction were sent away somewhere. There were rumors that these "Germans" hadn't been sent far, but had, in fact, been executed outside the city.

And so, I had to get through the next several hours of not knowing and only guessing about my fate, assuming the worst case, while convincing my loved ones at home, my husband and my mother, that this can't possibly be serious, and probably just a case of mistaken identity, which will become evident as soon as I report to the *Spetz-Otdel*. In a word, I was trying to persuade them of something I was absolutely not certain of myself.

Most importantly, there was Mama. She hadn't spent a day in peace in the years since my father's death, fearing that his identity and the reasons behind his imprisonment and death under Lenin would be revealed. I knew that those hours of not knowing, while I traveled to the regional city of the *Spetz-Otdel* (luckily, a tram ran there, we lived close by), and returned, would be torture for her. My husband was calmer about it, and I hoped that he could quiet her worries.

When I went home to change my clothes and told her that I had been called to report to the *Spetz-Otdel*, her legs collapsed beneath her and she sat down heavily, her head in her hands, speaking not a word.

"So now it begins, it has reached us too," was all that she could say in a half whisper after a moment of silence. It is hard to describe, after all these years, my feelings at that moment. Anyone who has lived through this or a similar event, who has survived Soviet rule, will recall it without any further description, and those whom this missed would not understand it anyway.

I arrived at the offices of the *Spetz-Otdel*. At the entrance, I was told which floor and what number room to report to, but not the name of the person who had sent for me. I approached the door in fear. Will I exit it again, and to where? Will I see God's light of day once more, or should I make my farewells to it now? The only calming thought I had was that if they wanted to arrest me, they would not have requested that I come here, they would have picked me up from work or at night from home, in the infamous car, the *Chernaya Vorona* (Black Crow).

I couldn't knock on the door, it was wrapped in heavy felt, with a plastic covering on top, which frightened me even more, causing me to think, "What happens behind this door that cannot be heard from without?"

I opened it slightly and asked, "May I come in?"

"Enter."

I walked into a well-appointed office with a beautiful rug on the floor, drapes on the wide window. It was furnished with a huge desk and a sofa. A portrait of Joseph Stalin hung on one wall, of course, and Nikolai Yezhov, then head of the NKVD, on the other. A balding, light-haired man was seated behind the desk.

"Sit. Your last name is Fediay?" he asked, without looking up.

"Yes. What is the matter, comrade? What do you need from me?"

"I, myself, don't need *anything* from you. Your government, your country needs you. Do you understand? We are cleaning out the land of all kinds of scum and riffraff which is still nested here and there, hiding from Soviet justice. Right now, we are focusing on the *belobandits*. Among them we are searching for a man with your surname, Vladimir Fediay. Do you know him?"

That was a full-frontal assault, one he hoped would put me off guard.

"No, I don't know him." But I was thinking that yes, my father had a brother named Vladimir, about whom he had no news for many years.

"Think. Remember. Maybe someone related to your father? Do you have a brother?"

"I don't have a brother, and if I did, then during the times of the *belobandits,* he would have been too young, because my mother and father got married just before the Revolution."

"Ah-ha. Well, then what about relatives, close, distant?"

I decided to tell the truth, because if they discovered something then I will be accused of hiding or falsifying information, and it will be worse for me. "My father had a brother, Vladimir," I began.

"See, that's better, and you said you don't know of him. Where is he now? Where is your father?"

"My father died a long time ago, and he lost track of his brother long before that, before I was born. No one knows what happened to him, but he couldn't have been a *belobandit* because he was a *Tolstovets*."

"And what is that?"

"A disciple of Tolstoy and his teachings on the nonviolent resistance to evil."

That response seemed to anger him. His voice rose. "You know what, don't think you can lead me astray into the woods with this talk of teachings, and anyway, who is this Tolstoy? I'm not certain. Does he share our ideology? Better that you tell me, where is your Uncle Vladimir now?"

"I don't know, comrade. I am telling you, he disappeared long before I was born. I am sure that the person you are looking for just has the same name. He has nothing to do with us. And even if he was my uncle, what of it? I don't answer for him or anyone else."

"That is true, but you can help us find him, you are a teacher, a member of society, an educated person who understands that we must rid ourselves of these enemies, that we must destroy them, wherever they are."

"I understand, but that is not my uncle, you are confusing us with someone else."

"So, do you have a photograph of your uncle? Bring it to me. If it is not him" (it seemed that some doubt had crept into my interviewer), "I will return your photograph, and the matter will be closed. But if it is him, then you will search for him, until he is found." He pronounced the word *search* with special emphasis, as if there was an additional meaning behind it.

It was decided that I should return tomorrow after I had found a photograph in the family archives of my uncle. I wasn't sure one of him had even survived. I rushed home with just a single thought in my head, was there a photograph of my uncle? Not for a minute did I doubt that the person they were looking for was not him, but how to prove that? I could bring him any photograph, of any person, and he could still not believe me.

I began to wonder, what did he really want from me? What if my uncle was just an excuse, and some other reason lay behind it? Why hadn't he shown me this "bandit's" photo, with which he wished to compare mine? The matter could have been decided more quickly.

I ran to catch the trolley. It seemed to move so slowly and make countless stops before I arrived at home.

After a lengthy search of old suitcases and trunks, I found a photograph of my uncle. By God, he didn't resemble a "belo" [white] or any color of bandit! His photograph showed him with his wife and his one-year-old daughter. It was dated 1912 on the reverse.

The following day, my mother accompanied me to the *Spetz-Otdel* building. She was somewhat relieved, although neither of us knew how it would all end.

I had to wait for a long time for my interviewer; apparently, he was busy with someone. I had stopped worrying, thinking *he will take a look at the photograph and will see that it's not him, and will let me go.* Finally, I walked into his office and proffered the photograph. He was angry, red in the face; the previous appointment had not gone well. Bad timing for me.

He took the photograph. "Hmm. It is possible that's him. In the next few days, we will be receiving some additional materials which will contain photographs, and then we will compare them and call you back in."

Again, I must wait! Again, the uncertainty of what is next. But what could be done? He was upset and it was unwise to counter him. As I readied to leave, he asked, "And by the way, this is your maiden name, isn't it? Are you married?"

"Yes."

"What is your husband's name?"

I told him.

Suddenly, he completely changed his demeanor and jumped happily to his feet, shouting, "So Alexander is your husband? It can't be! What a coincidence! Why didn't you say so earlier? We used to be friends and comrades. He was my instructor, we worked together. Yes, yes, together at the railroad depot. Sit down, sit. Tell me about him, how is he? He's my old friend, do you understand?"

But I didn't understand, and taken by surprise by his change of mood, managed only to say, "But my husband is a railroad engineer, and you, if you will excuse me, work for the NKVD. How would you know him?"

"I worked with him; I told you. He taught me how to operate a locomotive. I am happy to make the acquaintance of his wife! Please give him my regards, tell him from Sashka Apanchin. What a small world, eh?" And then, he added, handing me back the photo. "Here, take the photograph, I don't need it—this is not the person we are looking for."

I left hurriedly with my mother. At home, I told my husband the entire story. He wasn't surprised. He knew that this Sashka, a useless sod and an uneducated dolt with no technical skills, had switched over to a line of work more to his abilities. My husband knew of his decision and was nevertheless patient with him, staying on his good side.

"Something suggested to me that somewhere I might meet up with him again," he said. The only twist was the coincidence that the whole story of this imaginary *belobandit* would fall, by chance, into his hands.

We sat together, the three of us, and talked about how often in life chance can save the life of a person. Who knows how it would have all ended, if not for this coincidence stepping in to mitigate having a name in common with a supposed *belobandit*.

My mother had referenced this article, "Uncle Belobandit," in her journals and I had found the clipping of its publication in April 1975. She still had signed it with a pseudonym, so she must have felt some need to continue to cover her tracks, even two decades into living in the U.S.

In the same year, I had my own run-in with the KGB, and a random crossing of paths with the most famous agent of all.

17

My USIA Trip to USSR—1975

The London flight landed on the runway at Sheremetyevo Airport, Moscow, at night with a thud and rolled to a stop on the tarmac, bounded on both sides by the drifts and the snow-covered forests we had seen from the air on our approach. It was, after all, late January, the depths of winter—the Russian winter.

Looking out the small window, my heart skipped a beat. I was finally to set foot on Russian soil.

For the first time in my young life, I would see and experience Russia firsthand—not through the books, or movies, or fairy tales of my childhood, although the dark woods surrounding the airport seemed like they might harbor the wolves my mother had told me stalked Russia's forests.

"Your grandfather kept them at bay by carrying a flaming torch on our treks to the peasant villages," she had once mentioned. She hadn't elaborated on why they had been walking through the woods at night, but the image of his hand raised high, waving fire to keep away the wolves, had stayed with me all those years.

I peered into the dense thicket through the airplane window. I smiled to see that it was mostly white birches, as expected. No tree signified Russia to the émigré heart so much as did the white birch, and here was a forest of them.

Russia! It seemed impossible that I was here, and yet true.

My friend, Anne, who had sat next to me on the flight, nudged me. I could see in her widened eyes that she was equally enthralled by the prospect of Mother Russia, up close and personal. Like me, she had been raised in a Russian family; she had majored in Russian literature. Anne and I had known each other since summer camp days in the Adirondacks and had attended New York University together, living just a few blocks apart in Brooklyn Heights.

Fresh out of college the previous spring, we had both applied for jobs with an American government exhibit traveling throughout the Soviet

Union, relying on our native language abilities to be shoo-ins for the job. In the fall of 1974, we were accepted for a January 1975 departure.

For Annie and me, this was our first trip to the USSR. Our jobs with the United States Information Agency (USIA), which could rightfully be called the propaganda arm of the U.S. State Department, were for the first nine months of the exhibit tour. We would be attached to the exhibit as guides for its run in Tashkent, Uzbekistan, then Baku, Azerbaijan, and finally, in the summer of 1975, in Moscow, Russia.

The British Airways jet taxied to a halt in front of the terminal. Among its passengers, two dozen college-aged students, including Anne and myself, prepared to disembark into the cold. We waited while the aircraft steps were moved into place. Experienced travelers to Russia knew better than to expect a jet bridge and were bundling up for the descent down the stairs and into buses, which would take us into the terminal.

"I wonder how long it will take to get through customs with our diplomatic passports?" asked another newcomer. "It's usually fairly quick, but it's almost an hour ride to downtown," explained another student.

Our group had all gone through the FBI clearance checks, then the two-week training together in Washington, D.C., to become guides for the exhibit, but for some, it was not their first time to Russia, having studied abroad in the USSR.

Anne and I were feverish with anticipation. We couldn't wait to get into the city, check into the hotel, and get out for a walk in the streets of Moscow, no matter how late the hour. We were in Moscow! We would only be in the capital for a few days before we departed for Tashkent and the three-month stay, which would include mounting and then manning the 20,000 square foot exhibit of Technology for the American Home.

This USIA exhibit was the fourteenth since the famous 1959 "American National Exhibition," which had featured the impromptu "kitchen debate" between then–Vice President Richard Nixon and Soviet Premier Nikita Khrushchev, in which the two sparred over capitalism vs. communism and their respective achievements. In the press coverage, a lesser-known member of the Politburo, Leonid I. Brezhnev, was seen as having pushed himself into the photo of "Nik and Dick" in the mocked-up kitchen. Khrushchev came away impressed with Nixon, and subsequently hoped that Senator John F. Kennedy, who might be a lesser adversary, would prevail in the next U.S. election.

Clearing customs quickly, we were all loaded onto an "Intourist" bus, which proceeded to take us into the center of Moscow, to the Metropol Hotel, alongside Red Square. A spontaneous "Hooray!" arose from our group, seeing the colorful onion domes of St. Basil's Cathedral.

For me, the sight of St. Basil's was a fulfillment of childhood imaginings in real life. Fully illuminated at night, dramatic in its iconic representation of Russia, it eclipsed the squat mausoleum marked with the word Lenin across the front.

Writing to my mother later that week (she had been ecstatic about my trip, forgiving me for all previous transgressions in anticipation of my travel to her homeland), I described the details of my first walk in Red Square:

> January 22, 1975
>
> Dorogaya [dear] Mama!
>
> I cannot describe the incredible feelings I had at my first glimpse of Red Square—the Cathedral, the Kremlin walls, and the enormity of the square in front of me. We were walking across it, snow gently falling, and all around us we were hearing Russian spoken. But it wasn't just any Russian language, it was perfect, like a sweet melody to my ears. And everyone, all around us, each person we passed was speaking in this, my native language.
>
> It is hard to describe my emotions to you, the feelings which flooded me which said that "yes, these are all my people, this is my country." These faces, these couples walking arms locked together, these fur hats, this is all my own.
>
> We drew closer to the domes of the St. Basil's Cathedral and standing there, wondrously looking up at the multi-colored onion domes, we were approached by two young men, who struck up a conversation:
>
> "Where are you from? The Baltic Republics?" asked one. I would often be mistaken for Latvian or Lithuanian because of a slight accent in my Russian speech.
>
> "No, we're from America."
>
> "America? No, that can't be. You're one of us!" He replied, in disbelief. We hurried off, surprised to hear what would be repeated in the months ahead.

I wrote further about entering a cafeteria and sampling the appetizers of cheese, and a *pirozhok*, all familiar, but new to us here.

The following morning, a Sunday, we headed out to find a working church. St. Basil's Cathedral was an empty museum, its architecture, and colors for show only. No Russian Orthodox services were conducted there.

"Are you believers?" asked the Metropol Hotel's *dezhurnaya*, the floor nanny, when we asked where we might find an Orthodox liturgy. Her job was to keep track of the comings and goings of hotel guests, hold passports, keys. Her reaction was one of surprise at our request.

We nodded. She looked at us suspiciously but directed us to a cathedral in another district.

The church was filled mostly with the elderly women, heads covered in scarves, eyes closed in their private prayers, but there was much pushing and shoving and passing up of candles on the periphery. Anne, a churchgoer back home, was dismayed at the chaotic atmosphere in what she had expected to be quiet devotion. For me, just standing there in the incense-filled sanctuary and hearing the singing of orthodox hymns and the priest's invocations, was magical. I described the details in a letter to my mother.

A few weeks later I received a reply from her, which described how she sat and read my words aloud to my father.

> I cried, reading and re-reading your letter. Your father, too, was tearful. Why? Not because of some sorrow or grief. I cried on learning of your feelings when you first experienced that faraway land, which, regardless of its order and deplorable conditions, with genuine pride I still call my homeland.
>
> I cried tears of joy, my daughter, that even after the difficulty of resisting assimilation into this country, and the fact that you were born here, not in Russia, and that you came under the influences of American life, with its pluses and, sadly, minuses (I'm not sure which were greater), but that in spite of all this, your father and I were able to sow a love of Russia in your heart.
>
> Those seeds, which we planted in your soul during your childhood, reading fairy tales, stories and poems to you, the talks we had with you, always in our language about Russia and its people and culture, the summers, when you learned the songs and ballades, the special after-school lessons, taking it all together, those seedlings have finally born shoots.
>
> Yes, after all, you *are* Russian.

I think at that moment, my mother truly loved me, if not for being her daughter, then for allowing her to fully articulate the pathos of her exile. This was the Russia she had kept for so long in her dreams and memories, the Russia she wanted desperately to preserve, not only for herself, but for me.

Had I been standing at home in her study, waiting to be taken into her outstretched arms, she would have enfolded me in the close embrace I had sought so desperately throughout my childhood. I had finally pleased her.

In the months that followed, from Tashkent to Baku and then back again to Moscow for the final weeks of the exhibit's staging at Sokolniki Park, I would write to her my impressions of Soviet life, and of how I was reacting to the peoples and cultures I experienced.

She was sympathetic to my dismissal of Uzbekistan as an imperialist acquisition of the Soviet empire, having little to offer me as "Russian" except its rule. It was plainly Central Asian and Muslim. Azerbaijan was the same.

The American exhibit we manned was a magnet for the local populations to visit, with thousands waiting to enter every day. As guides, our jobs were to explain the exhibit artifacts and represent America. Standing for hours at our assigned sites, we had encounters with the local population, who were allowed to trek through the exhibit rooms.

The conversations with the exhibit visitors in those cities ranged from the mundane: "How much does it cost to buy a cup of flour in America?"

"What is the monthly wage of the American worker?" "Can an American *really* afford a home like this?" To more controversial subjects, often instigated by what the exhibit organizers called "provocateurs," the name given to visitors who were supposedly hired by the KGB to embarrass the young American guides with questions: "Why do you kill your presidents?" "Why is unemployment so high in America, under your capitalist system?" And even: "Why do you lynch your Negroes?"

Their prepared questions, shouted from the back of the crowd, were meant to put us on the defensive and undercut any promotion of the West to the general population moving through the exhibit. Later, several of the young guides fell prey to the KGB's more advanced tactics of isolating loners and creating compromising circumstances around them, usually after hours. Some were even sent home, for their own safety. Anne and I were followed wherever we went—we learned to recognize the faces who were keeping tabs on young, vulnerable Americans.

However, on the exhibit stand, our roles as ambassadors were to answer honestly and without fear of reprisal from *our* government, which as children of the sixties, we did with outright criticism of America's social and political policies of the 1970s.

The war in Vietnam was in its final agony. Saigon fell to the North Vietnamese while we were on tour in Baku, and public discussions at the exhibit raised Soviet citizens' eyebrows at the opinions held by some of us that the U.S. should not have been in Vietnam in the first place. Some well-meaning visitors even warned us that we might get ourselves in trouble with our bosses for expressing those opinions. Of course, we didn't, but rather earned much needed credibility with our Soviet visitors for our frank outspokenness about America's flaws.

However, after six months and thousands of questions from visitors to the exhibit, I grew weary of the absence of critical thinking about their *own* country. They refused to accept even the most provable facts, chalking them up to American propaganda. Almost always they parroted their Party line with the phrase—"but we have it better here"—as a counter. Sometimes that was said wistfully, hoping that I would concede that some aspect of their lives was indeed better than ours in America, as a matter of pride in their country. I would try to be gentle then, and not argue.

Not long after the exhibit opened in Tashkent, I was confronted with a question, which owing to my fluency in Russian, my name ("Lena"), and my immigrant heritage, was to be expected: "*Devushka* [young lady], it seems to me that indeed you are *Russian*, not American!" blurted out a young man, pushed up to the front of the roped-off exhibit stand. For some time, he had been asking otherwise innocent questions, mostly about my knowledge of pop music and familiarity with "Deep Purple." There it was again—the insistence that perhaps I was one of them.

"Well, I was born in the United States," I replied.

"But don't you want to return to your *rodina*, your motherland?" The questioner was sincere in his confusion.

When the question first came up, early in my tour, I was troubled by how to answer without hurting sensitive feelings. And, of course, there was my own ambivalence about the motherland and all it represented in my upbringing. I would deflect the query by mentioning all the wonderful Russian cultural sites I had visited. I would express my gratitude for the warm welcome we received in the visitor's city and the chance to travel and meet its citizens.

But by the end of six months' of searching in vain for the Russia I wanted to find and to feel a part of, I answered that question differently: "Yes, comrade, I want to return to my motherland, in fact, I can't wait to be back on her shores again." *And then the zinger.* "But it is America I long for, that is my motherland."

Some visitors would nod in understanding, saying that of course that was to be expected—a love of one's own country of birth. But it was evident that others were disappointed that life in their socialist paradise, compared to my capitalistic hell, was not more alluring. They had expected that perhaps a prodigal daughter might have wanted to return.

The closer I traveled to Moscow, away from the Soviet Socialist Republics of Uzbekistan and Azerbaijan, and back to the land of Russia proper, the more discerning the exhibit visitors became, often expressing the desire that citizens of the USA and the USSR might find common goals of peace.

Together we watched the Apollo Soyuz joint mission, which docked a spacecraft from NASA's Apollo program with the Soviet Soyuz craft in July 1975, fostering feelings of détente, if only momentarily. We were part of a global audience watching the exchange of U.S. astronauts and Russian cosmonauts in space, handshakes above us and on earth below.

But it was too late for me. I had lost all hope of finding myself even mildly kin to the "Homo Sovieticus" of the last six months. On the contrary, I was a confirmed American. My Yankee sensibilities were prevailing, running red, white and blue as I waited out the final months of the tour. I stopped writing home to my mother. I doubted she would understand my turnabout.

Only in Leningrad, where we had carved out a brief, two-day tourist visit during the "White Nights" of late June, did I allow the cultural gem of Peter the Great's city to seduce me. We rose early and rushed from our Hotel Leningrad along the canals to museums and squares, to the Neva River and the statue of the Bronze Horseman on its bank, named for the epic poem of Alexander Pushkin. Recalling the great Russian poet's words,

"I love you, Peter's creation," I acknowledged that this city, the most European in Russia, had cast a spell on me as well.

I walked through several galleries of the State Russian Museum, which housed masters of Russian 18th and 19th century art. One by one, the paintings that I had memorized in my childhood from my mother's art books, now huge and covering entire walls, beckoned to me. "Come here to Surikov's *Yermak Conquest of Siberia*, then come see Repin's, *Barge Haulers of the Volga*, and Shishkin's *Forest*." The canvasses, larger than life, were encased in glass panes. The effect was surreal—the glass reflected me standing there, mesmerized by the familiar painted images before me and the realization that I was finally in Russia, in the presence of the very art which had defined the aesthetics of my childhood.

Outside, I sat down on a park bench in Arts Square. Couples were strolling through the park, enjoying the day. There was less hurrying here than in Moscow, a tacit agreement to slow down. Two young men walked by, dressed in business suits. Later I would learn that my astrological birthmate, Vladimir Putin, at the same age as I, 22, was a newly minted KGB agent, just graduated. He was assigned to Leningrad during those days of summer, 1975. Although four young American women, albeit traveling on diplomatic passports, were not likely to be of much interest to KGB agents looking for bigger fish in Leningrad, who's to know?

A mightier observer of visitors gazed down on us. A large statue of Pushkin, his right arm outstretched as if to say, "Behold my city!" drew our attention. I accepted his invitation. But I was saddened by the thought that I had had to travel for six months to find what was dearest to me in Russia, and that it was all of a previous time, a long-ago golden age of arts and letters, architecture and music. What had *been* Russia a century before, that was my Russia.

I returned to the USA in the late summer and figuratively if not literally, kissed the tarmac at Dulles airport in Washington, D.C. The customs agent offered a "Welcome Home!" without knowing how much those words truly meant to me. Soon after my return, I married, moved to Connecticut, and started a family.

I would go back to Russia several more times, but never as anything but an *Amerikanka*.

18

The Last Days Before the War—1939

Before the war arrived in my mother's city in late 1941, her life consisted of working as a teacher of the German language in a local school, caring for Natasha and later, Yura, and trying to keep her marriage to Shura intact, a union which was characterized by marital discord brought on by his frequent unexplained absences.

Nadezhda, her mother, my grandmother, continued to live with the family and was an irreplaceable source of help in taking care of Tusya, as my sister Natasha was nicknamed, in the early years of her life. She took good care of her during the day, teaching her the alphabet, reading stories and poems to her while Tatyana was at work, and providing the comfort and attention of the Russian babushka. They slept in the same bed.

Babushka had never approved of the marriage to Budishevsky, insisting that it was a mistake, youth's folly, and urging my mother to end the marriage. She even went to the school administration to try and get a transfer for

Natasha (left), known then as "Tusya," with our Babushka, Nadezhda, who cared for her from her birth to adulthood. Circa 1939.

my mother away from the village of Mushketovo, but to no avail. "Leave him. We will manage," she advised.

But, as my mother describes, she did not listen to this counsel and still hoped that in time Shura would change, would come around and become more of a family man.

A particularly nasty fight was brought on by Shura's jealous rage over seeing Tatyana walking in the street with a group of teachers, side-by-side with a math teacher, while he himself was passing by with a girlfriend on his arm. They exchanged silent glares. Later, he confronted her angrily at home. He dragged her outside and hit her. Inside, he spared no swear words shouting accusations, all in the presence of Babushka and Tusya.

That was the last straw. The next day Tatyana went to the school administrator and begged him for a separate apartment for her, Babushka and Tusya. Luckily there was a two-room apartment available adjacent to the post office, in a teachers' residence building. With help from the school's porter, they moved out.

As she describes it, my mother should have called it quits on the marriage at that point. Babushka was happy that they had separated, and lobbied her to forsake him forever, arguing that she was still young enough to find a better match. Yet, as my mother wrote, "Who listens to their mother?"

Chastened, Shura started to come around, gifts in hand, and took an interest in spending time with his daughter. He paid 180 rubles a month in child support. He started to invite my mother out for the evening, courting her as he had before they were married, but rarely afterwards.

In all, they lived apart for a year and a half, after which Shura secured a larger apartment, away from his meddling mother, and persuaded Tatyana to join him. Their life took on a new, more positive turn as he devoted himself to his family. But even in those days of the late 1930s, it was a difficult time. Tatyana writes of obstacles in her way:

> Our government made much of the fact that women in our country were the smartest, most sophisticated, and above all, the most fortunate in all the world to be living in our socialist society. We were lucky to have the opportunity to become mothers under these circumstances, and to have the best care in the world. The details of that care depended on what the prevailing opinion was on certain issues.
>
> Before 1936, abortions were legal and were performed routinely in hospitals by doctors throughout the country. You only needed to have the required 25 rubles. During that period, the official Party line lauded women's right to make their own choice between having a family and devoting more of themselves to building the future of our society.

By 1936, the government realized its mistake. Because of the widespread availability of abortions, population growth had stalled, there were fewer schoolchildren, families had cut back to one or two children, and many remained childless. Something had to be done about this catastrophe, so the government outlawed abortions. Immediately following the decree, the Party line changed to reflect that Soviet women were the most fortunate in the world because they were protected by a government that cared enough about its citizens to outlaw abortions.

I remember just how fortunate a mother I was in 1939. Yura had picked the wrong time of year to be born. He was born at the end of September, 26 days after school had started. Having spent my allotted six-week maternity leave at home, I had to return to my teaching responsibilities at the local school. With Natasha it had been easier, she had been born in the spring and my leave took me up to summer vacation. By the time I had to go back to work, she was five months old, but this was a different story.

After six weeks I had to return to my classroom duties, even though my little son was still dependent on me. "Fortunately," our humanitarian-minded government had ruled that workers were allowed 30 minutes at lunch to nurse their babies. Whether that was enough or not, whether the child was brought to the worker, or she must run home to the child, that was the mother's concern. But with schoolteachers even that rule didn't hold. Classes couldn't be suspended or postponed for mothers, nor could schoolchildren be left by themselves. We had to make do at recess.

There was another law in effect in 1939: Being late for work by more than 20 minutes carried a prison term. Missing a day of work meant dismissal, trial, and exile to the gulag.

At the time, we lived in a railroad town. The house where we lived and the school where I worked were separated by twenty-seven pairs of train tracks, lined up next to each other and used for switching cars onto different rails. I had to dash across all of them to get home, nurse my son, hand him back to my mother, and run back, all during school recess.

It happened that one day he was sick and didn't want to nurse. I fussed with him. He cried but wouldn't eat. What was I supposed to do? The clock was ticking. Run off, not having fed him? He was still only nursing, not taking solid food. I couldn't be late, so I decided to make a run for it with only five or six minutes left to the recess. I reached the rail tracks. There was a freight train comprised of 40–50 cars on the tracks. But it wasn't just standing still, it was moving back and forth while the engineers coupled or uncoupled cars far in the distance. I couldn't climb through the cars. They were loaded and the heavy doors were shut. I froze in dismay.

Every time I wanted to make a dash under the cars, they started to move again, backward or forward. I couldn't circle around them, there were too many, nor could I get through them. I decided to risk slipping between the freight car wheels. I'd wait until they stop moving, then dash under the carriage, and hope that the train engineer hesitated a second or two before switching into reverse.

They'd stopped. I bolted. I was through!

"You're crazy!!" swore the signal man down the line. But I was already racing to school, without a glance backward. I ran up to the school, but I could see that the recess was over, the children were back inside. My students were watching me through the window as I hurriedly took the stairs, removed my coat, and entered my classroom. The principal was waiting inside for me already. He escorted me outside the
door.

"Comrade, you're late by six minutes. I'm forced to relieve you of your responsibilities. But we have no substitutes available here to stay with the children. Finish your lessons and we'll discuss this later."

Finish my lessons? Can you imagine how I "finished my lessons" that day? The children picked up on my panic, of course. The girls were sympathetic, it seemed to me. They knew that I had run home to feed my little son, and they sat quietly through the afternoon. But the boys were the opposite, they took advantage of the situation with rowdy behavior. I'll never forget that day; how I made it through to the last bell I'll never know.

After school, the discussion in the teachers' room turned ugly. None of my colleagues came to my defense; no one dared to support me. They were all afraid. Many of them were close friends of mine, but they couldn't take the risk of appearing to be against a law, however harsh it was. They all knew the price for going against the government. It was best to just stay quiet, unnoticed, looking down at the floor.

I managed to get off lightly that time, probably because I was only six minutes late and not the 20 which would have necessitated a trial and a conviction. The principal called the regional educational organization and learned that teachers were in such short supply that they couldn't find anyone to replace me. Instead, I was given a stern, written reprimand with a warning. It was posted in the hallway for all, including the students, to read. I wondered how many of them slavishly accepted its unfairness.

For me it was a wake-up call: This time you slipped through, but God help you if it happens again—it'll be the end for you.

Tatyana Budishevsky (married name, first marriage). At age 23 she was a mother to two young children and a teacher of the German language in a public school.

Life continued for Tatyana in this way for two more years, during which Hitler moved into Austria, Czechoslovakia, and Poland. However, he still honored the Molotov-Ribbentrop Non-Aggression Pact, signed in 1939, until June 22 of 1941.

Although she might have guessed that the Soviet Union would be next in the path of Lebensraum, the Nazi policy of annexing "living space" for the proliferation of the growing German race, my mother, living day-to-day to provide for her family, had little time to consider the growing menace of an invading army. That is, until it landed on her door-step.

19

Goodbye—October 13, 1941

At the outset of the German invasion of Russia in late June of 1941, dubbed Operation Barbarossa, my mother managed, against almost insurmountable odds, to retrieve Tusya, my sister, from the health sanatorium in Odessa and travel back home with her.

In the days that followed, three German army groups, numbering over three million soldiers, supported by close to a million more German-allied Finns and Romanians, moved the front line, which stretched from the Baltic to the Black Sea, rapidly toward the east. This was the largest invasion force in the history of warfare, over an 1800-mile front.

Hitler had been preparing for Operation Barbarossa for close to a year, despite his non-aggression pact with Russia. His intent was to mount another blitzkrieg to attain victory over the Soviet Union. Indeed, he stunned Stalin with his surprise attack. In the first few days of the invasion, the Red Army was easily overwhelmed. German units encircled millions of Soviet soldiers, who surrendered and were led on death marches into brutal POW camps. I would learn later that my father and my uncle, scooped up by the Germans in Belarus during a routine work brigade and mistakenly identified as Soviet soldiers, were among them.

During the summer of 1941, the German troops advanced further into Ukraine as the remains of the Red Army retreated. Before the invaders reached my mother's city, which was in the direct path of the advancing armies, residents were ordered by the local government to dig trenches on the outskirts, supposedly to prevent entry into the city—a laughable proposition according to my mother. She recalled that she was spared ditch digging, likely because she was the mother of two small children.

Shortages of everything—materials, food—sprang up almost immediately. Travel for civilians was barred.

"Everything for the front, all for the victory!" was the prevailing cry.

Tatyana describes a period of enforced vigilance during which nightly patrols, comprised of paired women from neighboring households were required to walk the streets during the night hours and report any suspicious behavior which might be staged by *diversanti*, that is, saboteurs. Her elderly mother and her partner typically rolled up to sleep on the outside earthen stove, unperturbed by the threat of supposed subversives.

As the armies from the west approached, now less than 500 miles away, there was an eerie quiet. But not for long. She wrote:

Yura (left), almost two years old, and Natasha, six years old, in July 1941. Shortly before this on June 23, 1941, Tatyana had returned from Odessa where she retrieved Natasha from the sanatorium during the Nazi invasion of Russia that started on June 22.

> The German Army kept getting closer to us—Kiev surrendered, the Dnieper River was crossed. The Soviet Army was retreating, in panic, without a fight. There were rumors that our government had surrendered Moscow, the capital, and had fled east to Samara.
>
> There were fantastic stories circulating, not credible enough to be believed. Some said that the Germans were bringing truckloads of bread for us, and all types of clothing to cover our naked, impoverished populace. (We were quickly disabused of this notion, when we saw what the Germans really had in mind for us.) Few had any faith in those rumors but did not want to think about what the actual reality might be of living under foreign occupation.
>
> Finally, the day of their arrival was upon us. There was no battle. The Soviets had left the city, destroying everything they left behind if they were unable to take it with them. They burned the warehouses of grain, they took all the foodstuffs they could, reasoning that nothing could be left for the enemy.
>
> Where it concerned the native population, most of us were left "to the mercy of the victor" by our Soviet rulers, who did not seem to care in the least for what happened to us. We had been instructed to leave, in any way possible, on foot if necessary, and evacuate with them to the east.

In the last days before the arrival of the Germans, the Soviets had dynamited the railroad tracks, sending huge pieces of tracks rocketing through the air, landing on our roofs, and breaking our walls and windows. A railroad tie fell on our outdoor pump, leaving us without water. The electricity had long since been turned off. We sat in the light of oil wick lamps; the availability of kerosene was a distant memory.

We realized that our government had left us to die.

When the warehouses had been burned, not everything was completely ruined. As soon as the Soviets retreated, the looting started. I admit that I too set off for the warehouse district with a small carrying bag, while others were pulling up with wagons. But when I saw some of my students there, doing what I knew to be illegal, I turned around and came back with nothing. I had only wanted to get some grain for our eight chickens, but I didn't even manage to do that.

As families of the railroad workers, we were given the chance to leave the city, not with our husbands, but on our own. The men would be moving the locomotives and supply cars elsewhere, away from the Germans so that nothing would fall into enemy hands. Shura was taking a locomotive east, to an undisclosed location. The families would be taken by rail to a different, unknown destination. We were to be allotted half a railroad car for ourselves and our possessions, and would be taken somewhere, no one seemed to know. Some said to Tashkent.

From left to right: Tatyana, Natasha (daughter) and Shura Budishevsky. September 1939. After October 1941, Natasha would not see her father again for 25 years.

Shura was not keen on our evacuation from the city. He argued that we should stay put, saying that the German occupation would be temporary, and if we left and then later returned, everything would be damaged or looted and we would have nothing to come back to, nowhere to live. He warned me that if we left along with thousands of other refugees, we might be worse off, maybe even starve in some far-off city. Men like him would not be able to help since they were being directed somewhere else.

Shura argued that our children were still young—Yura only two years old. Where would we go and how would we manage? We only had 750 rubles to our name. He was also concerned that his elderly parents were staying behind, afraid of the destruction of their house. I am sure that he was hoping that I would help them, with my knowledge of the German language. We decided that I would stay, along with the children and my mother.

On the 13th of October 1941, he took his leave of us. The goodbyes were difficult and Shura, usually the big and blustery man,

Tatyana and her two children, Natasha (standing) and Yura, July 29, 1941. Her husband, Shura, retreated east with the Red Army several months later in mid-October 1941, leaving her to fend for herself, her children and her mother under the Nazi occupation.

sucked in his breath and choked up bidding farewell to his children. Perhaps he sensed that he was seeing them for the last time.

He and I had tentatively agreed, however, that like some of the other railroad workers, he would drive his locomotive to a designated station, leave it there, and then sneak back home. Many of the railroad engineers did exactly that. But Shura didn't. He must have been worried—he was responsible for several locomotives, not just his own. And after all that was said, the pull of his family may not have been as strong, and in his mind, may not have warranted the risk.

We never saw him again.

And that was all that my mother ever wrote about her first husband, who, as I learned later from my sister, was drafted into the Soviet Army a few weeks later and fought at the Battle of Stalingrad, where over one million Soviet soldiers lost their lives between August 1942 and February 1943.

That my mother never saw Shura again, or learned of his whereabouts, despite attempts to locate him through the Red Cross, is not surprising. Postwar, after seven years' search, she was officially assumed widowed. He was presumed dead, along with the eight million military, and overall, 25 million civilian and military deaths of Soviet citizens during World War II. By many this is considered an understated total. Compared with the 418,500 losses to the United States, or Great Britain's 450,700, only China's toll during the war, 20 million, was even close.

Tatyana in the spring/summer of 1941. Judging by the smile, the photograph must have been taken before Hitler invaded on June 22, 1941, and completely changed her world.

Once the Germans invaded the USSR, there were no means of communicating from beyond the occupied territory back home. There was no way to get news to and from loved ones who had evacuated, no way to know their fate. Everything was under the control of the local German command; everything, including life and death.

20

Under the German Flag—Autumn 1941

"The Germans are in the market square!" shouted a panicked voice in a nearby yard. The words rang out mid-day on October 21, 1941, according to my mother's account. In only four months since the invasion had begun, the German Army had moved deep into Ukraine, crossing the 800 miles from the Polish border to Donetsk (Stalino), where my mother had remained. Soon after, German soldiers appeared in her front yard, and in the front and back yards of everyone else on her street in their town.

It was raining that day.

Everything was wet and muddy, dirt as only in Russia, where few of the roads are paved and trucks sink knee deep into the grime.

The mud stuck to the boots of the soldiers.

On our stoop there was a wooden basin, where we collected rainwater to wash our hair, since the city water was very hard and impossible to use for washing our tresses.

The Germans entered our yard, and without a second thought or asking permission, stepped into the water basin with their boots to rinse them of the mud and dirt. They had assumed that we had put the water there expressly for them to wash their jackboots. That was our first impression of them.

Three soldiers were immediately assigned billets in our apartment. At that time, I had not yet learned to recognize the insignias on their shoulders to distinguish their ranks as conscripted soldiers or officers. They demanded that we clear out and turn over one of our two rooms to them, which left us with just the other room and the kitchen. Some families only had one room, so we were lucky.

Once indoors, they quickly took off their boots and each soldier changed into a pair of bedroom slippers they had kept in their rucksacks. This greatly surprised us, because not only had it been years since we had even thought about such a comfort in our lives, but here they were carrying slippers with them into war! Later we would see that they had brought everything imaginable with them, down to the last item of personal hygiene.

They entered our room. My little son, Yura, just two years old, was sleeping nearby. One of the German soldiers walked up to the crib and stared intently at him.

I was frightened and stepped between the soldier and my child. Prior to the arrival of the Germans, there had been posters everywhere which depicted a sleeping infant with a German soldier poised menacingly over him with a knife.

I spoke up to the soldier in German, telling him to leave my son alone. He stepped back in surprise and answered that he had a child at home who was the same age, and he was reminded of him by looking at my boy.

When I explained to him about the posters, he started to laugh and gestured in a circular motion with his fingers by his temple, saying that it was crazy, all of it just Soviet propaganda.

It turned out to be that, for most of us. But not so when it came to the Jewish families among us.

My mother was not aware of what Hitler's plans were for her and her countrymen. As early as March 1941, before the invasion of the Soviet Union, Hitler had approved a policy to be carried out by Reichsmarschall Hermann Göring, called the Oldenburg Plan, which called for the total exploitation of the conquered territories in the east. The Plan, as Göring conceived and carried it out, included the expropriation of all food and all stocks of raw materials, especially oil, to supply the German Armies in the occupied territories and to be sent back to Germany for the war effort.

The expressed intent of this written policy of the Nazis was death by starvation of tens of millions of "racially inferior" Slavic people living in the occupied areas, and the extermination of "undesirable" populations of Jews and urban dwellers in large cities such as Kiev. This was to be an engineered famine, thus called The Hunger Plan by its architect, Herbert Backe, a German politician, agronomist, and SS functionary of the Third Reich, who with others, such as Heinrich Himmler, decided that a "surplus population" in Russia of 20 to 30 million could be cut off from food which could be used to feed both the invading German Army and the German population itself.

The Hunger Plan for starving the local population was conceived prior to the invasion and, in fact, became an essential condition of it, according to its planners, without which the assault on the Soviet Union could not succeed.

But at the time, my mother could only guess at what the impact of this "economic" policy held in store for her.

So, we began a completely different life. It was different politically, too—we started to hear new propaganda—a denunciation of the Soviet government, the taking down of all the portraits of Lenin and Stalin and the others—and presenting the successes of the Third Reich as victorious, the conquerors.

The food situation became horrific. The Germans had no intention of providing anything to the local population. They told us that we should have insisted that the food stuffs in the warehouses remain and not be taken away or burned by the Soviets, that we had allowed the looting and destruction to happen, and that we had only ourselves to blame for the shortages now.

Perhaps they were at least partially correct, but who could have argued with the Soviet powers when they were retreating? Our family—myself, my mother, our Aunt Marusia who had come to live with us when the war broke out, and the two children—was left with nothing.

We started out by butchering our chickens because there were rumors that the Germans were taking them for themselves, chasing down the hens in the backyards, grabbing the roosters and not giving them back. Shame! We hurriedly cooked up our hens and ate them.

And then what? What meager reserves we had were dwindling quickly.

Babushka hated the Germans for their ransacking of Russia's wealth and resources, and she despised them for their rudeness.

I will never forget an incident. When returning from work, I witnessed the following: A German soldier had entered our apartment and was dragging away our bed. My mother had gotten a hold of the other side of the bed and a tug-of-war ensued between the two of them, back and forth, while she is screaming at him in Russian, "This is *my bed*, you scoundrel, where are you taking it?" The soldier, paying her no heed, was using all his might to pull the bed out the door.

I addressed him in German. "What are you doing? If you don't leave the bed alone I will go straight to the Kommandant and report your conduct!"

He was stunned by this statement and dropped the bed immediately, retreating hastily out the door. He knew there was an order against marauding, that is, illegally removing personal belongings from the population.

Other houses were not so fortunate. My mother-in-law kept chickens for egg-laying. When the Germans arrived, she carefully locked the hens in an empty room and pulled the shades. As some soldiers tramped through their backyard, a rooster just had to fly up into the window and crow his heart out! All her chickens were appropriated by the Third Reich.

It was about then that the German occupying forces re-opened the schools. It was telling to see who had evacuated with the Soviets and who had stayed behind, as we had. Oddly, many had stayed.

When I walked into the school, my teacher-friends were surprised that I had not left, given that we would have been provided half a rail-car from the train yard as the wife of a locomotive engineer. The others did not have that opportunity and had no choice but to remain.

We started slowly reorganizing the school. But that didn't last long, because the Germans decided that the children of the local population needed to be taught only through Grade 4; learning to read and write would be enough. No more than that would be required of them. Consequently, those of us teaching the upper grades were let go.

By then, all our food supplies had been used up, so a group of teachers decided to go to the peasant villages in the countryside to exchange whatever we had in clothing or other items for food. We hired a horse and cart and rode out of town on it, and then returned walking, having filled the cart with grain.

A deep snow had fallen while we were out on our mission and the glaring whiteness of the snow on the fields hurt our eyes and reddened them. Our school principal had to wear dark glasses for several weeks.

But even those food stuffs were soon gone and once again I had to go off to the villages to exchange what I could for provisions. I had already bartered all of Shura's clothes and most of mine for a few potatoes. That was the only thing that was keeping us alive in the city, but I was down to my last dress.

The country folk, for whom life under the Soviet regime had been even harsher than for us, were willing to exchange anything to cover their bodies with something more than the potato sacks out of which they had fashioned their skirts and pants. Their hope was that in time, the Germans would dissolve the collective farms and let them till their own soil again, and that they would start to live a normal life, as before, during the good ole tsarist years.

On this trip, I was accompanied by just Shura's cousin Nina, a young woman. I dragged a sled behind me.

Once we were in the villages, we got separated from each other. I decided to return home alone, my sled laden with some grain, some potatoes which I had wrapped to protect them from the cold, and a goose, slaughtered but not plucked of its feathers.

As I was walking through a snowy field, I heard someone gaining on me and looked fearfully behind me. It was a man with a knapsack. He turned out to be a Soviet prisoner of war, an escapee from a German POW camp. His name was Nikolai. He helped me drag my load home and stayed with us a few days, taking turns milling the grain into flour on a hand grinder, which was difficult to turn. Then he left one night, disappearing into the shadows.

It was now 1942 and the Germans had been lording it over our poor homeland for almost a year. You could see their presence everywhere, on every corner. They behaved as if these lands were theirs by inheritance. Anything, everything that they could get their hands on, they grabbed and sent back to Germany. They robbed the peasants of any remaining supplies in the country. They dragged off what was left of any industrial machinery, even though most of it had been blown up or carried away by the Soviets, and shipped it to their war factories.

If anyone dared to politely question their tactics, they replied:

"It's the war. Germany needs everything for the front, for victory." And: "When the war is over, things will be better. There will be enough for all then."

Those responses didn't make it much easier for us, trying to survive day to day. It had been almost a year since Shura had left with the retreating Soviet army. Now, another factor came into play, a fateful one.

I knew the German language; I had taught it in the local school. Shura and I thought my knowledge of German might be of help in adapting to what we thought was a temporary occupation of our country, and then "our boys" would return and a normal life would resume.

But right then, I stood at the precipice of death.

21

Alexander, My Father—1941–1945

My father was not Alexander "Shura" Budishevsky, my mother's first husband, whom she married in 1931, with whom she lived in Soviet Russia, and about whom she was writing in her journals regarding the years preceding the war. The last time Tatyana saw Shura was when he left her and the two children in the city of Donetsk in October 1941 and moved eastward with the Red Army, retreating ahead of the German advance. The Germans soon occupied Donetsk.

As events were unfolding in Tatyana's life in Ukraine, a different fate was descending on another Alexander, this one Alexander Artemyeff—Sasha, as he was called in the family—who would later become my father. He was a 27-year-old engineer living in Belarus. Up until then, the lives of these two people, separated by a thousand miles, had been vastly different.

My father was born in 1913 and grew up in the village of Vidzy, which was part of Poland before Hitler and Stalin divided up that country in 1939. My father's Russian ancestors had moved there in the 1700s, during the reign of Peter the Great, as part of the exodus from Russia of the Old Believers, a splinter group of the Orthodox Church that rejected Patriarch Nikon's church reforms of the late 1600s. Thousands of Old Believers, *Staroveri*, were scattered throughout the world, including Eastern Europe and even Canada.

Growing up in Poland, Sasha did not live under the Communist regime, which was distinct from my mother's childhood and youth. He attended a Russian secondary school in Vilnius and received an engineering degree from a university in Warsaw. He and his two brothers, Leonid, who was two years younger, and Ivan, nine years his junior, were sons of a merchant landowner, Theodosius Artemyeff. When Theodosius suffered an accidental death in 1924, his young wife, Alexandra, was left alone to care for the family. The three boys grew up fatherless, but together with their mother continued to manage the orchards, farms, and livestock. Sasha left home to attend the university in Warsaw.

When the Nazis invaded Poland in September 1939, Sasha was in Warsaw. Hurriedly, he made the 400-mile journey home to Vidzy on his bicycle, returning to what had now become a Soviet-occupied territory under the two-year Molotov-Ribbentrop Pact, signed by Hitler and Stalin in August 1939. Sasha found that the family had no alternative but to turn their farmlands over to the new ruling Soviet authorities; all the farms were taken over for government collectivization. All Sasha, his mother and his two brothers were left with was their ancestral home in the village and a small plot.

Sasha, Leonid, and Ivan tended to their home and took care of their mother all the while suspecting, as did so many others, that Hitler would not stop with Poland and that war with the Soviet Union loomed inevitable. They were correct.

The Non-Aggression Pact Stalin had signed with Hitler lasted less than two years.

On June 22, 1941, the day of the Nazi invasion of the USSR, Sasha and Leonid, who had been conscripted as civilian non-combatants by the Soviets to be part of a construction battalion, were building an airport runway and fortifications on the border with Germany.

Leonid, my uncle, described it in this remembrance:*

> As we were busy with our morning wash-up, we saw planes in the distance, coming up over the trees. They were coming in our direction. As they dipped down towards us, their machine guns opened to strafe us on the ground.
>
> We scattered in a panic. I ducked under a wooden wheelbarrow, next to a political officer. The planes dropped several small bombs and then headed east. Only then did a voice come on the loudspeakers to announce: "*The enemy has treacherously violated our sacred borders! War!*"
>
> Our lieutenant, the battalion commander, gathered us up and announced that since we had no firearms, and no offensive weapons, we were of no value as soldiers, and that those of us who were local should return home.
>
> Sasha and I were about 200 kilometers from our farm. We set out in groups, hiding in the forest when we heard approaching planes.
>
> The Nazis blew up the bridges, so we had to ford the rivers. At

---

*Grateful acknowledgment is made to the following for permission to reprint previously published material: UNIFICATION: Excerpts from *In German POW Camp: Remembrances of a Prisoner of War,* by Leonid Artemieff, copyright circa 1999. Reprinted by permission of Unification, West Ryde, Australia. Translation by Helen Charov.

one crossing, a large group of soldiers, heading east, were wading into the river just as the planes suddenly appeared overhead with machine gun fire. The river waters turned red.

We walked for almost a week. In the villages along the way, women came out of their houses and brought out bread to us. "Here, son. Maybe someone will feed my boy somewhere."

On the sixth day, we were overtaken by a group of German soldiers on motorcycles. "Hands up! Hats off!" they shouted at us. And since we had shaved heads, they mistakenly took us for Soviet soldiers.

"*Los! Los!*" ("*Come on*!") We were commanded, herded into a group and taken to the nearby town, Suvalki, where we joined a thousand other tired and hungry soldiers and prisoners. We were denied any food or water. On the third day, each of us received a cup of dry flour. The powder stuck in our throats; we had nothing with which to gulp it down. Thirsting for a drop of any liquid, the prisoners would throw themselves face down into puddles after a rain. Anything for a drink of water.

We were formed into lines. "Jews—step forward!" And whoever did not obey was found out anyway when we had to drop our pants and exhibit our "passports." The Jews were led away. We were herded into the courtyard of a crumbling castle, where we tried to rest, worrying about what would come next.

The German guards dragged in a young Jewish woman. They ordered her to strip naked and dance. Her tender young body was luminous in the rays of the setting sun, as she shuddered from shame and disgrace. The guards, aroused, and with uniforms unbuttoned, screamed at her to circle faster. As she fell, exhausted, one pulled out his revolver and shot her in the head. She crumpled, in full view of the thousands of prisoners.

We waited for where we would be taken next. We were loaded into railroad cars and deported to Germany. Vanya, our youngest brother, said that right then our mother arrived at the prison site, having ridden on horseback all the way to Suvalki, over 200 miles. But we were gone, and what could she have done to save us? Still, what will a mother not try to do for her children?

We arrived in Germany and were unloaded from the train into a forest setting. There were no houses, not even a barbed wire fence, only four towers manned with machine guns and searchlights. The only building was a barracks for staff. Later this camp would be identified as Stalag 10, near Hanover.

We were lined up into endless rows, five men deep, and divided into groups of one hundred men. The "hundred" was the operative unit. The "hundred" received its rations of bread, a loaf each for eight men, which we had to cut into pieces with wire, since we had no knives.

The bread was hardly that—it was filled with sawdust and wood chips as filler. When each prisoner received his portion, he would turn away from the group while the rest of the slices were distributed. "Whose?" "The third one." Then, "the fourth," and "the fifth," until it was all gone. The bread ration was a matter of life and death.

Without a roof over our heads, the prisoners used their hands to dig out holes in the roots of trees, to shelter in the ground. When the autumn rains came, some of these *zemlyanki,* literally "earthies," collapsed, burying prisoners alive. Some prisoners reinforced their shelters with tree branches and twigs, ripped off trees, since there were no tools or knives with which to work.

All our razors or blades had been taken away, yet the fastidious Germans demanded that we shave our beards, so we used broken shards of glass, cutting into our faces, which bled. The criminals in our midst, who had smuggled in their own razors, shaved us in exchange for a bread ration.

Starvation drove us mad. There were instances of cannibalism. All the bark was eaten off the trees; anything made of leather was consumed.

By winter, we had built some barracks, housing hundreds of men in one building, but with no mattresses or blankets. We were lucky to have one overcoat for 5–6 men. We slept side-by-side to stay warm since there was no heat. But somehow life continued. A list of prisoners was compiled, by barracks, each man given a number to wear around his neck. No more names—we were called by our numbers.

The first winter in POW camp was brutal. The Germans were moving eastward and not meeting with any resistance. The Soviet soldiers did not want to fight, they retreated in panic. Thousands upon thousands of prisoners were taken, but the Germans were not prepared for such high numbers. The POW camps were overflowing, the rations were reduced further, there was not enough room in the barracks. Hundreds were left under the open winter sky to freeze to death. We were infested by lice. We scraped them off our shirts with our hands, then killed them by rolling over them with bottles or sticks.

The count in the Stalag 10 prison camp in the autumn was close to 35,000 POWs. By the spring, hunger and typhus reduced that to just a few thousand men.

I fell sick with typhus, with a fever of 42°C (107.6°F) and delirium. I lay semi-conscious for several days. Luckily, Sasha was there with me. By some miracle he did not fall ill and looked after me and other sickened prisoners. He bartered his watch to the cook for bread and a piece of fat. As Sasha described it later, he fed me some potatoes cooked in the fat after which my body temperature soared and he thought I was done for, but then I recovered.

Finally, the long-awaited spring arrived. The snow melted and the trees greened with leaves. Birds sang in the forest. We crawled out into the sun to warm our bones and shake the handfuls of lice out from inside our torn shirts. It was horrific to look at each other, skeletal, our skin pulled tightly over our bones.

We looked around, inquired about friends. Many were gone. Gone was Kazik, the Pole, who had a pleasant baritone and with whom, to pass the time and push back the sadness, we sang songs together in the fall. He had asked us to contact his mother with word of his fate, but we had lost his address. Forgive us, Kazik!

Gone were the engineers with whom Sasha and I had spent time sharing conversations and memories. So many were missing—thousands were piled into mass, unmarked graves.

One can only wonder at the persistence of Man. The conditions under which we lived would not have been enough even for cattle to survive, yet we persisted. This was not living; it was a brutal mockery of humanity. But we weren't considered human! Stalin had rejected the Red Cross, announcing that there were no prisoners of war, only traitors to the Motherland.

And since there was no one to whom we could turn for help or mercy, we were being exterminated. We weren't "human"; we were *Untermensch,* or sub-human, and Hitler's intent was to destroy the Slavic race. In *Mein Kampf,* he wrote that the Slavs must become the fertilizer for the plains of Russia to support the expansion of the German population.

Despair settled into the camp. There was no hope of survival. So why suffer these torments? Wouldn't it be better to end it all quickly? I recall a moment with this thought in my mind. All it would take was an approach to the barbed wire fencing and the machine gun would bring a swift end. The suffering would be over.

So, I walked closer to the wire border. And then I saw her. Just beyond the fence. Mama.

She was exactly as I had last seen her, kerchief tied around her face. The pain and longing were expressed silently in her eyes. I stopped then and did not move forward toward the barbed wire. She must have been praying to God for us. Her prayers were our salvation in the darkest moment of our lives.

I read these passages from my uncle Leonid's recollections of his years in POW camp and recalled that my father, Alexander, who had been there with him throughout the four years, had rarely talked about the war.

During my childhood in Brooklyn, my mother said that my father would be woken by nightmares in the middle of the night, and she would have to quiet him not to disturb Eugene and me sleeping in the next room.

Once, when we had touched on the Holocaust and the treatment of Jews rounded up into the POW camps, he related a memory from his days as working as a scribe in the camp.

"The new prisoners would line up to be listed on the rolls of the POWs," he said. "I was supposed to write down their name and assign them a number. If it was a Jewish sounding name, I would whisper to them that I could change it, right there."

"It probably didn't make a difference in the end," he added.

22

Summer 2001—The Decision of a Lifetime

Reading her story, I'd come to the point in my mother's life where she had asked me to stop and go no further with translations of her years in Russia.

I remember that day. It was in the summer of 2001. It was mid-morning, and we were in her library, the light streaming through the lace-curtained window over her writing desk. She was dressed in a beautiful green dress. Her hair was coifed in her usual short wave; eyebrows penciled perfectly, red lipstick. She was wearing matching emerald earrings and brooch. At age 84, she looked regal in her setting.

My mother had agreed to a Sunday magazine article I had been writing about her youth and early days as a teacher in Russia, drawn from the articles we had been working on together. We were waiting for a photographer, who was coming to take some portrait photos of her. The newspaper had requested a few photographs of her in her home and had dispatched a professional photographer to Sea Cliff for a photo shoot. He called to say he was running late.

Over the past several months, we had gone back and forth on word choices and fact checks of my translation. Her knowledge of the English language was adequate for an overall sense of the piece, and she made only minor corrections in the margins. She was pleased that I had shown an interest in her writing, and we worked together well.

While we waited, my father and I sat opposite her. She fiddled nervously with her hands, picking at her polished nails. He leaned over to me and said in a low voice, "Isn't she beautiful?"

There was no hint of anything except loving admiration for his wife of 52 years. He moved his head back and forth a little as if he was admiring a work of art. I looked sidelong at him with a raised eyebrow, surprised by his admission. I was not accustomed to hearing his outright expression of affection for her. "Yes … she is, even at her age."

"Just as beautiful as the day I met her," he added, not taking his eyes off her. We all knew that he had been smitten by her long ago in postwar Germany. In the refugee camp where they had met, he had been an amateur photographer, and had taken photographs of her in profile. Movie-star poses. I had seen some of them in the family albums kept on the shelf. He probably wanted to be taking photographs of her today, too, but was happy to just be there, admiringly.

His reverie was broken by the ring of the doorbell, signaling that the photographer had finally arrived. After the photographer took several dozen shots, including the Russian typewriter she had used to peck out her memories, my mother offered him the customary invitation: "Would you like a cup of tea before you go?" The photographer thanked her but demurred, walking out to his car.

We were left alone. After a few minutes, my mother spoke up. "Well, and what now?" she asked, turning to me.

"The article will be published this fall," I answered, "but I'm not sure of the date yet."

"I meant, after that, are you going to continue?" she added.

"I'd like to. There's a lot more to tell, isn't there?"

She paused and looked over at me sternly. "I don't need this. I just want the past to stay in the past."

I knew that we were moving into sensitive territory. "But there's nothing that you should be ashamed of, or reproach yourself for," I told her.

"Others may not feel that way," she answered, and got up and went into the kitchen.

I let it go. I knew she would be unhappy with me if I persisted in trying to convince her that her story was worth recording. But neither could I change it to make her feel safe in its telling. *Oh well,* I thought. *So much for that.*

My own life had taken a sharp turn with a divorce from my husband of 23 years. The summer camp romance which had blossomed into a full-blown courtship and marriage when I had returned from Russia had suffered through several crises, many of our own making. The Navy, with its separations, was no longer to blame. The stress of a failed start-up lay heavily on Alex, a brooding Russian, while I scrambled to keep the banks from foreclosing on our house by taking a job which required overseas travel. The extended absences didn't make anyone happy. Even the unexpected, miraculous pregnancy with the second child I'd always wanted only gave us a brief respite before disillusion led to dissolution.

As a single mother, I had to address the need to fend for myself and my young daughter, Katia. Like the women who had come before me, I was busy with the demands of work, survival, doing what I had to do to assure that what remained of my own family was the best that I could manage on my own. Of course, it was nothing compared to the travails of my mother's life, but it took all my energy and wits to keep it all together.

Put simply, life got in the way. It would be several years before I resumed where I had left off, and then I worked on it sporadically, alone. I didn't seek my mother's approval. But I vowed to find some way to tell her story. And I went on translating.

"Ya, ich spreche Deutsch"
("Yes, I speak German")

The Nazis learned that I speak German. Someone in town had been quick to let them know that I was a teacher of German and spoke the language fluently. I was sent for by the local commanding headquarters and ordered to report immediately.

I was away at the time, returning from a 35-mile trek, dragging a sled behind me laden with un-milled wheat, beets, and a few potatoes that I had bartered from peasants for what remained of our clothes. We had exchanged every last item, leaving us almost naked ourselves, but it was what had kept us alive up to then.

Upon my return, I learned of the summons from the Kommandatura. *And so it begins*, I thought to myself. *Now they won't leave me alone.* It was as I expected.

The Kommandant of our local German headquarters, a young Austrian whose surname was prefaced with *Von-something,* started in, trying to talk me into becoming a translator for them, explaining that it was useless to expect the return of the Soviet Army. He unfurled a map of the USSR on a table in front of me, and showed me where the fronts were: Leningrad was under a blockade. Moscow was in a pincer. Hitler's 6th army was approaching the Volga River.

When I admitted to him that my husband, who had left with the Reds, had strictly forbidden me to work for the occupation forces, warning me of my sure execution upon the return of the Soviets, the Kommandant started to laugh. He called in his staff officers and asked me to repeat my concerns. They all guffawed loudly at my naïveté.

The Kommandant gave me a few days to think it over, weigh the consequences, and return to the headquarters with my response. I came home upset—what should I do?

My family of five was on the brink of starvation. My two children, seven and three years old, were emaciated and constantly begging for food. They were like little baby birds in the nest with their beaks open, but I couldn't bring them anything.

My two elderly *starushki,* my mother and our aunt Marusia,

were swelling from hunger edema, and I too could not buckle my shoes any longer from the water collecting in my feet and legs.

There was nothing left with which to barter for food. I was down to a single change of underclothes and two dresses. All of Shura's clothes were long since exchanged for milk, beets, and grain, which Mama and I ground on a hand mill with difficulty.

The Germans promised to give me their soldiers' rations, and even more compelling, they offered soup from their field kitchen. Soup. It seems ridiculous to me to even mention a food that is now overlooked or omitted for the sake of weight loss, a lowly item of little or no interest. Was soup to decide the fate of our lives?

There is a Russian saying, "*Sitniy golodnomy ne tovarich*" (*The well-fed is not a friend to the hungry*).

We debated our dire predicament in a family council. What should I do? If I refused the offer of work from the Germans, if that was even possible, since there was a threatening tone to the request by the Kommandant, we would surely die. The children would die with us.

There are no words to describe the horror of watching someone die of starvation right before your eyes. Aunt Marusia was near death. She had started to lose her mind. Lately she had taken to running up and down the stairs, bursting into the rooms of our neighbors, and if no adults were present, grabbing food out of the hands of the children lying feebly in bed.

Friends from all over complained to us about her, begging us to keep her inside, under lock. There wasn't much I could do about her.

The thing was, my aunt was an excellent seamstress in her day. Women, and sometimes men, although not often, with sewing skills were able to sustain themselves by going into the countryside with raw cloth and thread and providing tailoring in exchange for food and a roof over their head. They would go from house to house among the peasants, sewing garments for them, their payment only in food, and thus survive.

I had tried to persuade Aunt Marusia earlier in the year to do the same—not to earn anything for us but just to have enough to support herself—but she had refused to leave us. "Whatever befalls you, will befall me as well," she said. "I will not leave you."

And so, her tragic end came in those next few days. I wasn't able to provide for her. Her death lay as a heavy sin on my soul for the rest of my life. When Mama and I were returning from the cemetery, having placed Aunt Marusia in a shallow grave, we wondered, "Who is next?"

We were both completely swollen. But giving our last crumbs to the children was risky. If I was to follow and die next, who would care for them?

Aunt Marusia's death pushed me toward a decision, either to die and let my loved ones die, or to go to work for the Germans and save my children, my mother and myself. In so doing, I would rip myself completely from my previous life, and have to put out of my mind the return of the Red Army and any hope of forgiveness for my cooperation with the enemy.

I wavered. The Kommandant summoned me again. "Well, have you reconsidered?" he asked.

I was silent, eyes down.

"If not, we will have to take measures. You have heard the term sabotage in war time? We are in power here, and we will do what we wish with you locals. I suggest you obey my orders."

I did. I went to work for the German Kommandant as a translator. This was the pivotal decision of my lifetime. From then on, my life was divided into before and after this decision.

After this moment, I would not even be able to think about staying on in my homeland if the Soviets returned. After this moment, I will have become their enemy. I would have to flee if the Red Army retook the city. I would have to retreat with the Germans, and never return.

23

Eintopf Suppe—1942–1943

I knew my mother would not want me to reveal what she had done to survive, when all she had done was fight to live another day. No matter how I phrased it, no matter how I tried to persuade her that under the same circumstances, if my children were in peril, I would have done much more to save them, with no regrets.

But she persisted in carrying a sense of guilt for having, in her mind, betrayed her motherland. All those years later, she was ashamed. All she was guilty of was using whatever means were available to her to feed my starving brother and sister, and to keep herself and her mother alive to watch over them. The consequences were life, over death.

The Kommandant showed his appreciation for my decision by giving me his own supply of cigarettes, on top of the customary soldiers' rations. He was not a smoker. That may not seem like a big deal, a pack of cigarettes! But yes, it was a huge help. Back then, cigarettes were a major, sought-after prize.

In the best of cases, smokers rolled up the dried roots of tobacco, *mahorka*, or cherry tree leaves, or other inferior foliage. German cigarettes were considered a finery and smokers were willing to give up anything for a quality smoke.

Babushka went out into the street and sold my cigarettes, part of my soldier's ration, and those that the Kommandant gave me, for a significant addition to what we began to receive in rations. Our daily ration was half a loaf of bread, a grandiose amount for the four of us, a few little pieces of cheese, some kielbasa which went to the children, and at times a small bar of chocolate. Of course, these were rations for one person and hardly satisfied the nutritional needs of my entire family, emaciated by hunger.

We were saved by the soup. The Germans called it *Eintopf Suppe,* meaning one-pot stew, which contained vegetables, grains, and even meat, but to us it was the Elixir of Life.

I befriended the cook in the headquarters kitchen, and he invited me to come after the meals were over and all the soldiers' mess plates had been filled. Then he would pour all the remains from the soup cauldron, including all the leftovers from the bottom, a veritable treasure, into my cooking pot.

In despair, I looked to the heavens and called out to my poor Aunt Marusia! Had you survived for just a few more days you would have returned to life! How many times did Mama and I anguish over your demise? But you cannot bring back the dead.

My children revived. We exchanged three cigarettes for a glass of milk for them, daily. They sprang to life with the vital nourishment.

But another worry lay siege to us—the cold. All the coal mines in the Donbas (the Donets Basin) where we lived had been detonated with explosives and destroyed by the retreating Soviet Army; many had been flooded. When the Germans arrived, one of the first tasks they undertook was to restore the mines, using the local Russian population as labor.

But all the coal from the reopened mines went to Germany. It was loaded into rail wagons, and under strict guard, the long echelons all moved westward. We didn't get a single pound of it.

Our winters are brutal and no matter how we wrapped up the children, when it was below freezing in our apartment, nothing could warm them. How were we supposed to live?

I decided to go and steal some coal from the coal wagons. At our railway station, there were always a few standing railcars filled with coal.

After dark, I stole my way between the cars with an empty sack tucked under my arm. Noiselessly, I pulled myself up on the coal car and quietly filled the bag to its brim, bent down low in order not to be seen.

And then a cry: "Halt!" A rifle was aimed straight at me.

What should I do? I jumped off the wagon. I walked up to the soldier, in tears. "Do you have children?" I yelled at him in German.

He was shocked at first to hear these words in his own language. "Yes, I do. So what?" he stammered.

"So picture right now, at this very moment, that they are freezing to death, their arms and legs are stiff with cold in your unheated apartment." I forgot all my fear in my rage.

"Picture that your wife doesn't have the strength to warm them, that she too is freezing, unable to fall asleep. Her breath alone is not enough to keep the little ones warm. Can you imagine that; can you see that or not?"

He shifted from foot to foot.

"So that is my situation, that is why I am here, and why I have no choice but to come and steal some coal, *our* Russian coal." And then I stepped forward toward him. "If you want to shoot me, go ahead and shoot. But it will be on your conscience for the rest of your life!"

The soldier backed up and lowered his rifle. It may be that he truly had children of his own in Germany, or that he was just a decent man who was forced to follow the orders to guard the railcars, but he not only let me take the bag of coal I had already filled, but let me come back several times during his watch to fill the bag up and take it home.

I was able to haul in enough coal to set my children up in front of our little stove and warm themselves. We cooked on that stove as well, so we were finally able to have hot meals. But how did other families fare, where no one spoke German? I don't know.

Our moral lives were deteriorating as well. There were numerous acts of extremism and rampages. Rumors circulated that the Germans were unmerciful when their soldiers were attacked. For each one that was killed by the locals, they would execute one hundred townspeople by lining up the population in the square and counting off every tenth person for a bullet in the head, regardless of guilt or innocence.

Before the arrival of the Germans, pickpockets were rampant, lifting your wallet in the blink of an eye. Once the Germans learned this, the order was given throughout the occupied zone to chop off four of the fingers of the thieving hand that committed the crime. The pickpocketing stopped almost completely, but at what cost? How many boys were left crippled for life? Perhaps not many, since soon after the word went out the petty thieves went quiet.

The worst aspect of our lives under the German occupation, was of course, the extermination of the Jews. At first, they were ordered to wear the yellow Star of David affixed to their chests, backs and sleeves. They all wore the stars in order to differentiate the Jews from the non-Jews. Then the rumors started that the Jews were being rounded up at night and sent off. Entire Jewish families were taken away. To where? No one knew.

The Jews were disappearing, and their houses were left vacant, soon after to be occupied by those who were working for the Germans. Thank God, I wasn't offered a move into a Jewish home. What would I have used as an excuse to refuse?

On one occasion, when I was returning home on foot from the

city center, which was over three miles from us, I witnessed a horrible scene: a group of Jewish men were being forced to march, just like a herd of cattle, driven by Germans wielding whips. I recognized our butcher, Shelkov, among them. He caught sight of me and started to cry, with a wave of farewell. I couldn't hold back my tears. His daughters had been my pupils before the war; they were such good girls! I knew his wife, too.

The Germans were implacable in this regard. It seemed that they had been hypnotized, convinced by their racial theory of the purity of the Aryan race.

There was a German officer who was billeted in our apartment—one of our two rooms was taken away and given over to him for living quarters, leaving the four us in the other, smaller room. This officer, who spoke Russian well because he was born and grew up in St. Petersburg, took a liking to Natasha, my six-year-old daughter, but couldn't stand the sight of my son, Yura. It was unclear why. He would always bring sweets to her, but gave nothing to him, as if he didn't even exist.

I asked him why he ignored my son, what was the reason for such different attitudes toward one versus the other, especially since Yura was a very affectionate and friendly little boy. "He's not Aryan," the officer said, without the slightest hesitation.

I was taken aback for a moment, unable to speak. "What do you mean by that?" I asked. "Both of them are my children."

"Yes, but the boy, it seems, must have inherited his non–Aryan skull, perhaps from some ancestral line. You can see that right away, just look at the shape of his head!"

I felt a wave of horror at his rationale. Clearly, I did not see anything blameworthy in the shape of my little son's skull and for a long time was offended to the depths of my soul by this judgment. I reflected to what depths must one descend in their idiotic, racist theory to believe that differences in bone structure determine the value of the human being.

On another occasion, I happened to strike up a conversation with a young German boy who was the assistant chef in the headquarters kitchen. Our talk touched on the Jews and their fate at the hands of the Germans. I said that I didn't agree with the theory that they must be exterminated. I expressed my opinion that Jews were people too, and why shouldn't they, as we, have a right to live?

The young cook flew into a rage. He definitely looked like he had been hypnotized. He started to scream and curse at me, saying that I understood nothing. I had to change the subject.

At the beginning of the German occupation of Donetsk, a large Jewish ghetto was set up and its inhabitants were kept without food or medical aid, with hundreds dying every day. In December 1941, the German command murdered several hundred Jews.

In April 1942, the liquidation of the Donetsk ghetto began. My mother wrote:

> The extermination of the Jewish families began in earnest. We learned that the Germans took the Jews to an abandoned coal mine that had been flooded by the retreating Soviet Army and executed them, pushing both dead and alive into the coal shaft. They didn't even bother killing the children, they just threw them down the shaft.
>
> There was talk that one of the Germans, an SS officer who was assigned to this duty, went mad. He had children at home and could not continue this process of child killings. Apparently, the Hitlerian hypnosis wasn't totally effective.

Before World War II, the population of Stalino, later renamed Donetsk, consisted of 507,000. After the war—only 175,000 remained. Most of these deaths were from starvation and disease. My mother survived and kept her children and Babushka alive. But the tide of the war was shifting, and a reckoning was coming.

24

The Battle for Stalingrad—1942–1943

The Battle of Stalingrad lasted for seven months, from July 17, 1942, until February 2, 1943, and was the largest confrontation between the Soviet Army and German and allied armies of World War II. There were huge losses on both sides; over a million Red Army soldiers were either wounded or killed and 800,000 Germans, Romanians, Italians and Hungarians suffered casualties, making it the bloodiest battle ever in warfare.

Stalingrad was a pile of rubble. From the beginning, Stalin refused the evacuation of any civilians, stating that the army would fight harder knowing that they were defending residents of the city. After all, it was a city which bore his name, which also emboldened Hitler to attack it. His army would succumb to undersupply, encirclement, and the brutal Russian winter.

The Soviet victory on February 3, 1943, finally stopped the German advance into the Soviet Union and marked the turning of the war in favor of the Allies.

During the winter of 1942–43, my mother was trying to stay alive in Donetsk, a mere 376 miles away from Stalingrad, the distance from New York to Pittsburgh. She had no way of knowing her husband Shura's whereabouts. He had been drafted into the army. Had he been able to take the locomotives further east to safety and was trying to make his way back? Was he in the battle? Was he even alive, given the rumors of thousands of war casualties on both sides? There was no communication or news about the ongoing front, since the Soviets had confiscated all radios from the local population prior to leaving, in order to prevent any contact with foreign influences, and the occupying Germans had filled the void with their own, always positive propaganda. My mother had foreseen the events that were coming.

By all indications, things were not going well for the Germans.
There were bombings of nearby villages, which had been unheard

of before, when the front was far away. An incendiary bomb even landed in our backyard one day. Soviet war planes started flying overhead with greater frequency and daring.

The Germans became quieter, even while their extermination of the Jews accelerated with every day, as if they felt compelled to finish their ghastly job.

In the second half of 1943, things started to really go badly for the Germans. We had word that the city of Kharkov had been re-taken, and later that other cities were being surrendered into Soviet hands. At the same time there were rumors, substantiated by witnesses who were crossing over the front lines, that the returning Soviets were mercilessly punishing anyone who by deed or word had aided the Nazis.

This meant our certain need to leave with the Germans.

But how? Would the Germans take civilians with them? That was the challenge, and it was then that the German officer who had been billeted in our apartment promised that if it came to a retreat, he would attach my family to his unit. It was a promise that he would keep.

On September 1, 1943, I abandoned the city in which I had lived for many years, where I had married, had worked as a teacher in the local school, where both of my children had been born. I left it forever.

We headed westward. Our unit crossed over to the western side of the Dnieper River, setting up in a small town called Kamenka. This was a typical Ukrainian village, with white thatched roofs and cherry orchards. It was famous for the poet Pushkin living and writing there, staying with the Davidoff family at their estate. The Davidoff homestead still stood, as a museum. Tchaikovsky was said to have spent time in Kamenka as well, giving it additional historical significance.

When we entered the village, it was overflowing with German soldiers, trucks and tents; it looked like an army garrison. We were able to rent a room from an elderly, disabled woman who was friendly and was kind toward us. She still remembered the last of the Davidoff family members, who lived on their estate before the Revolution.

The unit of our German officer did not remain there, but was ordered to return to Germany, and so we bade goodbye to our benefactor. We stayed on to determine what to do next. I had to find a job to support us. I had heard that there was an alcohol factory on the outskirts of the town that was under the management of the

Germans. So I set out to offer my services as a translator, not knowing if they had the need for one. Not only did they give me a job, but they also provided a small apartment at the factory for us. We left the warm hospitality of our elderly landlady, who was sorry to see us go as she had already gotten attached to my mother and the children.

There were two Germans; one a civilian, the head man, and the other a military man, was his assistant. Two other alcohol factories, within a few miles of Kamenka, were also under their management, but there were no Germans there, they were worked by Russians. I even recall one, named Romanoff. My job was to accompany the assistant manager to these factories to check on their production, shipments to Germany (which meant all of it), and to translate their orders to the local managers. We drove to and from these factories in horse drawn carts.

A month went by, and then a second one. We began to be warned of partisans who might stage attacks on the factory. I had only heard of the partisan movement, that they were about in the area, but in Donetsk the land was too flat, there was no place for them to hide. Here the surrounding woods provided them cover. They would attack the German-held factories at night and demand the turnover of significant amounts of their production. One night they even killed a night watchman—we heard the shots and the hand grenades—and since then we felt in danger by living and working on the site.

One day we were sitting in the office, when a German car pulled up and out stepped a German major. He went into the office of the assistant manager, showed him some documents, and requested that the manager provide him with a keg of pure alcohol. A keg? The assistant was surprised because that was an unusual amount to be requisitioned by the military. But he agreed and he told me to go with the major into the factory and secure the keg for him.

I started walking with him into the supply room when suddenly he addressed me in the clearest, perfect Russian language. He asked me how long I was there, and where was I from? This conversation seemed to me unusual for a German officer, although I was not surprised that he spoken Russian. But his words were somehow plain-spoken, with a Ukrainian accent.

However, his German language was impeccable as he explained to our German manager that he was from Silesia, that his wife and children were tired of the war, and that he wanted to return home. He was given his alcohol. His driver, also dressed in a German uniform, helped to load it into the trunk of the car, and they departed.

A half hour later the German radio blared the news that the day before a German major had been killed, his documents had been taken and his car had been commandeered, purportedly by a band of partisans. The German manager, when he heard this, stood stock-still, then bellowed, "Do you know that you went into the factory and supplied a partisan!"

"How?" I asked. "He was dressed in the major's uniform, and had his documents, but he was a partisan?"

The two German managers then recalled that there was a strange accent to the major's German, but it hadn't even occurred to them that he wasn't a German, but possibly was a transplant, a colonist.

I was shaken. He could have killed me right there for my work with the Germans, no doubt why he had asked how long I had been there, and why. But this time I had been spared, by the grace of God. Another month passed, and another.

The Reds crossed the Dnieper River, despite the Germans insistence that they would not be allowed that far west. The German Army retreated again, and with them we had to leave also, further and further away from those places we held dear. We moved to Mezherichka, another small Ukrainian town which also had an alcohol factory and where I tried to find work, but this time they had their own translators. We were billeted as refugees, awaiting what would be next.

I took out a map of Ukraine that I had bought in Moscow and traced the westward progress my mother had made in the few months since she had left Donetsk with her mother and her two young children. She had been lucky to have been attached to the German officer's unit. And then to have found work at Kamenka. She was resourceful, to say the least.

In 1943, she was a tall, attractive woman, 27 years old, and protective, like a lioness, of her children and mother. In the two years since Shura had departed with the Soviet Army and she had been left to manage on her own, she had taken control of her life and theirs. She had survived. She had faced down hunger and the cold. She had left her home and traveled some 400 miles to an unknown place, on the road to points further west.

She would have to pull on a reserve of strength that I would never be able to forget in the next chapter of her journey of survival.

25

A Close Call—Winter 1944

In the winter of 1944, during the retreat of the German army from the south of Russia, there was a constant shifting from town to town of the front lines, sometimes with no more than a railroad track delineating German-held territory from that reclaimed by the returning Soviet Army.

As a refugee in retreat with the German troops, my mother pushed herself and her two children, and Babushka, her mother, to stay well ahead of the ever approaching front. To be recaptured by the Soviet Army would have meant her immediate execution, and the certain death of her children and mother, since their survival during the occupation and retreat with the Germans would have been considered treasonous.

When I came up to this harrowing time in my mother's story, I struggled to put this tale of heroism into the context of the mother I knew.

> The Red Army had crossed over the Dnieper River. The Germans had to retreat again, and with them we as well, further and further away from our familiar towns and villages. From Kamenka, we pulled back to Mezherichko, where the Germans had no use for me. But one of the German administrators had to go check up on another factory in Malaya Viska, and he told me to come along to translate. It was dangerous to go there, it was closer to the approaching front. I left Mama and the children in Mezherichko and set off with him.
>
> We drove about 30 or 40 miles. When we got to the factory, everything was in order, there were no signs of any disturbances from the partisans. We should have turned around to go back, right there and then, but he decided to stay the night in the town. The local manager invited him. The manager's interpreter, a young Russian woman named Nadia, invited me to her apartment. We stayed up late into the night, talking about what fate awaited us and our unfortunate country. She was also far from home but had no intention of leaving Russia. She didn't believe the stories of reprisals by

the returning Soviets. After all, she reasoned, what choice did we have if we wanted to survive? She made it sound all so logical.

We fell asleep.

Suddenly, in the middle of the night, a thunderous crashing all around us awakened me. Either we were under bombardment or the front lines had moved into the town. I shook Nadia awake and we quickly dressed. This was January 1944, and it was bitterly cold. I had brought not only my own coat, but a second heavy overcoat and hat with earflaps. I was getting them on as Nadia dashed out the door and disappeared. I stepped outside the door after her when I heard the command at the end of the hall, in Russian: "Stop! Stop or I'll shoot!"

Instead of raising my hands in surrender and stopping, since I obviously had been taken for a man in my overcoat and hat, I ran down the hall in the opposite direction, hearing again the shouts of "Stop! Stop!" I don't know how I made it out of the house through the back door.

Outside it was getting light already. I started running across the yard, hearing the bullets firing past me into the dirt. I ran around the house straight for the root cellar and made it down the steps into the darkness below. There were several people crouching there already, including Nadia. She hurriedly whispered that the Soviets had suddenly burst through the German lines during the night and had taken the town, cutting us off from the German Army.

Impossible! What was I to do? My first thoughts were for my mother and the children—they were on the German side, I was on the Soviet.

All around us, the street fighting continued as shells exploded and gunfire strafed the pavement, continuing for hours. Soviet soldiers were rushing by, there was no sign of the Germans. We huddled in the cellar, no one willing to brave an exit. We sat there for what seemed a very long time, not moving. I couldn't think of anything but how to get away from there, how to get back to Mama and the children, and how not to get captured by the Soviets who would execute me on the spot if they discovered I'd come there with the Germans.

One of the women in the cellar was the cook of the local German factory manager, and when the firing finally subsided toward evening, she said we should go back to the house for something to eat and to spend the night. Maybe by then the Soviets would be beaten back. Nadia and I agreed and we ran out, running from alleys to doorways. Out in the open, we heard the approach of an airplane and before we could shelter, we looked up to see a Soviet warplane opening fire on us, the bullets whizzing by us on either side. One caught me in the coat sleeve, but since it was the outer coat, I wasn't hurt. We made it to the cook's house.

As we walked in, we saw the house was filled with Red Army soldiers. They looked horrible: dirty, ragged; they stank of unwashed bodies. Many of them had dressings that needed changing, from which drifted the stench of rotting flesh.

Another soldier entered the room. He had just been struck below the rib and his wound was gaping, filling with blood. One of the soldiers was actually a woman, a nurse. I wouldn't have noticed her if she hadn't spoken up. She was just as dirty as the men. She quickly circled the man's wound with a bandage, and in a few moments they were all gone out the door. We were alone.

I was overwhelmed by the day's events and the encounter with the Soviet soldiers, all the blood. I couldn't eat; I just sat there numbly thinking what to do next. I wondered what was happening to Mama and the children. If they had to evacuate further west with the Germans, how would I find them? How could I get back to them? I couldn't rest with all those worries on my mind—I had to get out of there. The cook told me how to reach the road which led to Mezherichko. I would have to figure out on my own how to cross back to the German side.

They retired, but I couldn't sleep—I had decided to leave, come what may. It was still dark when I arose, dressed and put on my two overcoats. I looked over at Nadia and the cook, sound asleep, not a care in the world.

I stepped outside into the dark. Quiet, no gunfire. I crept around the buildings, heading for the rail embankment, to where the cook had said was the road to Mezherichko. I refused to think about how I was going to walk thirty miles in my heavy clothes. I'd thought about dropping off the top overcoat, but feared freezing on the way if I had to stop. I pushed on, worrying only about where to cross the front lines.

The rail tracks were before me, but I couldn't just march over them. If they marked the front lines I would be an easy mark for the guard from either side. I lay down on my stomach and started to crawl through the snow up the rail embankment. Slowly, sluggishly, I dragged my double coats over the ground as the snow filled my pockets, my sleeves. I progressed a few feet at a time, until I reached the crest. I slowly crawled over it to the other side. It was easier downhill; I rolled the few feet down. At the cook's house the night before, it was rumored that the Germans were on this side of the railroad. It was confirmed the moment I decided to stand up and walk again.

"Halt!"

A German soldier rushed at me through the dark, probably taking me for a scout or a partisan. He was almost up to my face before he realized I was a woman, speaking in German to him. He demanded what I was doing out there at night and I briefly explained. He let me go. I almost ran for joy now that I was at least on the same side as the children and Mama.

But soon I realized that I was walking through a vast, snow-covered field with nothing around for miles and miles. The road, if there was one, was somewhere under several feet of snow below my dragging feet. Each step was an effort against the wind blowing in my face. Hunger and thirst began to gnaw at my insides. I walked, hoping that someone would come and pick me up; someone had to come.

As the sun rose, I looked around me. There was not a soul, not a house, not even a barking dog. I felt like I was the only being in the entire universe. I trudged on, thinking only about getting back to them safely. I never let the possibility of freezing to death right there, not making it back, cross my mind. I had to get back to my children. Someone would help me. I had faith that someone would come to my aid.

A dot appeared on the horizon, moving closer. It was a horse and sledge, coming toward me. As it approached, I could see a man and a woman seated inside. They were probably taking something to town, unaware that the Red Army had moved closer. Perhaps I would be able to persuade them to turn around and go back, taking me with them.

When they drew up close to me, I stopped them and asked them where they were bound and explained to them about the front lines. The man scratched his head for a moment, then turned the sleigh around.

I was saved! They put me in the back of the sleigh. I rejoiced, as now I was moving faster and closer to my loved ones. They took me only as far their village, but that didn't bother me. I knew I would be able to find some way to continue.

In the village, there were German soldiers everywhere, gadding about completely unaware of the fact that the Soviets had drawn nearer. I asked to see the Kommandant and was shown his headquarters. He was surprised to hear of the approaching front, but his attitude was that it was a temporary setback. He asked me what I wanted and arranged a ride back to Mezherichko. Before too long, two young soldiers came to let me know they would take me in their Jeep.

When I appeared in the doorway to our room, Mama collapsed. In the two nights I was gone, she had given up on ever seeing me alive again. She was filled with despair at the prospect of trying to keep her and the children alive. With me gone, she knew that she and they would all perish. But now I had returned.

The children rushed into my arms and I, too, started to cry, happy that we were together again. The next day we would move westward once more.

There is no more vivid image of my mother for me than the one of her walking alone across the snow-covered field in pre-dawn. She begins in the distance, approaching slowly, weighed down by the overcoats and hat flaps to the wind. As she draws near, her breathing is hard as she lifts each foot out of the snow and sets it down ahead of her. She is determined not to give up on getting back to her children. I have returned to this picture of her in my mind over and over and wondered each time how she could have kept going, not just on that night, but through the war, how she had the courage to get through it all.

26

February to March 1944

My mother's knowledge of the German language damned her to exile from her motherland, but had it not been for her ability to plead her case in German, she wouldn't have survived even the first year of the war. It had also saved her children and her own mother during the war. Whether it was stealing coal to provide life-saving heat in the dead of winter, or earning the extra rations of soup, or crossing over the front lines, her ability to speak the language of the occupier had saved her to survive at least one more day.

She surmised that the Germans, far away from home and hearing their native language, mistakenly identified her as one of their own and came to her aid, thinking her a German resident of Ukraine, a "kolonistka," a colonist, of which there were many. She wrote that the Germans always helped their own. It didn't hurt that she was a beautiful, dark-eyed young woman, a Scarlett O'Hara of the Eastern Front, not yet 30 during those war years. Her determination and commanding presence disarmed both field soldier and officer alike.

Hearing the insistent words of this young mother spoken in their native language, defending her right to save her children, must have made them wonder about the fate of their own wives back home. Less than decent types probably sought more, but she was a formidable woman, even when frail from hunger, fatigue and cold.

The sojourn in Mezherichko lasted a few more months, but by the middle of February 1944, the rumors of the Red Front moving closer were taken seriously by the Germans and they nervously started to prepare their retreat back to Germany, and my mother, the children and Babushka with them.

On the 18th of February 1944, my mother left her homeland forever, beginning a journey which would take her west across Rumania to Sudeten, an area which was occupied by the Germans in their Anschluss of Czechoslovakia, and into Hitler's Germany. The trip took more than a month, since the freight car they were allowed to board was given the lowest priority for movement west, the highest given to military trains, hospital trains returning with the wounded, even to soldiers on leave. Freight cars filled with refugees like my mother and her family were attached to trains only when convenient; they often stood still for days waiting for the next available hook-up to a line of cars. She wrote:

> The train travel was entertaining for the children, but for Babushka and myself it was full of anxiety and concern. We wanted to arrive at least somewhere.
>
> I met a woman who was traveling with her son to Vienna. Her name was Vera Schwab, and her son was about Natasha's age. Vera was from Kharkov. Her story was not unusual for the time.
>
> In the early 1930s, there were many Germans who came to Russia to teach skills for various industries to the local population. We saw them in the coal mines of the Donbas, and met up with them in their German classrooms, as well as in breweries.
>
> Vera worked in a brewery in Kharkov, and that was where a young specialist in beer brewing was sent to work from Austria. They met, fell in love, and married. A son, whom they named Ferdinand, was born.
>
> Everything was all right until the advent of the infamous year 1937, when thousands upon thousands of innocents were imprisoned or sent into the Gulag. Vera's husband was among them. He was sent away and she knew nothing of his fate.
>
> When the war started and the Germans invaded, Vera wrote to her husband's mother and sister in Vienna and they tried to persuade her to leave Russia. The mother-in-law wanted to see her grandson, the child of their only son who had perished in Russia.
>
> During the war, it was impossible for civilians to leave voluntarily; the borders were closed, except for the ordered mobilization of Russians for forced labor in Germany, but Vera was not forcibly removed to Germany because she had a child.
>
> Only when the Germans were retreating was Vera able to take herself and her son out of Russia. We found ourselves traveling together in the same railcar and became friends. Vera was an interesting, intelligent woman whose son, Feldshya (his nickname), was mischievous and misbehaved en route.
>
> Our train arrived in Schoenbrun, a little town in Sudeten. We were unloaded and all sent into communal showers, while our clothes were taken away for disinfectant treatment, a good thing since we had been besieged by lice. We had not bathed in a month and the railcar had been entered by soldiers who were dirty and

lice-infested. We itched miserably, so the disinfection was necessary. But how did the Germans conduct it? I cannot recall it without revulsion.

We were not treated even as humans. Here in Germany, Hitler's theories were in full force: only German men were men, and only German women were women. Everyone else were just cattle.

All the women were herded into a room with showers and told to undress. Our clothes were taken away to highly heated lice-removing rooms, *vosheboiki*, where extreme temperatures were used to kill the pests and nits.

Meanwhile, while we stood naked washing our bodies, two German men suddenly entered the room and started to walk among us, without the slightest restraint. I could not hold myself back and asked them what they thought they were doing, coming into a bathhouse where there were naked women washing?

One of them started to laugh and answered me, "You? Women? We know our women and for us you are nothing, empty places." Amused by that comment, his companion also laughed.

That was our first experience with true Nazi Germany. In our homeland, they had somehow kept themselves in check, they did not insult us, at least the women, but here in their own country, they didn't shy away from showing us their Nazi teeth.

We were billeted in an old house, several miles from the town, and Vera and I, since we knew the language, were given the work of creating a list of the refugees, a make-work project, but necessary because we had to earn our meager rations. We were subsequently moved to another town, where we were sent to work at a porcelain factory.

One day, Vera's mother-in-law and sister-in-law arrived and we bade farewell to Vera at the Vienna train station. That was where I parted with Vera, after a brief but memorable friendship.

Later, when I was living in Germany, we wrote to each other and I learned of her fate in her adopted country. She hadn't gotten along with her husband's parents and was living on her own, while working in a brewery, and bringing up her son.

One unfortunate day, during the aerial bombings of Vienna by the American forces, a bomb landed on the house where she was living. She returned from work to find the crumbled remains from which rose the cries of those buried in the rubble. With the help of others, she uncovered her son who, miraculously, was unharmed, but she had lost everything she had, and was left standing only in the clothes she was wearing that day.

When I wrote to her that we were constantly on the move from one town to another, she replied to me: "You still have the energy to move from place to place on this earth? I have none anymore! What will be, will be."

27

Waldenburg, Germany—1944

My mother and her family had been taken to Germany, to the city of Waldenburg, to work as OST ("East") workers. Fearful of the return of the Red Army, which was advancing, they had evacuated westward with the retreating German troops back into what was then Silesia, now mainly in eastern Poland.

The events I describe here, which are completely factual, without a trace of fiction, so shook me that to this day I recall them as some of the worst moments in my life, in what they may have led to in my fate, the fate of my children and my mother.

We—a group of refugees from Russia, which included families with women and children of various ages, even grandmothers—were brought by the Germans and settled into a camp of OST workers, which previously had been populated only with young men and women who had been snatched by the Germans and forced into labor in Germany.

Many, from their own description, had been grabbed off the street without warning and pushed onto trains in only what they were wearing that day. These kidnappings were performed by the local police, at the orders of the occupying German authorities.

At least those of us who had left our motherland "voluntarily" were able to take what clothing we had and whatever was precious to us in a few bags, and to carry with us at least some food supplies. And we always had valuable packs of *mahorka* cigarettes, the lowest grade tobacco, for bartering. But these provisions, however meager, and especially the food stuffs, which to the OST workers seemed like real riches, put us into an awkward and unfavorable position. We were envied, even though we tried to share with our neighbors.

It is well known that intrigue is born of envy. If you add to this the fact that many OST workers were patriotically inclined to favor Communist Russia, and found it impossible to believe that anyone would leave it of their own accord, as we had, the antagonism which developed between us and them became understandable. To this conflict was added another consideration—we started to lobby to have the OST patches removed from our sleeves, arguing that we had voluntarily come to Germany, not forcibly, and so could hope to be trusted.

The OST patch, as was well known, took away even the most fundamental rights and privileges. One couldn't ride the tram, for example, attend the cinema, or enter a restaurant. I will never forget how on one occasion, a female tram conductor forced me off the tram at the first station, and my seat was taken by a German woman and her dog.

The "privilege" of not having to wear the OST patch was finally granted to us, after much effort, even though we continued to live in the same barracks as the other workers, guarded by German Shepherd dogs.

Our new OST-less status brought another flood of envy and resentment. I was disliked especially because I spoke the language fluently and could express myself to the Germans. Because of my knowledge of the language, I had discovered that a young woman who was living in our midst and acting as a translator was using deceptive practices of interpreting for the Russians. Either she didn't know the language well, or she intentionally translated to the benefit of the Germans. Rumors circulated that she was collaborating with the Gestapo, but they weren't substantiated.

All of us, including myself, were working at a porcelain factory. My job, which was to glue the handles on to the cups, lasted 10 hours a day, on my feet, although one wonders why it wouldn't have been possible to glue the handles while seated. But not a single foreigner was allowed to sit, except for those whose work absolutely required it.

One day, the supervisor of my department called me in to tell me that I was required to report to the city police precinct-presidium, the Gestapo, and that I was relieved of my work for those hours I would be away—I would not be paid for them—and that I needed to go there immediately.

Suffice to say how this order worried me. I ran to the barracks to change and tell my mother, knowing that it would make her anxious and not give her a moment's peace until I returned. She would pace twenty times to the door and back, she would be consumed by worry, waiting for me, as she had been in similar cases during the "Yezhovschina" [the period in the USSR between 1936 and 1938 when Nikolai Yezhov was head of the NKVD], when I had been yanked around to the "spetz-otdels."

And so, having changed into a cleaner frock, I ran for the tram, which would take me to the police precinct. Thoughts raced through my mind during the short ride of a few stops: *What could this be about? What do they want from me? What could I have done wrong, a woman without a husband, concerned only with how can I feed my two children, my mother and myself on scant rations?*

Inwardly, I started saying goodbye to the crumbs of relative freedom I had come to expect, compared to the fates of those less fortunate and in more dire straits. God only knows how I made it to the precinct and entered through the felt and plastic-covered door, my knees barely holding me up.

At the table sat a tow-headed, balding man who was so pale he had no color whatsoever and no evidence of eyebrows or eyelashes, with ears that stuck out of his head like nobs, and a thin mouth, like a crack. After perfunctory questions about who I was, where was I from, and especially how did I know the German language so well, he showed me a letter from the German officer who had been billeted in our apartment in Ukraine for almost a half year, taking one of the two rooms we had lived in.

Immediately it became clear that letters in Germany, as in our motherland, were opened and inspected by censors, delivered first to the Gestapo before they reached their addressees. The letter was the supposed reason for requiring my presence. It behooved this Gestapo officer, as the watchdog of Hitler's law and order, to warn me that correspondence between the German military and Russian refugees was not allowed, and that I must immediately cease or be punished. The letter writer, I surmised, had already been advised of this through other channels.

After lengthy advice, while denying giving me the offending letter so to this day I don't know the contents of it, the Gestapo officer offered to walk me home, saying that he was headed in that direction. I was decidedly not thrilled at the prospect of a stroll in the company of this man. First of all, it held up my return home to allay the anxiety of my waiting mother. Secondly, and more importantly, I was ashamed and revolted by the thought of having to walk alongside him. Possibly he was known for his less than knightly vocation even among our community—what if we happen to meet someone on the way? What to do?

Well, then, if we had to go, we had to go. So along the way, chatting about this and that with no mention about the ill-fated letter, he said to me, as if in passing, "I'd like to ask you for some-thing."

I was put immediately on my guard.

"You live and work among Russians," he continued. "What is their frame of mind? How do they see the war, and their life here? How do they perceive Germany, and our rules and norms?"

He was using the word "they" in a way that didn't seem to refer to me, as if he didn't include me in "them." In his opinion, I was something else, someone closer to him than to my unfortunate compatriots. This angered me. *Why did he think that of me? Only because I spoke his language? What else gave him the right to say that?*

He continued, "Could you, from time to time, just drop in to my office in the evenings, or even to my home—I will gladly give you my address—and let me know what's new in the living quarters? At the factory?" He added, "We already know a lot about who and what is going on, but it would be good to confirm it."

I was struck by the sudden realization that *Aha! They already know a lot about us. From whom? Could the source be our young translator? Maybe the rumors circulating about her were true ... who else, if not her, could have tipped them off?* But I did not have time to analyze this. I was thrown into a panic by his request. I was numb from the unexpectedness of his demand, but I quickly came around to my first concern, which was to untangle myself from what I knew was at hand.

With everything I had, I started to fend off his suggestion. At first I argued that I had neither time nor interest in what others were up to, that my family situation required me to devote everything to my two young children, whom I had to school after a ten-hour shift at the factory, and that my worries and concerns for them precluded attention to anything else. My daughter was already of school age, but there were no schools for foreigners.

In a word, I tried every argument I could think of, but none of them appeared convincing to my walking companion. Then I risked—come what may—telling him that I was not suited for this kind of "work" and that I simply would not do it. I had never in my life participated in any denunciations and wasn't going to start now.

He again returned to his argument that he wasn't looking for denunciations but only for friendly conversations, the purpose of which was to protect society from any possible harm brought on by malcontents. He was almost appealing to my patriotic duty! And where would I have any inclination toward that, a Russian?

Then he even hinted at some threats regarding sabotage, but sensing that he didn't make any headway, he returned to promises of moving us out of our housing in the barracks, and allowing my daughter to attend a German school. I wasn't buying it.

We walked on, he pressing his objective and I refusing his pleas, until we reached our barracks and I saw the figure of my mother at the threshold, watching our approach.

I hurried forward, eager to quiet her with the report that I was all right, that nothing had happened. I wanted to bid a quick good-bye and get rid of my bothersome companion, but he held me back, insisting that I promise to at least help him with even the smallest, unimportant information, from time to time.

"Please understand, that we have so few people who speak both languages. It is difficult for us, with so many enemies," he said. "Germany is suffering hard times." He continued, "You came here voluntarily, we value that. See? You are not required to wear the OST badge." As if that had been because of his intervention. "You ought to help *us* with something, too!" he added.

Finally, when I was completely exhausted by his pleas, threats, and just his presence, we agreed that if I learned of something important, I would let him know. But if there were no word from me, then it would mean that I had heard nothing and knew nothing about anyone.

At the end of the day, I thought, what would be the harm of making a promise that I wouldn't have to keep? I hadn't sworn any oath or given him any pledge, thank God. I just wanted to get away from him, and forget that he even existed. And so we parted.

28

Inga—Spring 1944

What followed in my mother's description of the episode with the Gestapo officer seemed almost unbelievable, more a movie script than a retelling of yet another stop along her journey out of the dangers of wartime Russia to the relative safety of refugee status in postwar Europe. She had explicitly written at the beginning of this private chronicle that this was, indeed, a recounting of real events.

While translating this episode, I asked my sister, Natasha, who would have been nine in 1944, if she recalled a time when our mother had been called in to the Gestapo for interrogation and had walked out and escorted home by said tow-headed officer.

Natasha didn't remember the incident but she and I agreed that our mother was not one to embellish what was already a difficult period in her life. Fiction was not part of her canon. We knew that our mother was almost manic about never telling a lie. Moreover, her details were finely drawn—the names, the settings.

> It would be mistaken to think that matters ended with that.
>
> A month went by, a second... Life went on. I labored at the factory while Mama helped with schooling the children. The unending worry for a slice of bread, the crushing fatigue from physical labor, and the fear of the approaching Red Army pushed any other problems or thoughts to the back of my mind.
>
> Spring arrived. I had forgotten my visit to the Gestapo and whatever promises I had made. I didn't delve into the lives of my compatriots or interest myself in their politics, which probably didn't differ much from my own.
>
> My thoughts were focused on other concerns, namely, how to move further into Germany, toward the west, to where we heard rumors that the American forces were forging their way. For a Russian family, especially, there were complications, and for me, this was a constant source of worry.

One evening, a young man living in the barracks, who had occasionally done some household chores for us, came looking for me.

"There's a German woman outside asking for you," he said.

"A German woman? For me?" I asked. I walked out to see her standing there. She was an attractive young blonde, well-dressed.

She greeted me cordially, with a smile, and asked that we take a walk in the direction of the little woods behind the barracks. We started off together. "I cannot tell you my surname, you can just call me Inga," she said. "I was advised to seek you out, since you speak German and Russian, on a matter which is very secret; that is why I cannot divulge any names. And it isn't even necessary to know last names."

I was confused. Who was she?

"First of all," she continued, "I must ask for your word to keep all this in total confidence." She was creating an aura of mystery that fueled my curiosity.

"What is the problem?" I asked. "What do you want from me?"

"I have a friend," she admitted. "To be honest, he is my beloved. We have been meeting secretly and with enormous risk to both of us. Where and how I won't go into, but we are hoping, when the war ends, to be together. The fact of the matter is, he is a prisoner-of-war here."

She continued, "He is an interesting young man, from a good family, by his description, and well-educated. We are in love. Can you help us?" She finished in what seemed an authentic tone, even tinged with a suggestion of tears.

Inga's description of her lover as a POW sent a shock through me and immediately raised some serious doubts and confusion. Everyone knew how POWs were kept and guarded, everyone saw their appearance, when they were herded in columns to forced labor.

It didn't jive that this clean, attractive and well-turned out young German woman would keep company with a dirty, hungry, lice-covered prisoner. But there she stood with her request, right in front of me. I didn't have the time or the presence of mind to figure out if it was so, or not so.

"What do you need help with?" I asked. "He is, of course, being held in the POW camp?"

"Yes, unfortunately," Inga responded, now close to tears. "And here is what happened. We rarely see each other, and then only in special circumstances, which I cannot describe because, please forgive me, I cannot yet trust you, and I cannot tell you his name, either.

I came to our meeting place for three days in a row, and instead of my beloved, his friend arrived." She continued, "His friend told me, in broken phrases which were hard to understand, that my beloved is being watched and is not allowed to leave the quarters, and that he—the messenger—went outside with great risk and must return right away, in order to avoid any suspicion. But he is carrying a written message to me, which requires an immediate answer. He handed me a note on a slip of paper, and left hurriedly. The note, of course, is in Russian, because my lover has learned to speak in German, but not to read and write."

After this torrent of information, Inga opened her handbag and handed me a note. The expression on my face in reading this note would have appeared to anyone passing by as full of fear, surprise and confusion. I had never read, nor translated, the likes of its contents. I stood transfixed.

The note, which by the way was written in a chicken scrawl and contained numerous grammatical errors, read: *"Inga, I beg you, please hurry to get a pistol and plain clothes. Think how to get them to me. Yours, V."*

It would be impossible to describe my anxiety standing there with Inga, reading the note. It lasted only a few seconds, but horrific ones. Hesitating, as if to re-read the contents, I said to her, "You know, Inga, we are going to pretend that I never saw this note, that I know nothing and want to know nothing more about it. Go home and do not come back."

"I will leave as soon you tell me what is in the note, and you write an answer," she replied, and opened her pocketbook to fetch a pen and paper.

I didn't want to hear anymore and turned to walk back to the barracks, but what sounded like a low cry escaped from her. She grabbed my arm and held on to it. A deep sorrow was expressed on her face. She entreated me with a voice filled with tears.

I was scared and didn't know what I should do. I was afraid to translate the note because on the one hand, it might horrify Inga and present her with an impossible task, while involving me—an unwilling conspirator in an awful deed. On the other hand, sympathy, simple human compassion towards another woman, one like me—she seemed about my age—was pushing me to help her.

She promised me all kinds of support, saying that her father was well-to-do and she would reward me, that she had no one else that she could turn to, I was the only one who could help her, that she was at wit's end, and as a woman, could I not understand her position?

I listened to her as if in a dream, through a fog of thoughts and misgivings. *Was there really a prisoner-of-war who had written a note in Russian to this young woman? He had to know that a third party would read it. How could she, not knowing the contents of the note, turn for help to a complete stranger? Was this reality or a provocation?*

We stood opposite each other for seconds: me, dumbfounded, nervous, fearful and confused by feelings of sympathy, and she the supplicant, seemingly fighting for her lover and happiness. Finally, I said to her again, "Inga, the note contains an impossible, terrible request. You will both die if you fulfill it. I cannot be drawn into it, I have a family, children. Do you understand what that means for me? I am asking you to leave!" And with those words I handed the note back to her and started to walk away.

But she wouldn't let me go and begged me for help. She stuffed the note into my pocket and said, "Think on this, and I will come back in a few days, but I am begging you, help us and don't tell a single person about it. It will be our secret. And I will not leave my debt to you unpaid!"

At a loss to respond, I bid her goodbye without making any promises. The note stayed in my pocket. Strangely, Inga had stopped asking me to translate it. Perhaps she was, indeed, horrified at what might be the contents, or she was giving me some time to sort it all out, and later, in a few days, explain it to her. Perhaps she didn't want to pressure me further about it. Or, was there something else at work here, which I thought long and hard about when I returned to the barracks.

Of course, I took Mama into my confidence. I told her the entire story of Inga and read her the note of the prisoner.

She, who had lived through the years of Soviet rule, years that were not just ordinary, but years of Stalin's purges, court trials of the "enemies of the people," years of denunciations, entrapments and searches, was experienced and wiser than I was in sorting out the circumstances.

She didn't doubt for a minute that the entire thing had been staged by the Gestapo and that I was being tested for my loyalty.

I didn't agree with her! Why me? Why was I worth trapping? For whom and for what was I needed? In any case, we were both so nervous that we couldn't sleep. That night I paced the room from end to end.

The whole thing could end with me being sent to a concentration camp. Lesser crimes were punishable with imprisonment.

What would happen to my family if I was arrested? I was its only breadwinner.

But, what if it was true? Inga's pleading face was before me and gave me no peace. She had confided in me with such conviction, with such a desire to help her beloved, and her loved one was one of us, a Russian! Helping her I would be helping him. Were we so hardened by the war that we had forgotten any feelings of compassion for our fellow man? Everyone was aware of the plight of the prisoners-of-war, and all of us, even those of us who were hungry OST workers, helped when we could by throwing bread over the prison fence. But offering pieces of bread was not the same as risking arrest and execution.

What was I to do? How to act? I thought about the possibility that if this was a Gestapo trap, how in the world had Inga played her role so convincingly? She would had to have been an actress to show such genuine emotions, replete with tears and changing intonations.

And why was I the target? Me, who had never gotten involved in any political activities? I had always stood away from it all. What do they want from me? I cursed my knowledge of the German language, even though it had saved me on so many occasions and helped me to survive the years of the occupation. Thanks to my German, I had helped others as well. But here, in Germany, it had become an obstacle.

I wavered; I would arrive at a decision, then back away. I prayed constantly for God to show me the right course to take. In the meantime, I did nothing. Two days passed. God heard my prayers and my requests for Him to guide me in my indecision and confusion, and sent me a sign that was completely unexpected, and at first, almost hard to believe because it immediately resolved my doubts.

Two days after meeting with Inga, I was riding in a tram past the police station where I had been interviewed by the Gestapo officer, when I looked out the window at the place which had caused me so much worry and concern.

I couldn't believe my eyes! In front of the doors of the building stood the tow-headed officer and our Russian girl translator, chatting and laughing with each other. And together with them stood Inga!

At first I was struck dumb, and then almost gave out a whoop, but stifled my cry. My first thought was, Praise the Lord! You heard my prayers! You protected me again, as You had throughout the war! You guided me in my decision and took my hand away from translating the letter. And now what a burden had dropped from my shoulders. No Gestapo officer would now try to enlist me, seeing how unfit I was to serve them!

It seemed to me that the tram flew on wings!

Mama was glad. "I told you. I am rarely wrong in these matters. From the start, I thought that there was something not right with it," she said. "You are so young and naïve."

One thing was left unexplained, and to this day I wonder about it. What was the point of it all and who was responsible for putting it all into motion? The girl translator? Or was it truly a test that the Gestapo officer had put me through to determine my worthiness?

Soon after, "Other dreams, more surly still, and other cares, and other sorrows,"* eclipsed these events. Soviet forces were moving west toward Silesia.

Along with countless other refugees, I had to forcibly push the children and my mother and myself onto a train heading away from them, further into Germany, with no one even checking us for our documents or tickets.

I forever left behind Waldenburg, the city which had caused me to live through so much grief and worry, humiliation and captivity, and even fear for our lives.

---

*A quote from Alexander Pushkin's poem/novella, *Evgeniy Onegin*, Book VI, Stanza 43. *"Другие, хладные мечты, Другие, строгие заботы."*

29

The Last Train for Leipzig—February 1945

The number of foreign, forced labor civilians brought to Germany from more than twenty European countries to work in factories, munitions plants, and farms numbered in the millions at the height of the war. Of the estimated 7.5 million civilians, a third were from the USSR, specifically from Galicia and Ukraine, and along with slave laborers from Poland, were designated as *Osterbeiter*, workers from the East (OST). They had to wear patches designating them as OST and were forced to live in camps fenced with barbed wire and under guard.

Although my mother was not forcibly removed to work in Germany, as were many who were rounded up off the streets and trucked away without any warning, she ended up in the German OST camps once she had moved herself, her mother and her children westward to escape the return of the Soviet Army. She spent the better part of 1944 in Waldenburg, working at a porcelain factory, where the conditions were horrendous and the pay so meager that she, her mother and the children were always on the brink of starvation, their clothes worn to threadbare. But 1945 ushered in what seemed to be a hope for the end of the war.

> At the beginning of February 1945, the German front was being pushed back toward the west by the Red Army. From the west, the Americans and the British, together with the French, were advancing, pressing Germany into a vice. The Western Front moved closer towards us. Among the OST workers, there was talk about the next evacuation westward, but it still required a guarantee of the request, supported by documentation, that there was a work requirement to move. Without it, the pedantic Germans did not allow workers to leave.
>
> That was when an elder friend of ours, a fellow tenant from Donbas, responded to my plea for help and sent me a fake certificate, requesting my urgent presence in a Leipzig factory. With this

document, I resolved to get my release from the factory where I worked in Waldenburg. But it wasn't that easy.

The written request was helpful, but I was summoned to answer questions about where I was going, and why was I leaving, and was I really needed in Leipzig? I couldn't explain this to these fanatical Germans, whose belief was that their god, Hitler, was invincible. They insisted that all these military setbacks were temporary, and that the German Army would soon be reclaiming lost ground and cities—that it would be unnecessary to leave. They refused to talk about evacuation; it was useless to argue with them.

But for me, having lived through all of these retreats and re-takings, the surrendered and reclaimed cities, it was all too familiar, too personal, to subject myself and my family to the risk of staying on, a risk which might result in a tragic end.

The Red Army was approaching Breslau when finally, after concluding our war of words with the authorities, we were allowed to set out westward.

The Americans were moving eastward with the British forces, a fact that did not make us at all fearful, as did the specter of the Soviets' advance. We didn't stand guilty of anything in their eyes and relied on their humanity to treat us fairly. Unfortunately, we were bitterly mistaken, but that became evident much later.

We checked what baggage we had, not really expecting it to arrive at our destination but hoping at least for some of our belongings to make it. We set off for the train station with just knapsacks on our backs—me with the largest, Babushka with a smaller one and Natasha with a little one strapped to her. I don't recall if we carried anything in hand.

The train station was nearby, close to the factory, so we didn't even need to get on the tram since it was only a five-minute walk.

My God, what a sight! The station was under siege by not only Germans, but mostly foreigners looking to leave and go west. No tickets were being sold! Even in this normally orderly situation, panic was taking over. Suitcases, tied together belongings, crying children, the elderly, women (there were very few men), filled the station house, barring our entrance. Trains were being cancelled left and right, most likely depending upon from which direction the front was advancing on us.

I lost all hope that I would be able to push us onto a train, since they were arriving already filled with passengers from other stops. But we were already there, we had made the decision, and maybe somehow even under those circumstances we would be able to get a place.

The approaching front was hurrying us to get away; the realization that to remain was to tempt destruction.

When a train came to a stop, and everyone rushed to the doors, I somehow managed to get on board first, and then, standing on the train steps, pull the children through the crowd. It was especially difficult to get Babushka inside, she was heavy and hard to maneuver, the knapsack pulling on her, but the rush of people seemed to carry her forward on a wave of bodies. I'm not sure how I managed it—I still don't understand how I got them on board—other than God helped me again and preserved me to fight another day for their survival. It was nothing less than a daily battle just to live another day.

And so, we were away. We took a route that circled Breslau, even though in less troubled times the city route would have been the normal route, but now impossible due to the fighting between German and Soviet forces. Our route took us straight west to Gorlitz. The train took the turn for Zwickau, then stopped abruptly, and we were told it would go no further. Everyone was ordered to disembark.

At this station, matters were even worse than at Waldenburg—the Reds were advancing from Czechoslovakia and here, they were even closer to us. If we listened, we could hear the cannonade in the distance from where the front was.

I ran to the stationhouse to determine if there would be a train for Leipzig and was told that there was a freight train that was leaving shortly, and although it did not take passengers, it might be possible to hop it. All right, a freight train it would have to be then. But I did not know how I would get Babushka on board—the risers onto the freight cars were much higher off the ground than passenger cars, and freight trains often did not stop at the platform and had to be boarded from the rail bed.

I dashed out of the stationhouse, grabbed the children and Babushka, and at the direction of a railroad worker, ran toward the rail tracks where a freight train was ready to pull away. Luckily, there were one or two passenger cars attached to it and I ran toward them.

The train wheels were starting to move!

With little Yura in my arms I jumped on to the step, and Natasha, who was almost ten years old, and able to take it on herself, jumped up behind me. But Babushka, our poor Babushka, who had bad legs and was barely able to walk, was not capable of running.

The train was pulling forward as she was lumbering along, trying to reach the steps to get on.

I don't remember exactly, but I literally threw Yura into the rail car and returned to the steps, grabbing her arms as she started to fall away. With all my might, I pulled her on to the train as it started to pick up speed, managing to get her to cling to the steps, then into the car, by then semi-conscious.

I cannot imagine what would have happened had she not made one last effort to push herself closer to the train and I had not pulled her on board. As the train sped up, I would not have been able to get the children and myself off as it was already moving swiftly. She would have been left behind.

My poor, dear Mama! My companion and traveler through my life. My helper, my advisor—she would have faced a certain death without me. Not knowing a single word in German, not having any documents on her as to her identity—how and where would she have found us? We did not know where we were heading and into what circumstances, and where we might find refuge. To be lost in a foreign country, not knowing the language, in a time of war when approaching armies are on the horizon, what could be more horrible? For me it would have been the worst nightmare. It was enough that I had witnessed the death of my aunt, whom I had not been able to save from death by starvation.

But she had held on and was now inside the railcar. The car was not overfilled, and the children were able to sit down next to my mother, who was just barely coming to her senses. We were on our way to Leipzig. So were the Allied aerial bombers.

I have pictured this train scene in my mind over and over, trying to imagine my grandmother's valiant attempt to board the last train for Leipzig. Her kerchief is tied tightly to her head, her fragile eyeglasses are slipping down on her nose as she makes a superhuman effort to throw her hands up and be dragged by my mother onto the moving train.

At age 61, Babushka was hardly the model of health and fitness. Despite the ravages of hunger and malnutrition, she was a heavy-set woman whose legs were infirm from years of cold and wet conditions, improper footwear if there even was any to put on, only for going outside when necessary. But like so many elderly women during the years of Soviet rule, who had been left alone by the toll of the purges and then by the war's conscription, she was the rock that my own mother depended on not only for advice and comfort, but the daily care and education of her children, allowing my mother to work and to scavenge food. This was more than just the relationship of a mother and daughter. This was a lifelong partnership.

I didn't get to know my grandmother. She sailed from Bremen,

Germany, to New York City in January 1952, along with my family. Tired as she was and ready to quit after the refugee camps in postwar Germany, she still took the next steps of coming to America. She didn't have many of them left, however.

My recollections of Babushka are of visiting her in an unheated apartment in Brooklyn, where she lived with my older sister, Natasha, a few blocks away from our fourth-floor walk-up. My mother would take Eugene and me with her to attend to her bedridden needs.

One of the earliest memories I have, from age three, is my mother at the Russian Orthodox cemetery in Spring Valley, New York, where my grandmother was laid to her final rest on March 1, 1956.

It is a cold, gray day. We are outside on the grounds. I am next to my mother. She is in black, kneeling. She is bent over; her face is in her hands. She is weeping. I feel helpless to comfort her.

30

Leipzig—Spring 1945

"So it goes."

These are the words repeated by Billy Pilgrim throughout Kurt Vonnegut's 1969 novel, *Slaughterhouse-Five*. The title is taken from the name of the basement shelter where the novel's protagonist, Billy, an American soldier, was taken as a POW during the bombing of Dresden, Germany, by the Allied forces in mid–February 1945.

Pilgrim is based on Vonnegut's own wartime POW experience, captured by the Germans after the Battle of the Bulge (December 16, 1944 to January 15, 1945), and transported to Dresden, where a meatpacking complex was used to house him and a hundred other POWs. It was only the underground depth of Slaughterhouse Five, several levels below the street, that protected him and his fellow POWs from the 4,000 tons of incendiary bombs that were rained on the city on February 13–15 by the Allies. The bombings resulted in horrific firestorms which completely destroyed the city, incinerating everything at ground level, including more than 25,000 civilians, many of whom were refugees from the east.

In a passage from a later memoir, *Man Without a Country*, Vonnegut wrote, "I saw the destruction of Dresden ... I saw the city before and then came out of an air-raid shelter and saw it afterward." In *Palm Sunday*, he was more specific. "When we came up, the city was gone." As Billy Pilgrim puts it to Montana Wildhack, his lover-muse, "It was like the moon."

In Vonnegut's words: "There were too many corpses to bury. So instead the Germans sent in troops with flamethrowers. All these civilians' remains were burned to ashes." This experience would stay with Vonnegut for the rest of his life and inspire his first book, named for the place that saved his life.

Looking back, had it been published earlier, Vonnegut's *Slaughterhouse-Five* would have been required reading in 11th grade English by my English teacher, Bruce R. Mooney, following his favorite Southerner's *Look Homeward Angel* (Thomas Wolfe). But Vonnegut's novel wasn't published until the end of March 1969, at the end of my junior year in high school. Not even several years later, in 1972, when the movie was released, would I take an interest in the events described by Vonnegut. It completely escaped me then, and for long after, that my mother was huddled in a bomb shelter in Leipzig, just 68 miles away, less than a minute "as the plane flies," on the nights of the fire-bombing of Dresden of February 13 to the 15th, 1945.

My mother and her little family had arrived at the beginning of the month.

> The train brought us to Leipzig. We entered the train station's large waiting room and found ourselves among a huge crowd of refugees, waiting for an organization to take us to some sort of shelter. All of us, and we must have been in the hundreds from all over eastern Germany, sat and waited.
>
> We had no food with us, and nowhere to buy any. We started to get hungry and the children started to ask us for something to eat, but I had nothing to give them. It was especially hard on little Yura, who was still too young to understand what was going on. He was cold, he hadn't slept his normal times, and like every child under these circumstances, was whining.
>
> Hours passed. Finally, some people appeared and started loading the refugees onto trucks and taking them away. Somewhere around the fifth or sixth load, I was given a place with my family.
>
> We were taken to a school. All over Germany, the schools had been commandeered to become temporary shelters for refugees. We were surprised, and forced to admit, that even under the conditions of a massive evacuation, and the approach of armies from all directions threatening the imminent destruction of their homeland, the Germans organized the movement and shelter of refugees. They cared for them without interruption and housed them at first in temporary shelters, then placed them into privates homes, with food and provisioning. This could only have been done by the Germans, with their innate organizational abilities; elsewhere it would have been sheer chaos and impossible to expect help from anywhere.
>
> It was warm in the school. The desks in the classrooms had been moved aside and straw was spread on the floors for sleeping. A kitchen was organized in one of the rooms and we were immediately fed a hot meal of calorie-rich food, first the children and elderly, and then us, the women. There were very few men, mostly disabled and not qualified for the front.
>
> With our hunger allayed, we collapsed onto the straw. But sleep eluded us. With the advent of darkness, we were awakened by siren alarms triggered by the approach of enemy bombers, American

and British. We were ordered to go down into the basement of the school. For the first time, my family and I were subjected to real bombardments. When living in the Donbas, where we were bombed by the Red Army, those bombardments seemed like child's play compared to what was happening here. The bombs fell in clusters, whistling as they were dropped. They were preceded by the horrible sirens. It was hell.

We sat in the corner of the basement, packed tightly together, Yura in my arms, Mama next to me, and Natasha at my feet, with a knapsack of our stuff. Poor thing, she was so frightened that she shook uncontrollably.

The bombardment lasted only ten minutes in our area and then the planes proceeded to fly toward other targets, and we were given the all clear signal with a single long blast of the siren. We could return to our straw beds and lie down for a while.

I don't know how much time went by before we were awakened again by the alarm, again hurried down to the basement and it started all over again. Every time, I had to rouse Natasha and hoist a sleeping Yura into my arms. Sometimes it was only once during the night, on other nights it was two or three times.

It was said that the planes were flying to Berlin—which was bombed the most frequently—but we were given the siren alarm anyway, not knowing whether the Americans would drop a few bomblets along the way onto women and children sleeping peacefully on their straw beds in a school.

There was a small portable radio in the basement, and when it broadcast that the planes had turned for Berlin, everyone sighed with relief, that thank God, they were not directed at us.

We lived this way in the school for two or three days, after which we were distributed to houses. A few days after we were re-settled, the school was completely demolished by an aerial bombing raid. Had we still been sheltered there, we would all have lost our lives.

We were taken to live in a large manor, the villa of a factory owner by the name of Glockner. He was a self-made man, who had invented a process to replicate paintings. He received a patent for the process, then built a factory to grow the business, which made him rich. He and his wife lived in a large, two-story villa with a full basement and a mansard roof with two rooms, which was where we were billeted. There was no kitchen up there, and the heating did not reach us, either by design or the decision of Herr Glockner as to the need for providing heat for refugees.

The villa was beautiful! The furnishings were exquisite with every possible comfort. I had never seen anything like this before, and where would I have? In our proletariat nation? My entire childhood has passed in extreme poverty, under the difficult circumstances of fighting just even to survive. Surrounding me, everyone lived in the same way, perhaps a few slightly better off, like my aunt, but others way worse, like many of my girlfriends.

At the Glockners, I was allowed to use the kitchen in the basement to cook on a coal stove, and then to take the prepared meals up two flights to eat in our rooms.

There were bathrooms on every floor of the villa, but we weren't allowed to use them, only the one in the basement. This was especially difficult for little Yura, who was too young to undo his pants by himself. I would unbutton his fly upstairs and let him walk down the two flights of the Glockners' living quarters to the basement on his own. When Frau Glockner saw this, she was shocked and forbade it. Subsequently I had to walk down with him and undo his pants in the basement.

We had to deal with all manner of put-downs and humiliation from the masters, the Glockners, because we were Russian and considered not of their "race." There were many workers at his factory with the OST label. I heard stories about their work conditions from a young woman called Marusia, whom the Glockners had employed in their home as a servant girl.

Marusia, who was a very nice young woman with a good disposition, was continuously being put down by them and exploited from dawn until late at night, constantly on the go to be doing some kind of housework, although the house was scrupulously cleaned and the Glockners had no children; it was just the two of them. The mistress of the house was rude to her, physically pushed her around, forced her to do the same chore over and over, and fed her only table scraps.

During air raids, when we didn't have time to run all the way to the air raid shelter, fifteen minutes away, we would descend into the Glockners' basement and wait out the all clear signal there. Even then, when only God knew where the next bomb would hit and which corner of the basement would be the safest to shelter in, even here where it would seem we were all equally facing death, Marusia and my family were sent into the far side of the basement, where we crouched on wooden benches placed on the cement floor, while the Glockners were in a separate, more comfortable section.

Marusia described the exploitation of the Russians who worked at the factory. The workers had 12-hour days for a miserly pay, which couldn't buy anything. They were fed so poorly that they were swelling from hunger. Marusia thought herself lucky for having been chosen to work as a servant.

I was afraid to leave my family in the event of air raids and did not seek work, so we survived only on the ration cards given us as refugees, and selling off our dole of cigarettes.

Once, I took some time to take a tram into the center of the city, just to take a look around, and I was appalled at the devastation from the air bombardments. Some blocks were completely obliterated, not a single building remained standing, only the remains of the stones and bricks, laid low. It was possible to see across the city, a desert of rock. On the main square, there were the remains of a large building, completely burned down, with gaping holes for the windows where some walls stood. It must have been one of the main buildings of the city, but now only a skeleton. But its clock still chimed the hour with two life-sized figures hammering a bell! The clock still kept time

Monument to the Battle of the Nations, Leipzig, Germany. This was the 91-meter-high monument under which there was a bomb shelter where Tatyana, her children and Nadezhda (Babushka) took cover from Allied aerial bombing raids in February–March 1945. Dresden, which was only 58 miles away—one minute by plane—was destroyed by the Allied fire bombings on February 13–15, 1945, as depicted in Kurt Vonnegut's *Slaughterhouse-Five* (www.pixabay.com).

on the frame of the building; by some miracle, the electricity still reached the mechanism to make it work.

Our daily life was made miserable by the despotic Glockners, who kept putting new obstacles and restrictions on us. There was nowhere to go and no one to talk to. I didn't have a single person to talk to, not a single friend. Entire days were spent reading, when a book could be found, but mostly dozing, anticipating that the nightly air raids would deprive us of sleep during the night.

In most cases, we would just rush down to the basement, but at times we would be able to run to the public bomb shelter, fifteen minutes from us. The shelter was below the colossal Monument of the Battle of Nations, built in 1913, to commemorate the victory over Napoleon a hundred years before. It was a massive structure, underneath which was the huge bomb shelter.

The entrance to it zigzagged and there was a long corridor to the center, which opened into a big hall. There were benches in the hall, and it had lighting. I think that no bomb could have threatened this structure, since it would have been difficult to target the Monument itself, and to hit alongside it would not have affected those sheltering inside, because the stone walls were so thick. Sitting there, we did not fear for our lives.

Once, returning from an air raid that we had spent in the Monument shelter, we saw that the house next to the Glockners had been bombed. The roof had been flattened and lay on top of the rubble; the walls were gone. If the bomb had flown just a few meters further, it was likely that the Glockner villa would have ended up the same.

31

Stalag X Wietzendorf—1941–1945

On a cool spring day in 2008, I entered the United States Holocaust Museum in Washington, D.C., at 100 Raoul Wallenberg Place with the expectation that I could check it off from my list of places to visit in between conference sessions in the Capital.

It had been several decades since I had been taken to Washington as a child by my parents on their annual summer motoring trips. But that had been before the Memorial had been built in 1993 and the Holocaust Museum probably would not have made their cut of monuments in the late 1950s—Lincoln and Jefferson Memorials, Washington Monument—in the beautiful city.

Our motoring family continued south from there to Florida, stopping at gas stations along the way, which had designations for "Colored" bathrooms. The Civil Rights movement was yet to catch on and explode across our television set at home. Had the trip been later, my parents would not have ventured into Dixie.

This time, however, I was alone with several hours to spare and to learn more about the Holocaust Memorial Museum and its exhibits witnessing the deaths inflicted by Hitler during World War II.

Of course, the fate of six million Jews by Hitler's Nazism had not escaped me when I was growing up. Anne Frank's *Diary of a Young Girl* had been published in 1947 and formed the basis of every American child's perception of the persecution of Jews during World War II. Films like *The Pawnbroker* and later the 1975 TV miniseries *Holocaust* were early influences, but not until I sat rocking my infant son while reading Herman Wouk's *War and Remembrance* (1975), and then William Styron's *Sophie's Choice* (1979), did the latter fictional account of Auschwitz urge me to find out more.

At home, strangely, my father and mother, both of whom had directly experienced the brutality of Hitler's plans for extermination, there was little talk about it. My father would occasionally mention his trials "*v plenu*" in the POW camp, showing us how he would put his hand inside his shirt and pull out a handful of crawling lice. But not even he realized the extent of the numbers of deaths throughout all of the POW camps.

Later the following information would become widely known: The brutal treatment of Soviet POWs by the Germans violated every standard of warfare. Existing sources suggest that some 5.7 million Soviet army personnel fell into German hands during World War II … [of them] 3.3 million, or about 57 percent of those taken prisoner, were dead by the end of the war. Second only to the Jews, Soviet prisoners of war were the largest group of victims of Nazi racial policy.

This death toll was neither an accident nor an automatic result of the war. It was a deliberate policy of the Nazi state. German treatment of Soviet POWs differed dramatically from German policy towards POWs from Britain and the United States, countries the Nazis regarded as racial equals to the Germans. Of the 231,000 British and American prisoners held by the Germans during the war only about 8,300–3.6 percent—died in German custody. (*United States Holocaust Memorial Museum, Washington, D.C.*)

At the Holocaust Museum, I made my way through the halls until suddenly I was confronted with a display of a map, showing all the POW camps in Germany and Poland. I stood in front of the exhibit, wondering which one of the dozens of triangles shown on the map marked where my father and uncle had endured four years of the war, surviving the inhuman conditions imposed by the Nazis. Only later did I learn from my uncle's writing that their camp had a name, Stalag X, Wietzendorf, one of the largest camps established for Soviet and Polish POWs by the Nazis in the fall of 1941.

He wrote about the camp:

Kaput Command

The German word "kaput" means *destroyed, gone.* We were ordered to dig a deep pit in the woods behind the camp. The corpses were taken there. Since it was winter, the bodies were thrown down into it, and covered with lime.

In that first sub-zero winter, thousands of POWs died of hunger and typhus. Bodies were removed from the barracks and stacked outside. A special work unit, called the Kaput Command, was in charge of putting the corpses on a wagon and taking them out of the camp, then throwing them down into the pit, into the common grave. Our men told stories about Nazi soldiers who stood watch over the Kaput Command and ordered them to remove the gold fillings from the teeth of the dead before throwing them into the pit.

I will never forget the time when we were passing by a stack of bodies, and we heard a voice coming from among the dead, "Brothers, I am still alive!"

At Stalag X, the common grave contained more than 25,000 Russian prisoners of war. But how many more camps were there? Stalag X was the central camp for the region. Prisoners were brought here from other camps. The stories they told us! Supposedly, there were gas chambers in the other camps. I think it must have been in the concentration camps, where Jews were gassed and then cremated, but the accounts made us wary of any lice-killing shower halls we were forced to enter, lest they be something else.

On our clothing we had the stamped yellow letters, SU, for Soviet Union, but the prisoners deciphered it to mean *Skoro Umrem* ("soon dead")—there was so little hope to survive. And in reality it was so—thousands upon thousands ended up in common graves.

Stalin did not recognize prisoners of war. His Order No. 270, issued on 16 August 1941, during the Axis invasion of the Soviet Union, was that Red Army personnel "*fight to the last*," and announced that all prisoners were deserters or traitors.

The Soviet Union was not a member country of the International Red Cross. Prisoners from other countries received parcels from the Red Cross, while Soviet POWs received no support from anyone. Hitler's guards did what they wished, since there were no checks on them. German scientists used the prisoners like rabbits for experiments. It was said that there was a special barracks where a group of POWS was held for experiments to determine what was the minimal food required to keep from dying of starvation.

Our barracks held not just soldiers, but engineers, teachers, artists. There were also *zeks* (short for *zaklyucheniye*) who had been conscripted from Stalin's gulags to fight, and *urki*, the criminal element.

Sasha and I became friends with an engineer named Bragin, from the Caucasus. He was a wise and intelligent man. Usually, after the evening tea and before lights out, we would gather in groups to reminisce about our families, our loved ones—in a word, unburden our hearts through sharing. Engineer Bragin was a good storyteller and he talked about the Caucasus. He spoke of Lermontov, and Tolstoy, and raised our spirits with Pushkin anecdotes.

But most of the time the talk was of memories from home. Among the POWs were very young men, almost children. For all of us, the young and old, what we most missed was the affection of our mothers. In everyday times, we don't take notice of a mother's love, but here there were so many remembrances of mothers during those moments of despair and grief.

Mama! We owe our lives to you. In your sweet eyes is the light of eternal love. From my earliest years, I remember your familiar body, leaning gently over me. I hear your voice, always thoughtful and gentle. I feel the strength of your prayers, which saved us not once but many times. You understood the power of your prayers, you knew how to pray for God to show His mercy to your sons.

Looking into the past, I see the storms, shocks and misfortunes you suffered on your path. But there was also joy, happiness and successes!

In our history, the Russian Woman carried her motherly burden, responding to a higher calling to raise those who toiled, who worked, soldiers, geniuses who built our great nation. Mother! In your name is she our motherland, Mother Russia! And you, my mama, you are one of those mothers, to whom I bow in reverence.

The hungry, scorned prisoners, each in his own way, recalled his mother. The teacher from Siberia quietly recited a 1924 poem, "Letter to Mother," by Sergei Esenin, who was banned by the government but still widely read (trans. by A.Z. Foreman):

Ты жива еще, моя старушка?
Жив и я. Привет тебе, привет!
Пусть струится над твоей избушкой
Тот вечерний несказанный свет.

Are you alive and well still, momma?
I am alright. Greetings. Tonight
I hope your cottage is still bathing
In that ineffable evening light.

And in this ineffable light is the legacy of our Russian Truth, our strength and faith. We live by this light and with it we will prevail over the hard years. With this Truth, given to us by our mothers, we will bear our bitter Russian burden, we will preserve this Truth and pass it on to our children. And our wives, following on the example of our Russian mothers, will carry with them the same soul of motherhood and will pass it on to their children.

He, the prisoner, who thought this way, was able to retain his Humanity in the camp, he was able to withstand all of the suffering. Only those who were thus strong in their belief were able to survive.

I didn't find Stalag X named on the map at the Holocaust Museum, but later discovered a photograph of that camp with the "sod huts" of the

Alexander and Leonid Artemyeff were kept as Soviet POWs at Stalag X in Wietzendorf, Germany. Here is a view of the camp for Soviet prisoners of war, showing the holes dug into the ground that served as shelter. The camp was located south of Hamburg in northern Germany. Wietzendorf, Germany, 1941–42. (*Niedersaechsische Landeszentrale fuer politische Bildung* [Lower Saxony State Center for Political Education]. United States Holocaust Memorial Museum, https://encyclopedia.ushmm.org/content/en/article/the-treatment-of-soviet pows-starvation-disease-and-shootings-june-1941january-1942).

first winter, dug into the earth between trees. It gave me a picture of what my father and uncle had survived, and of the thousands who had perished. Hitler's strategy to exterminate the POWs played out successfully until he realized that the remaining POWs could be used for forced labor at factories needing help for resupplying his war effort, and all hands were sent out to build munitions.

Toward the end of the war, my father and his brother were working in a factory near Hamburg, under guard. The British forces were approaching from one side, the Soviet Army from the other. My uncle writes:

> Our German guards take us out of the city for the day work, and then billet us at a farm for the night.
>
> We are worried—who will take the village? The Brits? Or the

Reds? If it is the Red Army, then we will be threatened by repatriation and exile to Siberia, or execution, since SMERSH* (*smert' spionam*—death to the spies), is merciless in its reprisal.

Luckily, the British arrive first and take the village. The German soldiers guarding us surrender without the slightest resistance. The POWs scatter every which way, there is no rule of law.

Sasha and I return to Hamburg. Finally, in May, 1945, Germany capitulates. The war ends! Everyone is rejoicing at the victory. The POWs from England and France, and the workers from Holland return home.

The Soviet POWs and those who were forcibly taken out of Russia as OST workers are not celebrating. Many of the POWs and OST'ers run away to hide from the repatriation forces.

Roosevelt, Churchill and Stalin signed a shameful agreement in Yalta allowing the forced round up of all Soviet citizens to repatriation camps and their forcible return. The headhunt begins. SMERSH pursues groups and individuals, and how many tragic instances occur of deaths and suicides.

In one of the repatriation camps where the British forces had allowed SMERSH to pen up hundreds of Cossacks and their families, they were being loaded up on trucks to be taken away when they removed their hats and fell to their knees, singing.

"*Upokoi, Gospodi, dushi rab Tvoikh*" (Rest, Lord, Thy Servants Souls).

"What are they singing?" asked the British guards.

"They are singing the funeral dirge for their souls."

My father and uncle, having been citizens of Poland before the war, managed to avoid the repatriation. But for my mother, it was not so easy.

*SMERSH was an umbrella organization for three independent counter-intelligence agencies in the Red Army formed in late 1942 or even earlier, but officially announced only on 14 April 1943. The name SMERSH was coined by Joseph Stalin. Meaning: Death to Spies. Not to be confused with Ian Fleming's fictionalized SMERSH organization featured in Fleming's early James Bond novels as agent 007's nemesis.

32

Goodbye, Leipzig—April 1945

Day followed day. The front kept getting closer from both sides. The Americans were coming from the West and we prayed that they would reach our city before the advancing Soviet Army from the East.

No one knew where the armies might meet up. There were so many conferences—Yalta, Potsdam—where the Great Powers carved up Germany, deciding its fate in various pacts and agreements, but what would actually happen, no one could foretell. As usual during such an alarming and dark time, various rumors abounded in conversation.

Spring arrived with the coming of April. The days got longer and that lifted spirits. Everyone was awaiting the end. The Germans were coming to the realization that they had lost the war and would have to surrender unconditionally, caught in the vise of the two giants, America and the Soviet Union. Exhausted with the unremitting bombardments, food shortages and lines, the Germans awaited a resolution, it seemed, of any kind.

On the 19th of April, the city of Leipzig experienced one. Mid-afternoon of a sunny clear day, we watched from our third floor windows as three columns of U.S. Jeeps filled the street below us. Everything about the Americans surprised us: the healthy, rosy-cheeked faces of the well-fed soldiers, their beautiful uniforms, their calm and carefreeness since they advanced without any battle or the slightest opposition, exactly like the Nazis had moved in on us in the Donbas four years ago.

Most of all, we were amazed at how well they maneuvered their Jeeps, almost as if they were bicycles. This was the first time we confirmed the reports that Americans were born with a steering wheel in their hands; that all of America, from the youngest to the oldest, was on wheels.

A few minutes later, there were sounds downstairs and soon after a soldier of enormous size, fat as a hog, flew up the stairs into our apartment. He shouted loudly, "Pistole? Pistole?"

We understood that he was searching for firearms, and he

stopped short, seeing in front of him a mother, two children, and an elderly woman. No "pistole" could threaten him here. Glockner had the only firearm in the house, and it is doubtful that the cunning man willingly surrendered it. The soldier left our room with a nod.

The Glockners grew quiet, chastened. We noticed an immediate change in attitude toward us and Marusia. She was allowed to go out in the evenings to be with the other Russians who worked at the factory. Work hours were shortened and food rations increased. She laughed, saying that now the Glockners wanted to show themselves to be kind slave masters and make up for the years of abuse. That surely didn't happen since they had for too long humiliated the workers to be forgiven by them.

We were treated differently by the Glockners too, and we understood the reasons behind it and ignored their new advances towards us.

There was one joy that was immeasurable—the nightly bombardments ceased, allowing us to sleep uninterrupted through the whole night. The sounds of the ack-ack guns were silenced forever.

In the center of the city, there were still some scattered Hitler loyalists who were resisting, firing from their hiding places in the Rathaus (city hall) on the Americans. We heard that in the Monument to the Battles of the Peoples, where we had sheltered from the bombings, there were several detachments of Hitler's troops, although we never saw any German soldiers in the streets before. The Americans must have smoked them out quickly.

A new set of rules was imposed—the American order. At first there wasn't much of a difference, except that we could now go outside without the fear that in your absence during a bombardment, either your loved ones would perish, or you might die, separated from them. Under bombardment, we always used to sit close together, tight up against each other, thinking that if we are killed, then we all die together. Surviving for any of us, without the others, would have been unendurable.

I started to go out. There was a beautiful Russian church not far from us, which must have been built during the czarist times, since no new churches were built by the Soviets, they only destroyed them. Services were conducted on Sundays and holidays and the church was filled to capacity, with a choir conducted by a woman.

We started attending this church and a parish center next door where Russians gathered, and someone even played a piano. But most importantly, there was a library with a sizable collection of books. So finally! Finally! We were able to immerse ourselves in reading, as we had done earlier in our motherland, where a book was always the first friend to my mother and me.

A special social class of Russians visited the church and the club. Almost all of them were from the "old emigration," the intelligentsia who had exiled themselves after the Russian Revolution of 1917. For example, there was the librarian named Bukovsky, an intelligent, gallant man whose gentlemanly ways were surprising to me, having grown up with coarse Soviet social manners.

Everything about these people was new and interesting, and it was a pleasure to mingle with them, even though at first they seemed to distance themselves from on high. With time, I came to learn that most of them were from France and had been captured by the Nazis and forcibly taken to Germany as workers, similarly to our OST workers, except under better conditions—they had good jobs, lived in private homes and were not made to wear the OST patches. The Nazi attitudes toward them were different, too.

Despite that, these émigrés were overwhelmingly glad for the arrival of the American troops and the end of Hitler's domination, and were dreaming of their return to France. They understood right away that there would be no return for me and my family to the Soviet Union, that our fate was uncertain and what would befall us was known only to God.

An elderly man became interested in me. Sergei Lvovich Lusin, 72 years old, was from Paris. He took a liking to me and started walking me home. Soon after, he proposed marriage to me. He offered to take me and my whole family, sight unseen, to Paris as a way of saving us from the Soviet's repatriation, about which rumors had begun to circulate.

His proposal was not acceptable to me and I turned him down, delicately. I was only 29 years old at the time. To come together with an elderly man, one for whom I had absolutely no feelings, felt like suicide to me. Aside from that, I felt that since I had survived the war with my children and mother, emerged unharmed from all we had been through, I would somehow make do without the help of a 72-year-old.

The month of May, the most beautiful month of the year, thus came and went.

At the beginning of June, after Germany had surrendered and Hitler and his henchmen were dead, and the rest of his accomplices were being held at the Nuremberg trials, we heard some news on the radio. Saxony, including Leipzig, Thuringia, and some other regions, as was decided earlier at conferences with Churchill, Roosevelt and Stalin, were to be handed over to the Soviet command. Anyone who did not want to remain would need to leave this zone within nine days!

We would have to flee. We started to fret. Once again, we had to leave for somewhere. Again, we had to gather up our scant belongings and run. But where? Did we have anyone, anywhere, some goal, some place which we might at least potentially point to as a destination?

Along with many others in our situation, we had understood that things couldn't stay the same for long, that sooner or later would come a day when we would have to think about the future. We couldn't go into the camps for foreigners in Leipzig and other regions' cities because they were organized specifically for repatriation. French for the return to France of those who had been brought here, like my librarian friend and my suitor; Belgian for a return to Belgium, Polish camps for Poles.

The Allies—England, America, and France—burned with a desire to repatriate their people as quickly as possible and considered it their sacred duty to free them from their exploitation in a foreign land, from the slavery and discrimination they had been subjected to during the war, where they had been made to labor for their enemy. They wanted to quickly bring them back to their countries and their homes.

The Allies thought the same of us, the Russian refugees. It never crossed their minds that a huge number of us didn't want to and could not return to our homeland; that for many, it meant facing certain death. They just couldn't understand it. It wasn't really surprising, since never in the history of mankind had it been that someone torn from his familiar places and home, from the graves of his ancestors, from everything dear they had known in their childhood, their schooling, their youth—that a person not only would not want to go back, but would fear the return like a death sentence.

This could only happen because never before in history was there such a regime that devoured its own by the hundreds, thousands, millions. Stalin was firm in his position that there were no prisoners, only traitors to the motherland and anyone captured needed to shoot his last bullet into his head. For this reason, not even the POWs wanted to return home, but not seeing an alternative, they reckoned that it was better to go voluntarily, in which case they would be sentenced to 5–6 years in the camps—this after the cold and worse than cattle-like conditions of POW camp—than be repatriated by force and then be given a "ten-er," that is, 10 years in the camps, or more.

There were repatriation camps in Leipzig for Russians. But who found their way to them? The likes of Marusia and her factory friends. They reasoned that nothing would happen to them, that they had been kidnapped against their will in only the clothes they were wearing, snatched from the streets, the squares and markets, and transported to Germany. They were guilty of nothing.

If you used common sense, then of course, this was true. But did Stalin's *oprichniki* think this way? No. *How are you not at fault? Did you not collaborate with the enemy? Marusia, aren't you guilty of working for Glockner? Couldn't you have refused him?* She could have, but then what awaited her was a concentration camp in Auschwitz or Buchenwald.

As for refugee camps, other than for repatriation, there were none in Leipzig, nor elsewhere, I suspected. So with others who chose not to return, we waited. Our wait was not for very long. The political situation dictated our next move. We had to leave, go to wherever, at least get away from the eastern zone being occupied by the Reds.

Nine days was enough time. I was friendly with another family, Dr. Krivosheyev, his wife and daughter, and we decided to leave together. We were packed and ready to go in less than the allotted nine days. But before we left our abode at Herr Glockner, I had an interesting conversation with him. Despite his abusive treatment of my family and me, his rude and humiliating discrimination and constant insistence of the superiority of his race over ours, I still decided to give him some farewell advice.

I told him to leave everything—his factory, his villas (he had a second home outside of Leipzig where his daughter and son-in-law lived), and grab only what was most valuable and take himself to the American zone.

He laughed in my face when I told him that. He didn't understand that in the eyes of the Communists, he was a factory owner and an exploiter of the proletariat, and that especially the Russian workers would confirm this along with Marusia (she was already in the repatriation camp), whose labor had been backbreaking, day and night, in his household.

Glockner refused to believe me. He said that he had humble beginnings in the working class himself and was from a poor family. He had used his own mind to invent his machine and his own resources to build it, working tirelessly, achieving a patent. He wasn't a factory owner who had inherited his wealth, he had created it with his own hands.

I tried to persuade him, that having lived for a quarter century under Bolshevism and grown up under the power of the Soviet state, I knew all its rules and had been forced to learn its doctrines. I assured him that not a single Communist would care in the least that he had built his factory himself and did not inherit it. The most important fact would be that he was the owner, the exploiter, the capitalist feeding off of the workers, whom he had forced to labor, cold and hungry, for ten hours a day. His factory would be taken away, and at best, he would become just another worker; at worst, he would be jailed for his activities, especially since he had forced Russians to work for him.

He didn't listen. He just laughed at me. What can you prove to such a man? He was blind to the situation, unaware of communist dogma or lacking in his depth of knowledge of it, for which I am certain he paid dearly with his holdings and perhaps even with his life.

I felt no pity for him. He had drunk the blood of his workers, had enjoyed and fulfilled his life—now he would answer for it. We bade him and his wife farewell.

Dragging our suitcases to the tram stop, we boarded and took a seat to take us to the train. Arriving at the town square next to the train station, we saw that it was teeming with those who were leaving.

I left the children and my mother with our suitcases and went to buy the tickets. Dr. Krivosheyev went with me, and on the way we talked about to where we should try to procure passage. It really didn't matter, as long as it was out of the Soviet zone. We decided to try for Frankfurt am Main, having heard during the war that there was a large population of Russians there, and it seemed better to try and make our way there on our own.

We were sold the tickets, but with no guarantee if or when there would be a train in that direction. Perhaps there would be a freight train. I went back to haul our luggage to the train station. One of the suitcases, an old one of my father's, was very heavy and I had to lift it to my shoulders. I took Natasha with me to watch over it at the station and we started across the square.

Then I spied some Soviet soldiers walking toward us. Soviet troops were darting about everywhere now. They saw me with the suitcase on my back, and one of them said: "I swear, she's one of our Russian girls. No German woman would hoist a suitcase onto her back like that. She's running away from us."

I didn't look back at them, not wanting to signal that I had understood his words, and we made our way to the station. I brought over the rest of our belongings, and this time, Yura and my mother followed.

The train took a long time to come and we sat on our suitcases, waiting together with the doctor and his family, talking. They were also going somewhere, at random, wherever the train would take them, without thinking whether there was anyone there toward whom they might travel, and wondering what would be our fate.

The train was indeed a freight train, and we helped each other up into the car. We started to move slowly, and traveled quite far, until suddenly it stopped! The train went no further because the rail bridge ahead across the Fulda River had been blown up.

33

Repatriation Attempts—1945

> Roosevelt had brushed off warnings of a potential domination by Stalin in part of Europe, explaining, "I just have a hunch that Stalin is not that kind of a man … I think that if I give him everything I possibly can and ask for nothing from him in return, 'noblesse oblige,' he won't try to annex anything and will work with me for a world of democracy and peace."
>
> —*From Roosevelt to Truman: Potsdam, Hiroshima, and the Cold War* by Wilson Miscamble, 2007, Cambridge University Press

The mention of Roosevelt in our house was always with scorn. I didn't understand why someone who had led America out of the Depression, created Social Security for the aged, waged war against Japan, and was Churchill's ally against Hitler was reviled in my parents' minds. It was only when I probed them that they responded with the word—"Yalta"—and a litany of accusations about how Roosevelt had appeased Stalin with the agreement to allow the repatriation of Russian refugees and POWs from Germany. Churchill and the English didn't escape their wrath either for their collusion with Soviet forces.

My mother almost fell into the net which had been cast wide by Stalin's henchmen to gather up compatriots in postwar Germany.

The first DP "Displaced Persons" camp she entered in Germany was one for Polish refugees. She and her two children and her mother found refuge there as a way station. The camp director spoke Russian and was willing to register them as from Western Ukraine, Galicia, which had belonged to Poland before the war. Otherwise, they wouldn't have been allowed to stay. She described her brush with the Soviet repatriation forces while there.

> We were given a ration card immediately, which was quite ample. But the real bonus were the packages given out to each person. These packages played a critical role in our existence.

During the war, the Americans provided their armies with generous food packages. It was known that American soldiers were used to being well-fed at home and the government could not shirk its responsibility for providing for them abroad. In addition to that, some Americans were held in POW camps, and they could not be expected to survive in the horrible circumstances of Soviet soldiers in POW camps, where the USSR didn't concern itself about their fate.

American charities cared about American soldiers who had been captured and put into POW camps and sent CARE (Cooperative for Assistance and Relief Everywhere) packages to be distributed to them. Twenty-two charities formed CARE. People could buy a CARE package for $10 and have it shipped to anyone. The U.S. Army distributed them.

There was a huge amount of these packages. When the war came to an end and Germany surrendered, most of the Americans, beginning with the POWs, were sent home.

Thousands upon thousands of CARE packages were left in storage facilities and according to the orders of the American command, they were to be distributed to refugees like us. The CARE packages were remarkable! Each one contained chocolate, a sweet taste we had long forgotten, cocoa, cookies, rice, butter, coffee, condensed milk and other valuable food items. In addition to these, each package had no less than four packs of cigarettes, in most cases a brand called Camel. It was these cigarettes that gave us life. The price of a pack of Camel cigarettes reached 110 German marks, the cost of a train ride across all of Germany.

Folks started riding near and far "on Camel back," in search of where the conditions for life were safer and better. They speculated on the sale of coffee, which was the elixir of life for Germans, and for which they were willing to pay or trade anything for the real thing, not its surrogate. We were given the coffee in large quantities and it was also in the CARE packages. I remember bartering with a German woman—I exchanged a small jar of coffee for a pair of boots.

We literally came alive. The food, the CARE packages—four in total, one for each of us every two weeks—gave us money for the sold cigarettes, bartered clothing for the coffee. In a word, life returned. But there was the worry, what next? What would happen with the repatriation? The Americans were not going to keep us fed and housed forever. It would all come to an end sometime…

The refugee camps mushroomed. We knew that there were several camps nearby for different ethnic nationalities and there were rumors that in the south, close to Munich, there were large camps for Russians, which were well organized with schools, theaters and churches. They were their own "countries within a country," with a Russian administration and leadership, all of course under the supervision of the American forces.

Soon we heard that in our British Zone there were two large refugee camps established, named Colorado and Fischbeck, with sizable populations of Russians.

But here, amongst the Poles, we felt safer. They treated us well; they allotted to us a large room divided in half with dressers and blankets. In the other half lived a young couple, Edik and Maria. Maria took it upon herself to teach me conversational Polish, and Natasha attended the school, where she excelled.

My mother and I were not all that happy with our "Poletization," which was conducted by the Catholic church and required Natasha to attend Mass. But we were wary of seeking out our own, because the Soviet Repatriation Mission was active throughout Germany. People were turned over to their deaths, with no one defending them, no one standing up to oppose what had been the agreement between the Allies for the return of all Soviet citizens to their homeland.

We had to wait it out behind the Polish curtain of safety.

We had heard about the turnover of General Vlasov's troops to the Soviets, of the terrible tragedy at Lienz, Austria, where mothers and fathers had thrown their children into the Danube and followed them to their deaths; of the bloody suicides, preferring death to a forced return to the motherland.

The talk and rumors gave us no respite. We heard of instances where Russians were snatched right on the street, shoved into waiting cars, and taken to an unknown location.

What would happen to us? We went into town cautiously and those at home worried when we didn't return on time. We lived in fear of the "headhunters."

Someone related that up north, near Hamburg, Soviet troops had surrounded the DP camp and had already loaded the refugees onto trucks, but a local priest, Father Vitaly, stopped the process by running to the British authorities and asking them to intervene. Together they were able to get a stay for the refugees, and they were allowed to remain. Later Father Vitaly was acclaimed a savior and was much revered and loved.

Days passed, but the repatriation went unabated. Its zealots searched through the camps and cities, fishing out souls, preying upon them with every lie and coercion possible, rounding them up in trucks to be taken away.

One day, the block commander who was responsible for our row of barracks came running to me with the news that on the following day there was going to be a visit from the Soviet Repatriation Mission to search for Russians to be returned to the motherland. He advised us to go into the neighboring forest for the day and lock up the apartment. The Soviets would be told that it was occupied by a Polish woman and her children, who were absent temporarily.

We followed his advice. Early the next morning, we prepared sandwiches and coffee, packed a blanket to put on the ground, and made for the woods. Luckily, it was a dry and sunny day and pleasant to be out. We spent the entire day in the forest. Natasha took her school books and homework, and Yura ran about, but Mama and I kept looking around in fear that the "headhunters" were combing the forest as well.

We returned late at night to learn that the Soviets had indeed been there but had not completed their "work," and would come back the next day. We would have to spend another day in the woods. Well, what was to be done? We returned to the woods for another day in hiding; it saved our lives.

The children were given instructions, especially Natasha, in the event that Mama and I were taken away and we were separated from them. Rumors were that adults were put on trial and children were sent to orphanages. If that were the case, we told Natasha, that as the elder sibling, she should say that they had a father back home and repeat his name and surname, which of course she knew. We told her the exact address and locality of where he might be, if he was alive. For the time being, the danger passed and we calmed down, but only briefly.

Soon after that, Natasha fell ill. She had contracted pleurisy. There was no room in the camp hospital and she was admitted to the German hospital in town. Her condition was very serious and required a blood transfusion. Fortunately, it turned out that she and I had the same blood type so it was simple for me to provide her my blood, which the doctors transfused.

The crisis came when her temperature spiked and she lay semi-conscious in her hospital bed.

And then the Soviet Repatriation Mission descended on the hospital. They arrived in search of any Russian citizens who had been hospitalized. The German nurses told them that there were two: an invalid with both legs amputated and a 10-year-old girl.

They entered Natasha's hospital room. Despite her semi-conscious state, they started asking her questions. "Are you a Russian girl?"

"Yes, I'm Russian."

"Why are you lying here? We will take you to a good hospital and get you well immediately! We will come for you tomorrow. Be ready."

Natasha responded that she wasn't alone, that her mother and babushka would decide whether or not she could leave with them, and she would not go anywhere without them.

"Well, we will take them too!" (What beneficence!)

Natasha related all of this when Babushka came to visit her later that day.

I was in the refugee camp when suddenly I saw through the window that Babushka was running home. I guessed that something terrible had happened, since because of her infirm legs, she could hardly run.

We decided right then to take Natasha out of the hospital and bring her home the same day, and not to allow the Soviets to come for her the next day and take her away.

We returned to the hospital and started asking the German nurses to release Natasha to us, but they were unwilling because they needed the permission of the doctor, who was away.

So we dressed Natasha—her fever was more than 40 degrees Celsius (104 degrees F)—and took her under each arm to lead her out of the back door of the hospital. She could hardly walk.

Luckily, along the way back to camp, we saw the camp doctor in his car, and we stopped him. He took us the rest of the way and admitted Natasha into the camp hospital. The hospital physician there was an Englishman and when he heard the entire story about Natasha, he was outraged and told us not to worry, that no one would be allowed to take any patients out of his hospital.

We calmed down then, and Natasha spent the next several days recovering there.

The amputee invalid was "repatriated" the very next day. No one was there to defend him. He couldn't walk away on his own and he was taken. One can only guess his fate.

34

Displaced Persons Camp—Fischbeck, 1948

By the end of 1947, my mother, the children, and Babushka had moved several times into different DP camps, including one in an old castle called Ringelheim. In September 1947, my mother undertook teaching a small class of five or six children, including my sister Natasha, with the intent of returning them to fluency in Russian. During the war years, children had only the most basic instructions in the alphabet, if that.

This DP camp in Ringelheim was soon to be de-commissioned, once again forcing my mother to search for where to live. Thanks to contacts she had made at a teachers' conference in Hamburg, she was able to secure a teaching position for herself, and later, living quarters for herself, Natasha, Yura and Babushka, in the Fischbeck Displaced Persons camp in the north, near Hamburg, one of the biggest Russian DP camps in Germany after the war.

In the Fischbeck camp, my mother and her family were surrounded by other Russians who quickly took them into the cultural life of the camp. By the spring of 1948, they had settled into a daily life which included school, art, and as it turned out, love.

Fischbeck was a large camp with 15 barracks buildings, subdivided into 10–15 rooms each. The camp was a small city, with both an elementary and high school, containing classes of 15–20 students in each one. There were two large clubhouses, where there were theatrical productions, visiting artists, and art galleries. The camp had a hospital, with several doctors.

The church had its own building, with several priests serving parishioners, including Archimandrite Vitaly, the same one who had saved so many people from repatriation. In addition to the residential barracks, there was a main administrative building dubbed the "Kremlin," and in front of it a large open area that was named the "Red Square." The camp had a kitchen that provided full meals to singles and the provisions for families to cook their own meals in their barracks. My mother described the "little city":

Hamburg-Fischbeck Displaced Persons Camp where Tatyana moved with her children and mother in 1947. She met and married Alexander Artemyeff in this camp in 1949.

Tatyana teaching first graders in the Fischbeck Displaced Persons Camp school, 1948.

Hamburg Fischbeck Displaced Persons Camp 514 in Hamburg, Germany. The camp housed several thousand Russian Displaced Persons, including Tatyana and her family and her future husband, Alexander Artemyeff.

If it were possible to forget that you were in Germany and that you only had to walk a few blocks to be in the most typical of small German towns, you might think that you were living in a village in Russia.

It was the same in other DP camps scattered throughout Germany after the war. The Nazis had brought so many workers into Germany from the Soviet Union, and so many of them chose not to return. The result was that they accumulated into camps throughout West Germany.

Peoples from Holland, Belgium, France, and other countries that had been occupied by German forces used every means possible to return to their homelands at their first opportunity after the war ended. They were met with joy, with song, with embraces from their countrymen. They dropped to their knees to kiss their ancestral ground.

Our unfortunate people had no haven to return to in our native land, it welcomed them with an open door … to its gulags.

I haven't written a single word about the romantic side of my life; of course, I had one. At the time I was between 29 and 32 years old. I was an interesting and attractive woman, albeit somewhat exhausted, understandably, from all the toils of overcoming the war and its aftermath.

Along the way, I met a number of "possibilities" but they were all temporary—they didn't really suit me, or more likely I was not a good match for them because of my family situation. I won't hide that fact that my goal was to remarry, to find someone who would take upon himself the well-being of my family, to free me from this burden that I had borne for the war years, always on my own, all the difficult battles waged alone.

There was no return for me to Russia and to my husband. Who knew if he was even alive, if he had survived the war, or if he had taken up with another? It might have been like him to do that, while we sat shivering under the Allied bombardment.

My mother was categorically against my efforts to find someone with whom to tie my fate. She reasoned with me, "Why do you need a husband? You have done quite well both in supporting and bringing up the children. No outsider will be a real father to them. He will be a stepfather, with all the expected qualities. Devote yourself to them, live for them. Do you really need a man?"

She judged me by her own years of experience. When my father died, she did not remarry but gave up her entire life to my brother and me, and later when Fediay was killed, to me alone. But she had been widowed at the age of 40, while I was left without a husband at 25.

In the Ringelheim DP camp, I was courted by a Russian engineer / poet. Fortunately, the courtship did not result in marriage. I say fortunately because he turned out to have an egotistical nature and the manners of a cheapskate. Mama was timely in checking him out and warned me, but I had already taken note of it myself. He paid absolutely no attention to my children, as if they didn't even exist, which of course was hurtful. So, we parted and went our own ways, like ships passing in the night. He later left for Canada, where he married a woman with a daughter, with whom he didn't get along.

Here in Fischbeck Camp, I went out with a gentleman named Popliuko, but it didn't work out either due to differences in temperament.

Soon after I had settled in, the Russian Boy Scouts organized a campfire on the outskirts of the camp. There were a lot of Scouts in the camp, and they were led by one of the brothers Artemyeff, Leonid Feodosevich. Leonid had been a scoutmaster in Poland, where the brothers lived before the war.

I participated in the campfire activities by singing the Russian song *Ogonek* (Little Light), based on the same melody, but with my own lyrics written for the occasion. Everyone liked it very much and I was accepted into their circle. Natasha even became a Girl Scout.

At this campfire, I met the other brother, Alexander Artemyeff. At first, it was what was referred to as a "tip of the hat friendship"—hello and goodbye. But when New Year's Eve 1948 approached, Alexander invited me to greet it with him and others at the "Kremlin," along with the society *crème* of the camp population. He and Leonid were known in the camp as the "Bandit Brothers" and were part of a group called the *Solidaristi* (Solidarists), who organized the evening.

That evening marked the beginning of our courtship.

But it was a strange courtship at first. Alexander (Sasha) Feodoseevich was reticent to be open about our meetings. We met, at his request, outside of the campgrounds, where no one might see us together. What was presumed by a young woman meeting with an unmarried man? Whom did it bother? No one. Neither of us was trying to fool anyone, we weren't cheating—we were both free and

Left to right: Leonid Artemyeff and Alexander ("Sasha") Artemyeff. The "Bandit Brothers" Artemyeff, who were released from Stalag X Soviet POW camp in Wietzendorf when Germany capitulated and were living in Hamburg-Fischbeck Displaced Persons Camp 514 when Tatyana arrived.

independent. But for some reason Sasha was shy about our rendezvous and that was unpleasant for me.

Mama stepped in again. She didn't like him. For her, his manners were not up to par because he came from a simple family, even though he had been educated at a Warsaw university. His every gesture annoyed her. She complained that every time there was a need for some muscle, that is, a man's help in the household, we had to turn to Popliuko because Sasha shied away, likely because he didn't want others to presume or say something.

Regardless of her objections, I liked him and soon came to truly love him.

I liked him for his honesty and decency.

Perhaps it was because of his honesty that he was reluctant to be open about our growing relationship. He wasn't planning on marrying and he might have thought it dishonest to lead me on. He didn't want rumors about us flying through the camp.

We lived in a very open social environment. Everything that transpired was immediately known to all—it was impossible to escape that transparency—living in a "collective" as we were.

Left: Alexander Artemyeff, Hamburg-Fischbeck Displaced Persons Camp, 1948. Right: Tatyana Budishevsky and her son, Yura, 1948.

Tatyana and Alexander, courting.

Right to left: Leonid Artemyeff, Tatyana Budishevsky, Alexander Artemyeff. Alexander's birthday celebration, December 2, 1948. Fischbeck DP Camp, Germany.

Forces were at work to discourage us. To me they said: "Why are you going out with such an uninteresting man? You are a beautiful woman, and you will find a more prominent, solid husband from the intelligentsia!"

And to him, perhaps even the same advisers whispered: "Why are you getting mixed up with a family woman? You are a bachelor, you're as free as a bird right now, is it that hard to find an unmarried, eligible young woman? Why would you encumber yourself with an entire family?"

In a word, outsiders were trying to decide our fate.

Sasha hesitated for two reasons: he was ambivalent about my children and my age. I was three years younger than he was and perhaps he thought that three years were too few, not youthful enough. Every man wants to marry a woman younger than him, as did his father, who at age 55 took a 20-year-old bride. But the eligible younger women in the camp weren't all that interested in him or his brother; at 33 and 31, they considered them elderly.

But no matter the wagging tongues around us, we drew closer to each other. Our courtship lasted a year, including a summer sojourn in Lubec, from where we returned as almost an engaged couple, the formal announcement coming on the celebration of New Year's Eve 1949, once again in the "Kremlin."

Newly married, February 21, 1949, and creating a new family: Back row, left to right: Alexander, Yura, Natasha. Front row, left to right: Tatyana, Nadezhda (Babushka).

We were married on the 21st of February, 1949. From the first day of marriage, my life took a different turn. The burden that I had carried alone all those years was lifted from my shoulders. Almost intuitively, I started to remove from myself the responsibilities for many things. I now had a "back" behind which I could hide, which protected me. And what a difference I felt immediately with Sasha as my husband, from my former one. He showed such concern, love, and interest in my life, we had a common bond in everything.

35

A Mighty Resettlement of Peoples—1948–1949

By 1948 and the beginning of 1949, many of the DP's in Fischbeck had been assigned to leave for other countries. My father, Alexander, and his brother, Leonid, had already signed up to emigrate to Morocco.

My mother described the process of applying for and being accepted to leave Germany:

> The nations of the world, at the United Nations sessions, took it upon themselves to accept a few thousand refugees each to "unload" Germany, since it was burdened with its own Germans from its eastern regions. Many DPs who had left for England returned, unable to bear the conditions and regime there. Belgium took only the able-bodied to work in their coal mines. Other countries, like Colombia, Venezuela, Argentina, and Canada began to accept refugees. At the time, the United States only took those who had relatives who would sign affidavits of support.
>
> This "mighty resettlement of peoples" deserves its own volume in the story of the exiled. In the history of civilization there is probably nothing comparable to this exodus of people from their homelands. I say this because we Russians weren't the only ones who were relocated to foreign places overseas.
>
> People from other countries that had been seized by communism also migrated. They were fewer than us, of course, for two reasons. First, there were fewer of them in general, for example Estonians or Lithuanians. Secondly, many of these groups had only recently been put under the communist boot; they did not know yet what it was and believed the slogans of "equality and brotherhood" and other tempting communist propaganda. They did not believe us—we who had experienced this regime—and they trudged dutifully, some even enthusiastically, back to their native lands.
>
> Every day there was an updated posting in the office of which new country was willing to take refugees, in what quantity and on what

terms. All countries wanted a work force. Some announced different opportunities, while others were direct in looking for heavy work laborers with a contractual requirement to sign for two or more years. Australia was one of these. The demand was for workers who would chop out forests, or embed telephone poles along the coastline, or other heavy labor. Only a sufficiently able-bodied man could sign up for this kind of work. No one was taken at his word—each had to pass a rigorous physical exam performed by several physicians. These examinations were humiliating, reminiscent of the slave markets of the previous century.

There were quite a few who had signed for Morocco; they all departed, but Leonid and Sasha had declined to leave after Sasha married me. Leonid did not want to go alone, but all of us were not allowed to leave together because we had to now re-do all of the documents for a family. The brothers decided to stay on in the DP camp. Before they turned down the invitation from Morocco, Sasha attended classes to learn French, so that they wouldn't arrive in a country with no language skills whatsoever. He understood some phrases in French already.

At one point, I had signed up to emigrate to Argentina. I have no idea how I would fare there, with small children and an elderly mother, but I signed up anyway. There was a general psychosis to get out of Germany, to anywhere. I attended classes to learn Spanish, not knowing, of course, that I would need to know another language altogether.

Not many people were learning English at the time because few wanted to emigrate to England anymore, a country that was deemed exploitative and from which many disappointed refugees had already returned to the DP camps. Our friend Alexander Karmanov, an engineer from Leningrad with a degree in shipbuilding, was put to work sowing cabbage for a farmer as a laborer. That world renowned power, England—empress of the seas—couldn't find him a place in its numerous wharves?

The disenchanted returnees forfeited their exit fees, which were paid only once by the UNRRA (United Nations Relief and Rehabilitation Administration).

America was still unwilling to open its doors to mass immigration and only took those who had relatives living in the United States who would vouch for their financial support. This country, the richest in the world, was afraid that unfortunate refugees who were burning with desire to earn their own way and stop relying on all manner of UNRRA organizations, would lay a heavy burden on "poor America."

But even if it had been possible, Leonid was categorically opposed to going to America, and Sasha was of the same opinion, that the U.S. was a country of fast pace, crazily racing tempos, a country where the dollar was God and Tsar. People went over there to earn some money and then return home, not a place where one might live a normal life. Many people shared this perception, but regardless, they were still waiting for America to open its doors.

Even before Sasha and I were married, there were many of our friends in the camp who left for Australia on a two-year contract, but they were accepted without their wives or children. The conditions were that they would work there for a few months, up to a year, and then would be able to bring over their families.

Our family, which now had two male members, also signed up for exit to Australia. We filled out the paperwork immediately after our marriage but were not called to the commission in Wiendorf for two and a half months. In Wiendorf, there was a "transit" camp, a name which was given to it because no one lived there on a permanent basis. Refugees seeking deportation were sent there to pass the requirements of a commission for certain countries and were then sent on to await passage to their destinations, or if they failed the commission's requirements, largely for medical reasons, were required to return immediately to their DP camps of origin.

We were eight in all: Leonid and Sasha, myself, my mother, Natasha and Yura, and our friends, an elderly couple, the Popels, who posed as Leonid and Sasha's uncle and aunt. At their age, they were afraid of risking not being taken at all if they applied independently and would only be accepted as family members.

We arrived in Wiendorf to go through the examination by the commission. The commission approved only Leonid and me.

Sasha was rejected for health reasons. He and Leonid had spent the entire war in POW camps. Together they had survived the horrible conditions of the German POW camps on the Eastern front, about which an entire book should be written. Their experiences of this tragic period of their lives defied description. The Germans had shown their so-called humanity towards POWs no less than toward the Jews. Forced to live in holes dug out of the ground, in the open without cover, 35,000 POWs were reduced to 7,000 in a short time, dying of hunger or infectious diseases. Sasha contracted pleurisy. He was put in a hospital where there were no beds and the dying were covered only by their lice-ridden overcoats. One can only imagine the care in such a hospital. Sasha survived, thanks to Leonid, but the scarring on his lungs from the pleurisy remained, denying him a passing medical exam.

Mama did not pass the commission's medical exam either. During the 1930s famine created by Stalin in Ukraine, she had survived galloping consumption by what could only have been a miracle. Yura, who had just recently contracted tuberculosis, was strangely overlooked, either because he was a child and not being evaluated as labor-worthy, or because he was so young that the scarring had healed over sufficiently to be hidden from the x-raying. The elderly Popel couple were rejected as well.

The question of whether Leonid should leave for Australia, alone, presented a dilemma. By then, we considered ourselves a family. Sasha and Leonid were close brothers, born less than two years apart, growing up together. They were captured together by the Germans and survived the war together. It seemed irrational to be parted now when better times had finally arrived. The separation would appear to be forever, considering the geographic location of Australia on the planet.

Leonid wavered. Of course, he could refuse to go. The night following his acceptance by Australia, he couldn't sleep, pacing the room from corner to corner, thinking, weighing whether he should depart for such a far place, unable to make a decision.

Sasha kept silent. Instead of saying just a single word, "Stay!" he said nothing. If he had only said, "Stay with us—what will be will be—but we will remain together," then Leonid would have stayed.

But the silence convinced him that his brother was indifferent to him, that with his own family now, his own personal interests, he wasn't concerned with his brother's fate.

But that wasn't so. Sasha just didn't know what to advise him in this critical decision, how to affect the destiny of his brother. What if the future here in Germany boded misfortune, and he had talked his brother out of leaving? No one knew what lay before us. All anticipated, some even hoped, for a war between what used to be allies and were now rivals. Everyone wanted out of Germany and considered anyone who managed an exit to be fortunate.

If Sasha counseled Leonid to stay back, God knows what his fate would have been, and he might have blamed Sasha for it. Conversely, if he supported his leaving that might turn out badly as well, because no one knew how a foreign country would welcome newcomers and what sort of life awaited them.

So, Sasha chose to remain silent and to leave to his brother the full responsibility for deciding his own fate.

Leonid sailed. He first took a train to Italy, then by ship through the Suez Canal to the Red Sea, to the Indian Ocean with a stop in Ceylon, where he was offered an elephant in exchange for some souvenirs, then through Malaysia and finally to Sydney, Australia. On board was an acquaintance, Galina Fomin, and her daughter, Larissa, who was four years old at the time. Galina was to be reunited with her husband, Nickolay Fomin, who had already emigrated to Australia several

Farewell party for Alexander's brother, Leonid Artemyeff, leaving for Australia. The two brothers would not see each other for 25 years. Top, left to right: Alexander, Tatyana, Leonid. Seated, left to right: Yura, Nadezhda (Babushka), Natasha. Spring 1949.

Alexander, expectant father, putting together a baby carriage. Hamburg, Germany, 1950.

months before on a two-year contract to cut sugar cane on plantations. They sailed the high seas for 27 days.

The brothers would not see each other again for 25 years.

Despite Uncle Leonid's attempts to bring over his brother and family to Australia, which he started after several months' arrival, and numerous more examinations by the exit commission, my father and mother were not given permission to emigrate to Australia to join him. They were reconciled to staying in Germany on a permanent basis by then, but decided to give one more try, one last chance to leave for America.

Then my mother learned that she was expecting a child. She wrote:

> Sasha went almost out of his mind for joy. Before we were married, Sasha had stipulated that he wanted to have children. He couldn't picture a future without children and mine were not enough for him. They were already grown—Yura was 9 years old, and Natasha was 14—when we married. Of course, they understood that he wasn't their father.

Eugene Artemyeff, born December 23, 1950, in Hamburg, Germany, with Tatyana.

The plans for America were again delayed because pregnant women were only allowed to fly across the Atlantic, not sail, and a family of five was too many to be afforded that luxury. The child would need to be born and be old enough to travel by sea. Once again, they traveled to transit camps for medical exams.

My brother Eugene was born on December 23, 1950, in a Hamburg hospital. He was a restless infant and kept his parents awake at night, keeping him quiet so nearby refugee families could sleep.

A year later, my parents and their young son, together with my older sister and brother and grandmother, were finally granted passage to America. The DP camp in Bremen was the last stop before they took a train to where the ship for their crossing was docked. On board, my mother recalls the bittersweet departure:

> We were leaving the Old World for a new, unknown country beyond the sea. What awaited us there? What kind of life? Was it worth it to abandon our "Old Lady Europe" where we had lived through so many misfortunes, but also so many happy years? Where we had been born, schooled, and in whose ground lay the bones of our ancestors? Would we ever return to this land?
>
> The ship slipped away from the dock in the evening hours. City lights illuminated the fading buildings as we moved away. I stood on the deck in heavy thought. How would I be greeted by a new, unknown life, new people, new environment? A new language, that I would have to learn, whether I wanted to or not? And how far can one be expected to wander over this planet?
>
> I recalled the prophecy told me by a fortune-telling neighbor of my childhood: "You will go far, far away—to the opposite end of the earth."
>
> This was that very journey to the other side of the world. I watched sadly as the fog-shrouded shores of Europe melted away in the last rays of the setting sun.

36

Coming to America—January 1952

January 2, 1952. The ocean voyage aboard the USNS *General Muir*, a battered and poorly heated military vessel, was cold and dreary. It was a difficult passage for everyone except my older sister. I asked her recently what she remembered of the sailing, and she happily reported, "I wasn't seasick at all." She spent the entire time working in the children's kitchen by day, feasting on cooked chicken, which had previously only been available in celebration of my brother Eugene's first birthday. By night, Natasha "danced my way to America!" because the young sailors on the crew were allowed up to the salon in the evenings. At age 16, she was ready to seize every chance to have a good time.

The others didn't fare so well, as my mother described:

> The ship started listing back and forth once we were in the English Channel. Sasha turned out to be the most affected by it and he suffered with seasickness the entire passage—10 long days—during which he couldn't even get up from his berth or have anything to eat except grapefruit juice, which I brought him from the kitchen.
>
> Everyone on board had to work on the ship because the passage itself was free. Whoever did not work was not allotted any rations. Sasha would not have been allowed to eat, not that he could, in his state of sea sickness. Mama was not well and was even taken to the ship's hospital. Yura, however, was not seasick.
>
> Little Zhenya [Eugene] fared the best of all of us, except that he was surprised that having recently learned how to walk and already doing it well, now he was unable to stay on his feet because of the boat's rocking from side to side.
>
> I was not forced to work because I was caring for a small child. After the first night in the English Channel, I felt better; it was likely that my body adjusted to the motion.

The USNS *C.H. General Muir* brought Tatyana and her family to America on January 11, 1952 (http://www.navsource.org/archives/09/22/22142.htm, U.S. Navy Photograph).

A storm came up in the Atlantic and the ship started to list heavily on the waves. Mama, who was sitting on the deck in only canvas shoes, completely soaked her feet, after which the weakness in her legs worsened considerably. It was frightful to sit on the deck and watch the ship rise above the waves one moment, and then the sea would wash over the deck on the downside.

On the tenth day, we started to see the shores of America. As we approached New York City in the morning, I saw the long-awaited Statue of Liberty. My heart started to beat faster. We were stepping into the New World, into the unknown. Everyone on board poured out onto the decks to see the Statue and to take photographs of her from the ship.

Closer and closer we came to the city. We saw a road along the coastline with an almost unbelievable number of cars being driven on it, speeding one after another. Never in my life had I seen such a vast number of moving cars on what I later learned was the Henry Hudson West Way.

The ship docked at 23rd Street. We weren't let off for some time, owing to the checking of documents and meals, which took almost an entire day. It was evening by the time we disembarked.

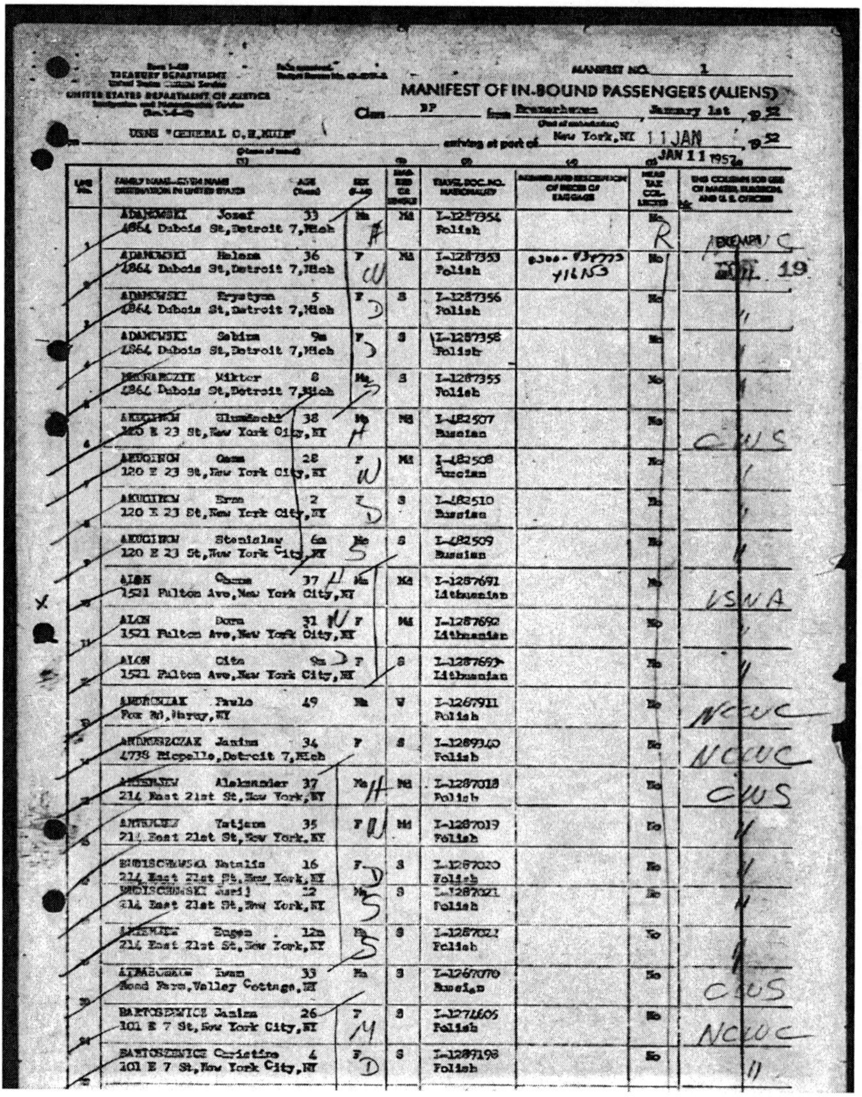

MANIFEST OF IN-BOUND PASSENGERS (ALIENS)

Manifest No. 1

USNS "GENERAL C. H. MUIR" — Class DP from Bremerhaven, January 1st, 1952 — arriving at port of New York, NY, 11 JAN 1952

Family name–Given name / Destination in United States	Age	Sex	Married or Single	Travel doc. no. / Nationality
ADAMOWSKI Josef, 4864 Dubois St, Detroit 7, Mich	33	M	M	I-1287354 Polish
ADAMOWSKI Helena, 4864 Dubois St, Detroit 7, Mich	36	F	M	I-1287353 Polish
ADAMOWSKI Krystyna, 4864 Dubois St, Detroit 7, Mich	5	F	S	I-1287356 Polish
ADAMOWSKI Sabina, 4864 Dubois St, Detroit 7, Mich	9m	F	S	I-1287358 Polish
... Wiktor, 4864 Dubois St, Detroit 7, Mich	8	M	S	I-1287355 Polish
AKUGINOW ..., 120 E 23 St, New York City, NY	38	M	M	I-482507 Russian
AKUGINOW ..., 120 E 23 St, New York City, NY	28	F	M	I-482508 Russian
AKUGINOW Erna, 120 E 23 St, New York City, NY	2	F	S	I-482510 Russian
AKUGINOW Stanislaw, 120 E 23 St, New York City, NY	6m	M	S	I-482509 Russian
ALON ..., 1521 Fulton Ave, New York City, NY	37	M	M	I-1287691 Lithuanian
ALON Dora, 1521 Fulton Ave, New York City, NY	31	F	M	I-1287690 Lithuanian
ALON Cita, 1521 Fulton Ave, New York City, NY	9m	F	S	I-1287693 Lithuanian
ANDRUSZAK Pawlo, ...	49	M	W	I-1267911 Polish
ANDRZEJCZAK Janina, 4738 ..., Detroit 7, Mich	34	F	S	I-1289340 Polish
ARTEMJEW Aleksander, 214 East 21st St, New York, NY	37	M	M	I-1287018 Polish
ARTEMJEW Tatjana, 214 East 21st St, New York, NY	35	F	M	I-1287019 Polish
BUDISCHEWSKA Natalia, 214 East 21st St, New York, NY	16	F	S	I-1287020 Polish
BUDISCHEWSKI Jurij, 214 East 21st St, New York, NY	12	M	S	I-1287021 Polish
... Eugen, 214 East 21st St, New York, NY	12m	M	S	I-1287022 Polish
... Iwan, ... Farm, Valley Cottage, NY	33	M	S	I-1267070 Russian
BARTOSZEWICZ Janina, 101 E 7 St, New York City, NY	26	F	S	I-1271605 Polish
BARTOSZEWICZ Christine, 101 E 7 St, New York City, NY	4	F	S	I-1289198 Polish

Passenger Manifest for USNS *General Muir* showing Artemyeff and Budishevsky members: Alexander, Tatyana, Natalia, Yuriy, and Eugene Fediay was lower on the list.

We found ourselves in a big open plaza. Since we were emigrating under an affidavit from the Council of Churches, which had supposedly found a job for Sasha as an electrician in the State of Indiana, we would somehow have to find our way there. We had no idea how or with whom.

Left to right: Yura (12 years old), an unidentified man, Tatyana with Eugene in her arms, and an unidentified woman, as passengers on board the USNS *C.H. General Muir.*

While we were sitting on our suitcases in the plaza, with people from various organizations coming and picking up families, and the number still waiting becoming fewer, I spied a familiar face behind the barriers, that of Misha Ganusevich. He had lived at our Hamburg-Fischbeck DP camp, and we had kept up a correspondence with him here in America from Germany.

I walked up to the fencing where he stood, elated to see his familiar face. It turned out that he had read the passenger manifest in the newspaper and had come to meet us, seeing us on the list.

When I told him that I didn't know what our next steps would be, because according to the affidavit we were to go to Indiana, but we did not know when or by whom we would be taken there, he laughed and replied, "You're not going to any Indiana! I shall be your sponsor and you will go with me!"

"How can that be? Can anyone be a sponsor?" I asked him. "After all, it wasn't you who sent us the affidavit? What do we do about the company in Indiana that is awaiting an electrician?"

I had supposed that America had the same rules that we had been accustomed to in Germany. There, if you were given written instructions to go a place, that's where you went, and nowhere else.

The Germans were orderly in that way. But here it was not like that at all, it was complete chaos.

No one from the supposed company in Indiana had arrived for Alexander Artemyeff, no one was meeting us, and it was clear that the affidavit was just a pro forma document used to allow us to emigrate.

We gathered our belongings and followed Misha, saying not a word to anyone. When we left the plaza, we realized that there was a problem. Misha was without a car, so what would we do for transportation, especially with a one-year-old child? We were chilled and hungry, having sat for some time on our suitcases in the cold.

Misha decided to call one of his friends, Sasha Deriugin, who had a car, to ask if he would come and pick us up. Deriugin arrived in a while with his wife, Ira, in their car.

He still could not take all of us, so we took our places in the automobile (he and Irochka were clearly very proud to own it): Sasha, myself, Mama, and Natasha, with Eugene on my lap. Misha took Yura on the subway.

We had no idea where we were being taken, but on the way, Deriugin said that he was driving us to the club of the Solidaristi, in Brooklyn, where we would be sheltered until an apartment could be found.

In spite of our hunger and tiredness, and having just arrived from a crippled and broken Europe, Deriugin and Irochka took us a roundabout way through the center of New York City, evidently to shock and impress us with the nightlife of the City, this giant of the world.

They drove us up Broadway and the first impression took our breath away. The advertisements, the neon lights, spilled over everything. On one large building—and this was especially memorable—there was a billboard for Camel cigarettes. Our very own Camels! Our ration saviors! On the billboard was depicted a huge head of a man, with a large, gaping mouth from whose depths he exhaled puffs of smoke every 3 to 4 seconds!

On another building there was a waterfall displayed, the lights running down from the topmost roof onto a lower platform. An eagle, all alit and the size of a three-story house, was flapping its wings to proclaim the high quality of Budweiser beer!

We were dumbfounded and surprised—we didn't know which way to look. Sasha and Ira Deriugin succeeded in their mission to wow us with the never-before-seen sight of a city unharmed by war and burning bright with all the different colored lights of the rainbow.

Times Square in 1952, the night view Tatyana witnessed on arrival in New York City on January 11, 1952 (Top: www.oldnycphotos, with permission from Brian Merlis. Bottom: Library of Congress, Farm Security Administration—Office of War Information photograph collection).

It was very late when we finally made it to the Club; Misha arrived with Yura momentarily. A Club meeting was just finishing up and we met some of the members. A family we knew from Fischbeck, the Fedorovs, offered to take Yura, where he spent the next two weeks until we had set up an apartment. Lydia Vladimirovna Treml, who worked at the Tolstoy Foundation, offered to host Mama. The rest of us were made comfortable to spend the night at the Club. Mattresses and cots appeared from somewhere, and we fell asleep peacefully.

The following day we were again filled with surprise. Upon rising, we looked out the second-floor windows of the Club and were astonished! Automobiles, cars everywhere we looked, lined up on both sides of the street as far as the eye could see—not a space between them to walk through, long strings of them. At first, we thought that we had landed in a part of the city devoted to government offices. In Europe, only the government buildings had so many automobiles parked nearby, not so on residential streets.

There was another family living at the Club, also recently arrived and awaiting a move to an apartment. The Polchaninoff's grandmother brought some porridge that she had cooked for their child, Misha, and she motioned to us that she had made a double portion, one for Zhenya. She enlightened us as to the parked cars—they were all private automobiles of the people living in the houses on the street. The houses were attached, side by side, without garages, so the residents had to keep their cars on the street near to their homes.

We were astonished at this information; never in our lives had we ever seen or heard anything comparable. We had been told that America was "on wheels," but to such a degree that it was difficult to even pass between the parked cars? We had never even imagined it.

Our drivers, the Deriugins, and Misha Ganusevich, loaned us a small amount of money to "get a start" with our new life—that is, to buy some food. We asked the Polchaninoffs where we might buy some provisions and how to go about doing that, with no knowledge of English. They told us, to our delight, that we were in a German speaking neighborhood where German was spoken in all the stores and even Russian was spoken in some Jewish-owned shops.

In addition to that, there was a store where you didn't have to say anything at all, you just took a cart, wheeled it around the store taking what you needed from the shelves, and only paid at the very end, without having to have uttered a single word. We didn't believe our ears!

"How could you take whatever you wanted down from the shelves? What if we fill a shopping cart to the brim?"

"Well, then you pay for all of it." We had never heard of such a thing. In Europe, there was not this level of service yet.

Natasha and I went off in search of provisions.

Sasha, who had equipped himself with a map of the underground subway system, had already been instructed yesterday as to how to board the subway, where to go and with whom to speak. There was no time to waste! We had to start in right away to look for our "sources of existence." Sasha had busied himself with his job search since morning with the help of friends, who, even though they themselves were newcomers to New York, knew some basics and could help with at least some advice.

Natasha and I went off to the stores. We were surprised by the prices. A pound of potatoes cost the same as a pound of apples! In Germany, that would have been a miracle—apples there cost four times that of potatoes! We didn't understand it. Were the potatoes priced dearly or were the apples that inexpensive, 5 cents a pound? The German greengrocer just shook his head when we told him about the prices in Germany.

We went off to the store where "you didn't have to speak," where we were, indeed, completely dumbstruck. There were rows upon rows of food products, everything available, take what you want and place it into a wheeled cart. After all the malnutrition, hunger, and constant lack of food, the queues, the minuscule amounts of anything edible, the supermarket seemed to us a paradise.

No one rushed you to decide, or hurried you along, as if to say, "Go ahead, walk around at your own pace, choose what you need." But the problem was that, not knowing the language and not having the ability to read the labels, we could only guess at the contents of the boxes and bottles from the pictures. We saw packets with the word "Borden's" where there was the likeness of a smiling cow and started to look for boxes with a smiling pig, to signal that it was lard. But we didn't find it, so we had to "settle" for butter, which was familiar, from the German words *Die Butter.*

We returned to the Club, where there was a kitchen to prepare food, and made soup. Of course, we had yet to find out what sort of income we might earn and whether we had spent a little or a lot, and what it would cost us to pay for necessities like food, shelter, and clothing.

Things became clearer in a few days, when Sasha found work which paid him $1.13 per hour. The apartment we rented, a third-floor

Helen's first Christmas, January 1953. Left to right: Helen (three months old), Tatyana and Eugene (two years old). Brooklyn, New York.

walk-up with no heat, cost us $23 a month for three rooms, a kitchen and a bath. It took my breath away to think that I could live in an entire apartment, finally! After years of wandering and living in a single room, sometimes even sharing that room with others, we would have an apartment with a bath! A friend loaned us $46 for the first month and security, and vouched for us to the landlord, who included some used furniture that his mother had left behind.

Yura started junior high school but encountered bullying from the other students because of his German clothing and eyeglasses, a not very American style. Children can be so cruel—they beat up on him—and we were forced to buy him all-American outfits but failed to replace his broken glasses. A girl who had lived in Germany for a while served as the interpreter to and from his teacher.

Natasha went to work in a factory, packing book matches. We both applied for jobs there, but for some reason they didn't take me, only her, and her income helped us a lot in supporting herself and Babushka. She worked more than eight hours a day and it was hard for her; she was only a 17-year-old girl. Due to her workday, she couldn't attend school and was left without a formal education.

After being turned away at the match factory, I stopped looking for work because it turned out that I was expecting. A second child was not exactly welcome under our uncertain circumstances, and I even considered terminating the pregnancy, but Sasha was against that. As fate would have it, I carried the baby to term.

On October 5, 1952, we were moving from one apartment to another, in the next building, to give us a little extra space. I had shuttled furniture down three flights of stairs and up two to the new apartment when the birth pains started. My friend called an ambulance, and I was surprised and worried when a police car pulled up—I didn't know that in America the police arrive first, followed by an ambulance, and that the police are trained in the delivery of babies!

They took me to Kings County Hospital and 15 minutes later I gave birth to a daughter, Yelena. It was recorded by the doctor, after he tried to make sense of a foreign sounding name, as Helen.

Epilogue

June 2007

I walked into my mother's room in the rehab facility with my daughter Katia and we gasped. There lay my Mama, almost unrecognizable, her small frame blended into the bed sheets, the gray-haired face disappearing into the white pillows of the elevated headboard.

In just a few days, barely a few weeks, her condition had gone from talking and moving about her house, where she had still lived independently a year and a half after my father's death, to what were the final days of her life. A mild stroke, which my brother detected in her absence of speech one morning two weeks ago, had led to another one a few days later, and now, here she was, barely able to look around, let alone make herself understood.

Katia would admit to me later that she had not believed it was Baba Tania at first, the change had been so rapid to who could only be described "the ancient one." In a way, the end that was so quickly approaching was merciful, not prolonged with breathing tubes, IVs that she would have undoubtedly ripped out, beeping machines.

My sister Natasha had warned me to make the trip down from Connecticut that day. "Don't dilly dally," she had told me on the phone the day before, her optimism of past years now replaced by the reality that Mama would probably not last the week.

I walked up and sat on her bed, taking her hand in mine, not saying a word. Her dark brown eyes were watery, and it was hard to tell if she was "out of it." Before being moved to the rehab facility, while still in the hospital, she had sat up, eaten, even tried to talk with difficulty with Natasha and my brothers, Eugene and Yura, unaware that she was slurring her speech, but a second stroke had weakened her 90-year-old heart beyond normal functioning, and now she seemed far away, inside herself. I was surprised when her frail hand gripped mine.

"Mama, do you know who I am?" I asked, more to make conversation than with any real hope for an answer. She directed her gaze towards me, and our eyes met. We sat like this for several minutes. I knew the time was past for any platitudes like, "We'll have you out of here in no time, Mama." It was enough to just sit and hold her hand, and her eyes seemed to focus in on me. At least I imagined that they did.

Katia was too scared to get any closer, the shock of seeing her grandmother decline so quickly had affected her. She remained in the doorway. She had said her goodbyes the week before.

I sat quietly, then stroked her cheek as I brought my face closer to hers. "*Spasibo,* Mama," I whispered.

I had said thank you to her so many times before, with birthday cards, with gifts, that if she had heard me this time, I am not sure she attributed anything more to it than usual. For me, however, this time carried a greater import, knowing that it might be the last time I could tell her thank you for having given me life. So it was not "goodbye" that I uttered, but *spasibo*, closer to her ear.

We were interrupted by a young doctor appearing in the doorway,

Left to right: Tatyana and Alexander Artemyeff, Helen Charov, circa 2004. Alexander Feodoseevich Artemyeff (1913–2005), was married for 56 years to Tatyana Borisovna Artemyeff (1916–2007). Helen Charov, their daughter, lives in Moodus, Connecticut.

with a woman who introduced herself as the resident physical therapist. He spoke loudly to my mother, from the doorway. "How're you doin', kid?"

Katia and I winced at the presumed familiarity of his greeting. *Kid? Who was the kid here?* My mother did not acknowledge him.

"Mrs. Artemyeff, good morning!" chimed in the therapist in a thick Long Island accent. Katia rolled her eyes and signaled she was going back to the waiting room.

The doctor motioned to me for a conference on the other side of the room, my back to the hospital bed. The absurdity of discussing my mother's proposed physical therapy plan, that of getting her into a wheelchair, forcing her to try and stand, even walk, didn't register immediately with me until they suggested she be started on it that afternoon.

I knew they were just doing their jobs, but it seemed ludicrous, even cruel to put her through the motions to check off someone's list of administered "health care." I argued with them that she was beyond the need for any physical therapy, barely able to turn her head from side-to-side, and that the family was prepared for the end to come soon.

"But look at her," said the physical therapist, and I turned around. My mother, with great effort, had lifted her hand off the bed and was holding it out to me. I knew then that she had recognized me, perhaps had even heard me, had known it was her youngest child, her daughter. I went to her and embraced her in my arms.

Index

Numbers in ***bold italics*** indicate pages with illustrations